D0867145

Exploring Sacred Landscapes

Exploring Sacred Landscapes

Religious and Spiritual Experiences in Psychotherapy

Mary Lou Randour

Editor

Columbia University Press

New York

Columbia University Press
New York   Chichester, West Sussex
Copyright © 1993 Columbia University Press
All rights reserved

Library of Congress Cataloging-in-Publication Data

Exploring sacred landscapes : religious and spiritual experiences
  in psychotherapy / Mary Lou Randour, editor.
      p.   cm.
    Includes bibliographical references and index.
    ISBN 0-231-07000-4
    1. Psychotherapy—Religious aspects.
  2. Psychotherapy—Religious aspects—Case
  studies.   3. Psychotherapy patients—Religious life.
  4. Psychotherapy patients—Religious life—Case studies.
  I. Randour, Mary Lou.
    [DNLM: 1. Psychotherapy.   2. Religion and
  Psychology.   WM 460.5.R3 E96]
  RC489.R46E95   1993
  616.89′14—dc20
  DMLM/DLC
  for Library of Congress   92-49511
                                                      CIP

⊗

Casebound editions of Columbia University Press books are
Smyth-sewn and printed on permanent and durable acid-free
paper.

Printed in the United States of America

c 10 9 8 7 6 5 4 3 2 1

Contents

Contents

Exploring Sacred
Landscapes

Introduction

O ur intent here is simple: to encourage clinicians to consider the significance of spiritual striving and religious experience in their patients' lives. We propose, and hope to illustrate in the following clinical papers, that spiritual and religious material can provide vital information about the psychology of an individual. Religious concerns can often shed light on the nature of object relationships; the central questions in an individual's life; the ideas and values that have shaped and influence character; and how one addresses, or ignores, questions of mortality and ultimacy. Our attempts to "listen with a third ear" (Reik 1949) to another person and to uncover repressed conflict, denied need, neglected hopes, and unmourned losses cannot ignore any aspect of that person's life.

In order to establish a rationale for this book with its purpose of encouraging clinicians to consider religious experiences in psychotherapy, I shall discuss here what makes religious experience so vital in psychological formation and functioning. In the section following I provide a brief review of the historical and ongoing relationship between psychoanalysis and religion. The last section briefly describes the clinical case papers (which focus on the developmental courses of treatment), and the essays that conclude this book. The two essays, one written by a theologian with clinical experience and the other by a clinician and an academic with theological interests, reflect the overriding themes of these papers and their implications for clinical practice.

The Significance of Religion for Psychological Life

Religious questions and experience encompass the most vital needs, passionate hopes, and existential longings of us all. Meissner contends, and I agree, that "there is no area of human endeavor or existential involvement more profound, more far-reaching, more full of implication and significance than religious experience" (1984:6). There is a human need

1

to make meaning, a need emanating from the capacity to recognize one's own mortality and to see the possibility of ultimacy and transcendence as a response to this experience of finitude. This is our uniquely human "burden of understanding" (Langer 1963). Beneath the shadow cast by our mortality, we reach to understand why we are here, the meaning of our lives, the purpose of our being. Awareness of our mortality presses us to more deeply and authentically consider the value and meaning of our lives in particular, and of all life in general. To paraphrase Voltaire, if religion did not exist we would have to invent it.

The emotional significance of religious and spiritual concerns and their power to shape personality is considerable. Religious experiences interact with one's internal cast of characters at all levels of development, with "God" (however understood by an individual) playing a formative role in this internal theater (McDougall 1985). A person's current relationship with God, and the developmental course of that relationship, can shed light on other significant object relationships and can also suggest how she or he copes with narcissistic deprivation and conflict. I illustrated this illuminating capacity of religious experiences to reveal the nature of object relations in an earlier paper written with Julie Bondanza (Randour and Bondanza 1987). In that paper we provided clinical detail on the interplay between a female patient's God object representation, other object representations, and her sense of self. We discussed an intervention that, making use of an idealizing transference, demonstrated the relationship between a concept of God, God object representations, other object representations, and her self representations. (A concept of God is distinguished from a God object representation in that a concept of God is rational, conscious, associated with secondary processes, and resides in the cultural arena, whereas God object representations are emotional, usually unconscious, linked to primary processes, and private.) In this case the therapist's understanding and use of religious experiences facilitated the differentiation of self and objects and furthered self-integration.

It is obvious, but needs to be said, that these religious questions that touch the deepest core of human existence are always understood, interpreted, and experienced psychologically (James 1982). Our experience of a relationship with God, which most of us have early in life (even if we later renounce or discard that relationship), follows a course similar to other significant relationships. The actual interactions we have with important other people are "taken in" or "internalized," constituting our representational world (Greenberg and Mitchell 1983). The internalized images—of our experiences with actual others and with others we can only imagine—may create an expectation of how others will respond to us; closely related to how we experience our selves, these images may act as persecutors or seducers, or be sources of security and love. Whatever function these representations serve, we all interact not only with the people in our "actual" (public) lives but also with all those others who now form a part of our internal (private) lives. In fact, this internal cast of characters that populates our psychic landscape creates the reality we live in as much as the consensual reality we live in with the actual others in our lives. While God may never be experienced in actuality, God is encountered symbolically, mythologically, and imaginatively and becomes an important other in our lives.

A relationship to God is bound by the same psychological conditions as any other object representation: it develops out of our earliest relationships; it is bound to self representations by affect and behavioral expectancies recalled in the context of one's current needs, desires, fantasies, and conflicts; and it may differ in its accessibility to consciousness and in the ability to be synthesized, so that it may remain unconscious, stand in opposition to other representations, or be defensively denied (Randour and Bondanza 1987).

Most important, God object representations operate in a continual dialectical dialogue with other self and object representations throughout the individual's lifetime, with the potential for ever more complex elaborations. This potential for ever-increasing complexity in object representations is always in the service of psychic equilibrium (Piaget 1970) or self-cohesion (Kohut 1977).

When we learn about our patients' religious experiences we are gathering psychological information. We will learn more about our patients' psychic functioning, ego strengths, and how they defend against psychic pain when we understand the role of spirituality and religion in their lives. For example, a patient of mine signaled the status of his object relations and his way of handling psychic distress with the initial telephone call requesting therapy. He explained that one of the reasons he wanted to enter therapy had to do with his relationship with God. As treatment progressed he described how he was troubled because he consciously wanted to believe in a newer image of God, a benevolent female. All his conscious strivings were toward that goal. Despite this conscious desire, he was plagued by an image, inherited from a fundamentalist background, of a harsh, punitive, judgmental, male God. The difference between these two images seemed irreconcilable to him; in fact, he had no interest in attempting to integrate them. I knew that his inability to imagine the possibility of the two opposing images of God interacting revealed the same defensive split in his other early object relations. Achieving greater complexity, elaboration, and integration in his representational world would require paying attention to both his God object representations and his other object relations, and understanding the interdependence between them.

I have concentrated on describing how concepts of God and God object representations can play an organizing role in the development of object relations. But not all religious and spiritual experiences are God-centered, although I would argue that all are object relational. For some, what begins as a concept of God, usually as a rather concrete being, evolves into increasingly more complex notions of divinity (Fowler 1981). However, a child's first experiences with religion, usually beginning at age two or two and a half, cannot be interpreted beyond the cognitive developmental capacity of that child. Childhood God concepts are typically fairly simplistic and lack articulation. Since the organization of object relationships moves from simpler organizational schemas to more complex and elaborated configurations, the early God object representations are also simply formed. In time, it is likely that the child's God concept will go through many different transformations. While some adults maintain a rather unelaborated God concept, others will have created an adult version of God that is more abstract, deanthropomorphized, and sophisticated. Some transformations of the original God concept may be so evolved that the original version is unrecognizable and no longer referred to as "God." For example, in my earlier study of women's spirituality (Randour 1987), some of the women referred to God as a process, a higher ideal, or an experience of transcendence. Mary Daly (1978), noted for her renaming, suggests *God* is a verb. The possibilities are many.

A God concept can provide the first clue to the developmental level of a person's object representation. While it is common for a God concept to exceed in sophistication and articulation that of the God object representation, a fairly unelaborated God concept points to a God object representation of similar developmental status. At best, the continual developmental articulations of the concept of God will parallel increasingly higher levels of complexity in the God object representations. But this is not always the case. What is relevant for the clinician is that great psychological distress can result when a gap exists between the conscious idea of God and the internal representation of the experience of God. Such a gap usually indicates some impeded development of the God object representation in that its articulation has not kept pace with the individual's conceptual understanding of God.

Two Systems of Thought: Opposing or Complementary?

The theoretical framework for the clinical cases and essays in this volume is psychoanalytic in orientation. With this psychoanalytic perspective, the following discussion enters into a historical stream of discourse between psychoanalysis and religion that has long been infused with suspicion and hostility.

The "mutual antagonism" (Meissner 1984:vii) between these two systems of thought is the inevitable aftermath of the successful effort of psychology to distinguish itself from metaphysics and philosophy by declaring itself a science in the late nineteenth century. Gay describes this time—when Freud was developing his ideas—as one in which intellectal passions and fierce competition between opposing concepts prevailed. "Biologists, pedagogues, journalists, politicians, all were deeply immersed in battle. Wherever the historian looks, he discovers tensions over the nature of God and the power of churches." (1987:8).

While some, notably Williams James, wrestled with the tension between psychology and religion, Freud had no ambivalence about religious belief. He declared religion the "enemy," and he remained unalterably convinced that theological thinking and scientific thinking were absolutely and irrevocably incompatible systems. (Peter Gay's book *Freud: A Godless Jew* offers a compressive analysis of the effects of Freud's atheism on psychoanalysis.) Freud's well-known position was that religion is an illusion based on neurotic needs. This attitude came to be largely adopted by the psychoanalytic community. Freud contended, Meissner notes, that "religious illusions were a dragon to be slain with the hard sword of science" (1990:98). Freud was not, however, opposed to art; he endorsed the redemptive power of art, conceived in fantasy and illusion, to lift the human spirit.

William James was a contemporary of Freud's: his classic work *The Varieties of Religious Experience* was published in 1902, two years after Freud's seminal *Interpretation of Dreams*. James, too, was developing his ideas at this turning point in intellectual history, but unlike Freud he was able to propose a system of thought that encompassed both systems. When forced to choose, he resolved the conflict between his respect for science and his spiritual interests—Gay thinks a little "desperately" (1987:30)—by "placing his bets on the will to believe."

Since that antagonistic beginning, some psychoanalytic theorists have been able to value religious experience. Most notable, of course, is Jung, whose name seems synonymous with the field of psychology and religion. However, other important psychoanalytic theorists have also displayed varying degrees of receptivity to religious thinking. Adler (1965) was open to the psychological possibilities of religious belief and Rank's (1930) exploration of the nature of the soul—or as Kainer (1984) describes it, the spirit of the self—seems to me a highly evolved God concept. Winnicott's conception of transitional space as a place for creative activity and as belonging to "arts and to religion and to imaginative living and to creative scientific work" (Winnicott 1971:14) has attracted a number of writers (McDargh 1983; Meissner 1990; Randour and Bondanza 1987; Rizzuto 1979). The positive significance of art and religion has also been supported by Kohut (1984) and Guntrip (1957).

Despite this impressive list of significant psychoanalytic theorists who have, to varying degrees, demonstrated an openness to religious experiences, a wall of resistance still surrounds psychoanalysis proper when it comes to religious concerns. In his paper in this volume Tim Kochems challenges this tendency of clinicians to isolate religion from other clinical material. In the same vein, the theologian Hans Kung (1990) compellingly and forcefully argued that psychoanalysis is defensively ignoring the role of religion in a patient's life. Turning the tables, Kung wonders if psychoanalysis is not repressing religious material. Conceding that there is much merit in the psychoanalytic critique of religion, Kung contends that religion has responded and has adapted itself on the basis of this critique. He claims, however, that psychoanalysis has not reciprocated by showing any curiosity about the formative influence of religion and religious and spiritual experiences in human life. Kung asserts that what sex was to the Victorians, religion is to psychoanalysis. Although the intellectual leadership provided by psychoanalysis was instrumental in encouraging a more enlightened attitude toward sexuality, this same intellectual system continues to ignore the fertile field of religious experience. Much like Pfister, a Lutheran minister who entered into a lifelong dialogue with Freud, Kung argues that the common ground between psychoanalysis and religion is that both seek to help suffering individuals.

Contemporary Voices in the Dialogue

The papers in this volume follow in the tradition of those in psychoanalysis who have found merit in understanding how religious experiences and ideas bear upon psychological development and functioning. (See, for example, Fromm 1967; Goldenberg 1990; Guntrip 1957; Leavy 1988, 1990; Loevinger 1984; Meissner 1984, 1990; Pruyser 1960, 1968; Ricoeur 1970; Rizzuto 1974, 1976, 1979; and Stern 1985.) Each of the contributors here assumes that religious content has potential clinical significance, and each writer demonstrates in some detail what this significance is. It is this deliberate clinical focus that distinguishes the papers in this volume from other work in the area of psychoanalysis and religion.

Most of the discussion to date has been an abstract analysis—removed from the clinical level and clinical aims—that needs some interpretation before it can be clinically useful. With this volume, we hope to assist in building some of the necessary bridges between the metalevel and clinical practice. Because the literature at the metalevel of analysis lays a conceptual ground for a clinical focus and complements a clinical orientation—albeit with interpretation—it is useful to briefly review its major foci. Although this body of literature can be organized in a number of ways, for purposes of this discussion I suggest three major approaches: integrative, expansionist, and appreciative.

Meissner, who is both a Jesuit priest and a psychoanalyst, is most notable in the attempt to integrate psychoanalytic and religious concepts through his self-described effort "to reformulate the issues in terms of the fundamental images of man that prevail in the psychoanalytic and religious perspectives" (1984:191). He has also delineated the conceptual tensions between these two competing systems of thought, with the recommendation that we dialectically live within that tension. In a later work he continues this line of thought by extending Winnicott's formulations of transitional phenomena (1990). His purpose is to define a "conceptual space that provide[s] a medium for a dialectical resolution of these tensions between the subjective and the objective," and between religion and psychoanalysis (1990:96). Leavy's work also attempts to find the connecting concepts between psychoanalysis and religion (1988). Reflecting on what psychoanalysis and religion have to tell us about the human condition, he characterizes human suffering, loving, hating, and mourning as relevant to our degree of affinity with God. Unlike Meissner, whose discussions on the topic of psychoanalysis and religion eschew any personal statement of belief, Leavy's analysis of the common ground between psychoanalysis and religion emanates from his stated perspective as a Christian believer.

The second approach is represented by those who seek to expand psychoanalytic theory by including a religious perspective to gain an understanding of the human experience. The latest such effort is Smith and Handelman's edited volume, *Psychoanalysis and Religion*, (1990) with contributions by academic philosophers, religious studies scholars, clinical psychiatrists, and practicing psychoanalysts. In that volume, for example, Leavy develops concepts of reality—a basic preoccupation for psychoanalysis—that include religious experience. By introducing and elaborating on how religious experiences can be considered a part of reality, Leavy pushes against some of the theoretical limits of psychoanalysis, encouraging an expansion and redefinition of those limits.

Spero's contributions dominate the third approach in the literature—the possible value, or appreciation, of religious experience. Spero, who is Jewish, is explicit about his faith. Going one step further than many of his colleagues, he challenges the theoretical position that posits God only as a psychological product of interpersonal relationships (Spero 1985a, 1985b, 1985c, 1990). He contends that we cannot ignore the possibility of an entity that also "enters into relationship with and promotes the development of the self" (1990:55), and he offers a model for "conceptualizing the parallel and overlapping aspects of anthropocentric (human-and-human) and deocentric (human-and-God) object relationships" (1990:54). Others also support the position that religious belief can have some value. Smith makes a case for the possibility that either religious faith or nonfaith can be nondefensive. He concludes that "mature trust, mature faith, whether specifically religious or not, allows . . . for the endurance of inevitable suffering." (This is a position shared by Kohut [1984] who observes how faith provides courage to some in the face of grave danger.) Smith seems less sanguine about the claim that faith opens up the possibility of "love, joy, and peace that surpass understanding." This, he offers, "remains for most of us, most of the time, more problematic" (1990:38).

Rizzuto's work is an important exception to the underemphasis on clinically relevant analyses. She expands psychoanalytic developmental theory with her careful, documented articulation of the development of a God object representation. The importance of her work to an "experience-near" level of analysis (Kohut 1984) is demonstrated by the extent to which the writers in this volume have relied on her thinking and by the fact that the title of her essay was used as the title of this volume. (If the symbol of Freud as the "father" of psychoanalysis has been used to explain his historical position, certainly Rizzuto is the "mother" of all attempts to explicate a developmental and clinical psychoanalytic theory of religious experience.)

One of the purposes of this volume is to encourage a clinical and developmental focus in the discussion between psychology and religion. In this as well, we draw our inspiration and direction from Rizzuto. The discussion here is derived from clinical observations. Using theory to organize the discussion, the writers offer rich clinical detail supplied over the course of treatment. The clinical detail focuses on the development that occurs within the context of psychotherapy where the motivational edge for such development is associated with some religious or spiritual dimension. Whether the contributor uses psychoanalytic theory, structural stage theory, or Jungian psychology as a guide to understanding, all share a developmental focus. While any one definition of development may be shaded by different nuances in theoretical orientation, the Bloom-Feshbachs' view that continued development "requires further self-definition with increasing degrees of separateness, autonomy, and relatedness" (1987:2) is one that encompasses all the positions taken in this volume. Using spiritual or religious themes that arose in therapy, each contributor illustrates development within treatment with a clinical case, each highlighting a particular clinical topic, such as transference, countertransference, symbolization, and structuralization.

In this volume we do not intend to integrate religion and psychoanalysis or necessarily encourage any type of reconciliation. Ours is a pragmatic effort: we aim to show clinicians how they might use an understanding of spiritual and religious influences in their clinical work. We hope to show by example, and in very practical ways, the clinical relevance of spiritual and religious expression.

The Contributors

Ana-Maria Rizzuto begins the discussion with her paper "Exploring Sacred Landscapes." Once again she reminds us that an individual's religious understanding is a private reality, and that one person's private God is not everybody's God, and not the God of official religion, but one "created and found, transformed and refound in the private reality." She demonstrates the diagnostic value of taking a religious history and also offers technical assistance. Reflecting on the dynamic motives of the appearance of religious themes in psychotherapy, she gives examples of how God is used, e.g., in the service of regression, progression, avoidance, resistance, for companionship, or as an oedipal object. Rizzuto closes her discussion with a clinical example of how the successful completion of a treatment involved a critical examination of a woman's personal beliefs.

The clinical uses of transference and countertransference are central to all psychoanalytic therapy, whatever its theoretical leanings (Gorkin 1987). The centrality of transference and countertransference as sources of information and as potentially transformative arenas of experience, also applies to an examination of religious and spiritual material. In "Countertransference and Transference Aspects of Religious Material in Psychotherapy: The Isolation or Integration of Religious Material," Tim Kochems proposes a useful conceptual tool with his articulation of the "isolation of religion." He characterizes such isolation as a bipolar phenomenon in which religion is either devalued or treated as special. In either case religion is regarded as "untouchable" and there is a refusal to integrate religious experience into one's entire psychological experience. As an alternative to the isolation of religion, Kochems proposes a model of interaction and relationship, which he demonstrates with a clinical case study. Detailing the beginning phase of treatment, he identifies the existing God object representation of his patient, links it to primary objects, and then traces how, in the context of transference and counter-transference, this God object representation was elaborated, resulting in the formation of a new God object representation (and a successful treatment).

The role of transference and countertransference in understanding religious and spiritual dimensions of psychotherapy is the topic of Nancy Kehoe and Thomas Gutheil's paper "Ministry or Therapy: The Role of Transference and Countertransference in a Religious Therapist." This time, however, the focus is on the dual identity of the therapist as a psychologist and a nun, and the effect of that dual identity on treatment. The authors delineate the special quality of this particular dual identity, which distinguishes it from other dual identities such as parent and therapist. The religious professional is associated with a "ritual aura" and is often expected by the patient to actively offer healing. Additionally, the nun's expectations of herself are based on a long-standing tradition of self-sacrifice and assistance that infuse her identity as a nun. These expectations of a religious person operate in a dynamic tension with the professional standards of a psychologist, which emphasize the significance of boundaries and limits. Using a clinical case study to center their discussion, Kehoe and Gutheil describe how the inherent tensions in a dual identity both create problems and offer potential for treatment.

In "The Use of Religious Imagery for Psychological Structuralization," Martha Robbins discusses technical considerations in using religious imagery to facilitate psychological structuralization. She presents a detailed description of this process with a clinical case study of a two-year treatment using hypnotherapy. In the therapeutic process of structuralization, she traces her patient's use of four predominant religious images: the Christ light, the Madonna and Child, the prodigal son, and Jacob wrestling with the angel. With each successive image, representing the four phases of treatment, Robbins describes how her patient's images are related to the parental imagos and corresponding self representations, and how these self and object representations evolve into more mature psychological structures.

Representing a Jungian perspective and also using hypnotherapy, Robert Goodman proposes in "Myth and Symbol as Expressions of the Religious" that these unconscious expressions are movements toward a larger psychological and spiritual unity. Goodman argues that expressions of symbol and myth from the unconscious are religious experiences for three reasons: they are spontaneously generated by the individual; they contain both personal and universal meanings; and they contribute to the person's development toward integration and wholeness. He uses clinical case examples, each characterized by a hero/journey myth, to illustrate his point that religious and spiritual strivings are a "human, constructing, meaning-making process." In addition to this discussion, he delineates and illustrates a recommended stance for therapists in working with symbols: welcoming, facilitating, and amplifying.

In "Religious Imagery in the Clinical Context: Access to Compassion Toward the Self—Illusion or Truth," Sharon Daloz Parks explores how religious phenomena help or hinder access to the patient's "hidden strength," perhaps each therapist's only ally. In the therapeutic encounter she wonders what "hospitality" the therapist gives to exploring images of power, value, and affection that center and shape life. These images are religious, she proposes, and in the therapeutic encounter an imaginative constructing of reality takes place. She questions how we as therapists join this meaning-making activity, how we function as part of an individual's "community of confirmation or contradiction." Using two clinical case examples, Parks explores whether a compassionate image of God can reconcile the alienated self.

In finding the spiritual dimension of the creative will, R. G. K. Kainer conceives of and describes the transcendent moment in therapy. In "The Transcendent Moment and the Analytic Hour," she proposes that transcendence is the moment when the self is transformed to a higher, more creative level of being. In the transcendental moment the individual triumphs over those destructive internal images that had previously impeded the creative potential of that self to "go beyond." Framing transcendence within the analytic matrix, Kainer suggests that the essential transcendent medium is one of empathic connectedness. Using clinical case examples, she illustrates two different forms of this transcendental empathic connectedness: through vicarious introspection and through the acceptance of the patient's projective identifications.

The concluding section contains two essays, each reflecting on the shared implications of the clinical papers. John McDargh, writing from the vantage point of a theologian with clinical interest and experience, encourages us to develop a psychotheological perspective, i.e., an intentional, self-aware position on the relationship of the person to ultimacy.

To assist clinicians in this process he describes three "contemporary psychotheological listening perspectives in psychotherapy": spiritual reality, God-relational, and faith-relational. McDargh suggests that what is critical is not whether the clinician evolves a belief system that is based on established traditions or remains agnostic; what is essential is that the clinician critically reflect on his or her own psychotheological perspective so that the normative bearings it provides for the conduct of psychotherapy is made clearer.

Gil Noam and Maryanne Wolf conclude the discussion with their reflections on the relationship between psychotherapy and spirituality. They write from the positions of a clinician and developmentalist, with an interest in, and appreciation for, religious concerns. After reviewing the origins of the tensions between the two conceptual systems of psychoanalysis and religion and noting the recent trend to bridge the gap between these systems of thought, Noam and Wolf sound a cautionary note. An antagonistic separation between psychoanalysis and religion is detrimental to both, since each can be informed by the other. However, they propose that there are advantages in maintaining a separation, which they proceed to delineate.

Each author, then, sketches one of the shapes in the intricate contours of a sacred landscape. This sacred landscape, the metaphoric space where psyche and spirit converge, is a terrain that remains largely unexplored by clinical psychoanalysis. Yet it is a terrain rich in possibilities for understanding not just the human mind but also the human heart. With the variety of "maps" suggested by this collection of essays, we hope to invite others into this exploration.

References

Adler, A. [1933] 1965. *Superiority and Social Interest*. London: Routledge & Kegan Paul.
Bloom-Feshbach, J. and S. Bloom-Feshbach. 1987. *The Psychology of Separation and Loss*. San Francisco: Jossey-Bass.

Daly, M. 1978. *Gyn/ecology: The Meta-ethics of Radical Feminism*. Boston: Beacon Press.

Fowler, J. W. 1981. *Stages of Faith: The Psychology of Human Development and the Quest for Meaning*. San Francisco: Harper & Row.

Fromm, E. 1967. *Psychoanalysis and Religion*. New Haven: Yale University Press.

Gay, P. 1987. *A Godless Jew: Freud, Atheism, and the Making of Psychoanalysis*. New Haven: Yale University Press.

Goldenberg, N. R. 1990. *Returning Words to Flesh*. Boston: Beacon Press.

Gorkin, M. 1987. *The Uses of Countertransference*. Northvale, N.J.: Jason Aronson.

Greenberg, J. and S. Mitchell. 1983. *Object Relations in Psychoanalytic Theory*. Cambridge: Harvard University Press.

Guntrip, H. 1957. *Psychotherapy and Religion*. New York: Harper & Row.

James, W. [1902] 1961. *The Varieties of Religious Experience*. New York: Collier.

Kainer, R. G. 1984. Art and the canvas of the self: Otto Rank and creative transcendence. *American Imago* 41(4): 359–72.

Kohut, H. 1977. *The Restoration of the Self*. New York: International Universities Press.

——. 1984. *How Does Analysis Cure?* Chicago: University of Chicago Press.

Kung, H. 1990. *Freud and the Problem of God*. New Haven: Yale University Press.

Langer, S. 1963. *Philosophy in a New Key*. New York: Harcourt, Brace and World.

Leavy, S. A. 1988. *In the Image of God*. New Haven: Yale University Press.

——. 1990. Reality in religion and psychoanalysis. In J. H. Smith and S. A. Handelman, eds., *Psychoanalysis and Religion*, pp. 43–59. Baltimore: Johns Hopkins University Press.

Loevinger, R. J. 1984. *Working with Religious Issues in Therapy*. New York: Jason Aronson.

McDargh, J. 1983. *Psychoanalysis Object Relations Theory and the Study of Religion: On Faith and the Imaging of God*. Lanham, Md.: University Press of America.

McDougall, J. 1985. *Theaters of the Mind*. New York: Basic Books.

Meissner, W. W. 1984. *Psychoanalysis and Religious Experience*. New Haven: Yale University Press.

——. 1990. The role of transitional conceptualization in religious thought. In J. H. Smith and S. A. Handelman, eds., *Psychoanalysis and Religion*, pp. 95–116. Baltimore: Johns Hopkins Press.

Piaget, J. 1970. *Genetic Epistemology*. New York: Columbia University Press.

Pruyser, P. W. 1960. Some trends in the psychology of religion. *Journal of Religion* 44: 113–29.

——. 1968. *A Dynamic Psychology of Religion*. New York: Harper & Row.

Randour, M. L. 1987. *Women's Psyche, Women's Spirit: The Reality of Relationships*. New York: Columbia University Press.

Randour, M. L. and J. Bondanza. 1987. The concept of God in the psychological formation of females. *Psychoanalytic Psychology* 4(4): 301–13.

Rank, O. 1930. *Psychology and the Belief in the Soul*. New York: Barnes, 1961.

Reik, T. 1949. *Listening with the Third Ear*. New York: Farrar, Straus.

Ricoeur, P. 1970. *Freud and Philosophy*. New Haven: Yale University Press.

Rizzuto, A. 1974. Object relations and the formation of the image of God. *British Journal of Medical Psychology* 47: 89–99.

——. 1976. Freud, God, and the devil and the theory of object representations. *International Review of Psychoanalysis* 31: 165–70.

——. 1979. *The Birth of the Living God: A Psychoanalytic Study*. Chicago: University of Chicago Press.

Smith, J. H. 1990. On psychoanalysis and the question of nondefensive religion. In J. H. Smith and S. A. Handelman, eds., *Psychoanalysis and Religion*, pp. 18–42. Baltimore: Johns Hopkins University Press.

Spero, M. H. 1985a. Theoretical and clinical aspects of transference as a religious phenomenon in psychotherapy. *Journal of Religion and Health* 24: 8–25.

——. 1985b. The reality and the image of God in psychotherapy. *American Journal of Psychotherapy* 39: 75–85.

——, ed. 1985c. *Psychotherapy of the Religious Patient*. Springfield, Ill.: Charles C. Thomas.

——. 1990. Parallel dimensions of experience in psychoanalytic psychotherapy of the religious patient. *Psychotherapy* 27(1): 53–71.

Stern, E. M. 1985. *Psychotherapy and the Religiously Committed Patient*. New York: Haworth Press.

Winnicott, W. W. 1971. *Playing and Reality*. London: Tavistock.

Exploring Sacred Landscapes

Ana-Maria Rizzuto

L ife is a journey between birth and death—two unavoidable and unfathomable events. This mysterious and compelling reality calls forth the creative myth-making powers of the human pilgrim. Intuition, hope, and fear, based on experiences with natural events and mental landscapes, guide the traveler to the sacred dimension of life, conceived as a separate realm beyond the senses. The secret beyond one's limited temporal existence compels us to find meaning in the acts of life and to be encompassed in a network of affectionate links. The young child's question, "Where do I come from?" is later followed by the query about the dead beloved grandfather, parent, friend, or pet, "Where did he go?" The child, like the human unconscious according to Freud, has no way of imagining the absence of existence of a known living being. No human being can avoid dealing with the appalling dimensions of what precedes and what follows life on earth. In their efforts to answer the child's persistent questions, human societies give the pilgrim a context, a "before" life and an "after" life, beyond her or his alloted lifetime. Whatever the answer, nihilistic or mythological, it is by definition a sacred, religious answer about another reality. In this sense everybody has a religion and is religious, whether one adheres to a public religion or has created private beliefs to find personal meaning in life.

The undeniable fact that all people have their own sacred landscapes as explicit or implicit context for their lives has been ignored by clinicians. Many patients undergo lengthy psychotherapeutic treatments without ever attending to the beliefs coloring the background of their experiences. Psychotherapists are not trained to listen to the religious dimensions of the patient, who in turn does not mention religious feelings and thoughts. It is only in the bizarre delusions of paranoid patients or decompensated schizophrenics that the patient's religious ideation and feelings claim central stage. Such pathological religiosity, even if meaningful in the context of a personal history, lacks the subtlety of everyday religious feelings and beliefs. "Everyday" private religion results from the individual's progressive attempts to locate her or his personal experience of a particular family and historical situation within the frame of reference of parental and societal beliefs, particularly the religious convictions of her or his social group. Religion is always a component of social and personal identity, a way of placing oneself among one human group and of finding an individual niche within the group. Self-understanding and self-definition must include a religious dimension even if it is to reject religion, to extricate the person from a familial and societal web created by religious affiliation. Being a regular or deviant member of the community of believers always has deep psychological significance. It bespeaks achieved or failed identifications, quality of object relations, social integration, and is an indicator of the person's sense of being part of a larger group, beyond individualistic concerns. Organized religion is not the only institution to provide the opportunity for psychic achievements: professional associations, political parties, interest groups, and sport institutions are examples of other societal groups that provide a sense of participation and belonging, be it real or imaginary. Religion is, however, the most important and enduring institution providing a sense of identity and belonging in the majority of societies existing in the world today. Precious information about the psychic reality and functioning of a person may be obtained by exploring the manner in which the individual integrates her or his beliefs with private and public reality.

In the human developmental process each child has to create anew as a psychic reality the parental world of objects that brought that child to life. That human world is and will be the most important reality, the very tissue that constitutes her or him as a particular human being. The essential parental responses of physical care, love, respect, and individual recognition provide the foundations for the child's psychic growth and for the integration of a progressively more complex reality. When the time comes to interrogate the world about the "before" and "after" dimensions of existence the child must necessarily use the images, impressions, and experiences accumulated in her or his short life to flesh out the divinities offered by the parents in answer to her or his inquiries. I have described the developmental process of forming a God representation in my book *The Birth of the Living God: A Psychoanalytic Study* (1979). There I show that the formation of private God representations is a process that occurs in dialectical integration with the formation of self representations. A person's private God is neither everybody's God nor the God of official doctrine but the only God that particular individual is able to have. Such a God has been created and found, transformed and refound in the private reality of love and hope, fear and freedom, acceptance and rejection, experienced with primary caretakers. God, created as a transitional representation in the process of psychic separation from mother and father, soon acquires a powerfully convincing reality, a sense of unseen presence, capable of caring relatedness, painful indifference, or frightful punishment. Once created, God's watchful presence, protecting or persecutory, becomes a fact of psychic life so real that no human power, not even the wishes of the child God-maker, could make it disappear. Belief, once established, requires major psychic shifts to be changed.

This brief overview suggests that the type of God and religious belief a person has, is a precious document of the individual's psychic vicissitudes during development. Obviously, I am not talking about religious formulas or official dogma but about their private adaptation to a personal religion as the source of deeply-held convictions about the nature of things. A brief example may illustrate the point. A young Jewish man was certain that God had cursed him for being too demanding of his mother and more than normally insistent that she devote all her attention to him. He envied Jesus, who had his mother "all to himself," but was terrified of the certain death that, in his opinion, came with having what Christ had. The young man had given religious form to his personal oedipal drama.

No human being can have a religious faith without coloring it with touches of personal history. Great mystics, centuries before psychoanalysis, always insisted that the inner perception of the transcendent God needs purification of its sensory qualities if it is to approximate the existing divinity. For the therapist, God's attributed human liabilities and the religious context in which the believer places the divinity are an invaluable spontaneous projective test capable of revealing, in subtle and personal meaningful detail, the story of the believer. Taking a religious history and learning to understand and explore the patient's religious convictions and experiences give depth to the therapy by attending to all aspects of psychic life: physical, social, interpersonal, creative, and spiritual.

The technical handling of religious material varies according to the moment in treatment. During the initial interviews information about religious convictions has considerable diagnostic value and must be included as a routine part of a first assessment of the patient's predicaments, conflicts, and clinical diagnosis. The exploration of personal beliefs also provides an overview of the human and transcendent universe in which the individual locates her or his personal drama. During the course of treatment, religious issues emerge as part of the patient's psychic efforts to deal with conflictual and transferential wishes. Religious guilt, devotion, rejection, or intensification of religious feelings voiced by patients are frequently directly related to the types of changes they are undergoing as a result of the treatment, in particular those that pertain to transferential feelings. Finally, during the termination period, the issues of separation and the experience of coming to the end of a journey frequently bring up concerns about death, departures, and the need to be on one's own. Many patients at this point reflect upon their religious beliefs and their stance about the unknowns in human life.

Taking a Religious History

During the initial interviews the patient frequently makes spontaneous remarks about her or his beliefs; references to death in the family, conception of children, birth, confirmation, marriage, diseases, and accidents are frequently presented in some religious context. These remarks reveal fears and hopes, wishes and conflicts, together with an overall picture of the patient's sacred landscape. Sometimes they indicate that the person is struggling with contradictory convictions, frequently between an official religion and personal beliefs incompatible with it. The therapist needs to take note of the context in which the remarks appear, as well as of their wording and the affective tone of their enunciation. A devout Jewish man described how he went to temple regularly and how much he appreciated his religion. Later he complained that he had no spare time, perhaps not even time for treatment. He was very busy and could not see me during the week, and he could not see me on Saturday because he was not supposed to drive until sundown. His voice changed at that point, indicated anger and resentment. I asked him if he was very observant of the Jewish laws. He said it was very important *for his family* that the Sabbath be observed. This very simple exchange revealed his secret resentment of family traditions and his disclaiming responsibility for obeying a law he seemed to blame for his lack of time. A conflict of angry submission and of ambivalence about responsibility for his own behavior pointed in the diagnostic direction of an obsessive, angry man whose ambivalence about committing himself to life and relations was equally present in his religious life.

The therapist needs to be ready for the unusual. During the first hour of therapy, a young woman related the death of her mother. She cried and said she missed her mother very much and that she did not know where her mother was now. When asked where her mother could be after death she said that *she cold not imagine any place* for her mother. She had been raised by militant atheists and all her childhood questions about religion had been answered by both parents saying there is no God, heaven, or hell; she was not to dwell on those questions. She said she needed to place her mother somewhere, to feel she was someplace after death. The exchange revealed her difficulty in mourning her mother, in separating from her psychologically, as well as past inhibition by her parents of her efforts to create a religion for herself. Later in the treatment she revealed that at age seven she frequently locked herself in her room and prayed, "Please let there be a God." During the treatment she had a dream in which her mother gave her implicit permission to have some belief. In the dream she saw her mother sitting on a flying oriental rug, smiling at her and waving her hand while saying, "Bye, dear. I am going to heaven." The dream was very vivid and convincing, and while it portrayed the obvious fulfillment of a wish, it also provided her with an abode where she could locate her much-needed mother. The therapist's tactful listening to her search for a geography for the dead, and the respectful investigation of her wishes, provided the occasion for the patient to have a resolution dream that brought her peace of mind.

Great flexibility is required of the therapist. The patient's spontaneous remarks about religion need to be fully respected as a psychic reality that must not be challenged. The therapist may choose to explore them. To do so the therapist needs to enter the internal logic of the patient's beliefs without judging what they mean. Their meaning is always private and can only be learned from the patient. The therapist needs to suspend disbelief to enter the patient's private universe. A young man assured the therapist that the entire source of his misfortunes was that God had cursed him at birth. He did not notice the contradiction of seeking treatment to avoid the consequences of God's malediction. The therapist asked him for details about his cursed condition, specifically God's motive for cursing him, the nature of the curse, when he became aware that he was cursed, and his feelings about being the object of God's wrath. The investigation revealed a highly competitive oedipal man who was convinced that his arrival into this world was a great threat to his father, whom he considered much inferior to himself. Later he revealed that as a young boy he had sworn to himself that he would never be like his father, but would be much better than him, a real man.

Many patients do not talk spontaneously about religion at the time of their evaluation. Some believe the therapist does not want to hear about it, while others declare religion a private realm they prefer to keep to themselves. Such exclusion announces difficulties because the patient may use his religion to displace or avoid distressing transferential feelings, or to hide shameful aspects of his life. There was a time when therapists were reluctant to take a comprehensive sexual history, fearing the patient's indignation. Present-day circumstances make the taking of a sexual history a compelling clinical obligation. Religious matters do not have such compelling practical urgency. Their clinical significance lies in the therapist's commitment to attend to the fullness of the patient's life as a physical, spiritual, and social being. Technically, the inclusion of questions about religious upbringing, practices, and beliefs conveys to the patient the notion that psychotherapy is a very serious undertaking involving the exploration of the *entirety* of psychic life. In due course the patient comes to see that psychic problems color not only human relations but also exchanges with the divinity. A patient may discover that her praying is not a free action but is subject to similar compulsions as other aspects of her life, driven by a pathological sense of duty. A successful psychotherapy may, as a result of the exploration of religious and other issues, help the patient achieve more freedom in her spiritual life as well.

The questions to be asked in the initial interview are those pertaining to development circumstances, such as parental belief, religion of each parent, religious practices at home and within the community. It is important to know the patient's experience of religious landmarks such as baptism or circumcision, first communion, confirmation, bar mitzvah or bat mitzvah, marriage, and funerals. Much can be learned from such information about the lifestyle of the family of origin. Disorganized families tend to have strong beliefs but limited church attendance and social religious integration. This does not provide the growing child with the opportunity to attend religious services that may help modulate the family's sense of not belonging. A strict, very orthodox upbringing may enhance the sense of identity and the strength of concrete beliefs but it limits the child's need to doubt and question, to rebel and find personal convictions. Submission and fear may engender resentment and the inability to express it. A family's lack of any religious participation in a community where most people belong to one denomination may engender a sense of shame and isolation, of being different from other children. The converse can be true: if the community is lukewarm or directly critical of overt religious practices, the child of a religious family may feel ashamed of being different from other children. In short, issues of identity, self-definition, social integration, and the pride or shame that accompanies them are illuminated by the answers about religion in the family.

The taking of a religious history provides its richest information when it focuses on personal psychodynamics by attending to the beliefs the person has about herself or himself as a specific individual facing the divinity and human existence. Here the therapist needs great tact, convincing respect for the patient's revelations, and a gentle persistence to get the patient to talk about such private matters. The question about religious affiliation can be asked directly as part of identificatory information. Such a factual attitude prepares the patient for further questions within the context of the original answer. The therapist needs to be ready to ask the informative questions when they appear naturally related to the subject matter. A patient may be repeatedly talking about the *premature* death of a parent. After investigating how the patient means *premature,* the therapist, always within the context of the patient's disclosures, may ask about the circumstances of the death and the manner in which the person explains the untimely death. At that point the therapist may inquire about prayers or religious services before or after the death. Tactful questions may reveal how the patient perceived God's intervention and intent in the death of the parent. God may be accused of cruelty directly or in a veiled manner. The patient may imagine the parent as being near God and may feel that prayers allow some contact with the deceased. Guilt may appear in the form of self-accusations of not having prayed enough. Death wishes may be hidden behind the feeling that propitiatory prayers on behalf of the parent might have changed God's decision. Revenge may disguise itself in attributing the death to God's punishment of the parent for something that frightened or frustrated the patient. The death of a parent is always such a momentous event that even patients who have declared having no religious convictions at all may benefit from a question about where the parent is after death.

Similar questions can be asked when the person refers to major life events like birth, marriage, decisions about career, or historical events such as war, natural disasters, or public catastrophes. The therapist tries to learn about facts, attitudes, motives, and the feelings the patient has about all those moments in which the normal course of life brings all human beings to an encounter with the sacred dimensions of existence and the social organizations that shape the rites of passage from one age or state to the other. Frequently the patient finds in the answers the opportunity to disclose personal myths barely known even by the patient. A young woman believed that her mother named her Mary as a direct hint that she should be totally asexual. A borderline woman feared as a child taking her first communion because she was afraid to chew the body of Christ. Guilt may appear in relation to God. A middle-aged woman disclosed tearfully that when she made her marital vows God knew she was intentionally marrying the wrong man. She deserved to suffer at the hands of her husband because she had lied to both God and him. World disasters reveal in the attribution of their causes the frame of mind of the interpreter. A young man who was struggling with his disowned homosexual wishes said emphatically that AIDS was God's proper punishment for gay men. Many other examples and more subtle questions could be brought to bear because people's interpretations of events in religious and other ways are inexhaustible. The therapist must be ready to question and examine the ways in which the patient relates to God, to organized religion, and to religious beliefs and practices in the context of the patient's private and universal sagas.

To be able to ask pertinent questions the therapist needs a certain knowledge of basic religious dogmas and practices. In the absence of such information the evaluator may directly ask the patient a question such as, "Is that the way your denomination requires it?" Most people are willing to instruct the therapist who asks an honest question. It is important that the evaluator not reveal her or his beliefs, or avow any particular religious dogma. This is not a matter of principle but of technique. Any objective statement on the therapist's part may inhibit the patient from revealing private feelings that go against recognized dogma or moral consensus. If the therapist talks about something as benign as God's love, it may close the possibility for the revelation of the private conviction that God hates the patient, or is terribly unfair. Rage against God the Father for Christ's crucifixion is not uncommon among children who have felt or fear their parents' cruelty. Many women today deeply resent a male godhead whose power seemingly distills every discrimination they have experienced. The therapist's abstinence from revealing any belief gives the patient latitude to expand freely on wishes, hopes, and complaints. It gives the therapist room to take nothing for granted, following the patient wherever necessary. A young man was certain he had made a pact with the Devil. Careful questioning revealed that he had watched a television program about someone who had made a pact with the Devil. When he saw the Devil on the screen he felt compelled to ask him for his help to kill his hated father. Thereafter he felt that the Devil had accepted his request as a pact and would demand its fulfillment. The young man had felt impotent rage toward his father and believed at the instant of "the pact" that only the Devil could control his father. A great panic came over him when he felt the Devil would "force" him to commit the murder. He ran to the hospital asking for release from his pact. He was not able to acknowledge his own murderous wishes. He needed projection and the paradoxical protection of the strong Devil to be able to control his own rage. The respectful acceptance of his story and the progressive clarification of issues without any statements about the reality of the Devil or the pact, was what he needed at the start. Discussing in great detail what the Devil might or might not want gave him enough psychic space and time to create a relation with the therapist and slowly explore his side of the story. The "Devil" served him well as a figure for displacement of unbearable patricidal feelings.

Religious Themes During Treatment

Religious themes frequently emerge during the course of treatment. Psychotherapy and psychoanalysis as clinical theories have much yet to learn about the meaning of religious associations during treatment. Careful documentation is required of clinical cases where the appearance of religious themes is related to transferential feelings, conflictual and regressive situations, and defensive moves. Such data would permit the creation of a clinical theory of the psychodynamic meanings of religious themes. An initial attempt to understand such matters starts from what is apparent. In the Western world religion has a well-defined godhead portrayed in a direct, even if disguised, anthropomorphic manner. Wishes, demands, feelings, motives, and intentions are attributed to God and given full credence. A God conceived in this manner has all the attributes of a human object. As such God can be used by the believer as any other object is used in the psychic realm, where wishes and defenses carry out the complex choreography between hope and fear, love and hatred, closeness and distance. In studying these matters the therapist may encounter two types of phenomena. The first is the dynamic process of when and how God is brought to the psychic forum. The second is the type of God representation and the transformations it undergoes during treatment.

God's Appearance During Treatment

Like all other human or imaginary objects, from parents to pets, God *never* appears in conscious associations without a dynamic motive. God's presence may take the form of a silent companion or a watchful vigilante. God may serve as a powerful defense against involvement with the therapist. God may be the depositary of displaced transferential love, hatred, or any other affect that feels too dangerous to express in the treatment situation. God is always an available alternative object for any affect or ideation that for dynamic reasons needs to be displaced without delay. Not only God but a full retinue of angels, saints, and souls of the deceased may be called to psychic duty at moments of transferential or psychodynamic need and appear in dreams and daydreams, as well as in spontaneous or official prayer. God's archenemies, the Devil and his fiends, can also be called on to take any evil the patient cannot bear.

A distinction must be made between God, the Devil, and their followers as a psychic representation in the mind of the patient, and any transcendent reality that may exist and correspond to such representations. A therapist, competent to understand the workings of the human mind, is not called upon to pass judgment about reality, either human or divine. The patient's psychic reality is what matters. If factual reality is to be found, the therapist has only one job: to assist the person to discover on her or his own the nature of reality. Any other attitude is indoctrination, whether about psychic processes, the world at large, or transcendent dimensions of life. Individuals in conflict need to find their own way with themselves, other people, the universe, and existence itself. Such a task is difficult and lonely, even in the company of a caring therapist. The clarification of this issue is indispensable: without it the therapist would find it strenuous to follow the patient along many difficult, bizarre, or confusing roads. Both patient and therapist need the respectful freedom of true explorers.

The joint search by a therapist and a patient for alleviation of the patient's psychic pain by discovering its private meaning awakens hidden hopes and dormant fears. The will to obtain help is obstructed by the fear of self-disclosure to an authority figure with imputed powers to deprive, humiliate, hate, hurt, or even kill. It is also hampered by longings to satisfy closeness or attain love and admiration. Fears and longings are in turn enmeshed in the unavoidable and usually subtle battle of wills and secret or overt competition about who gives and who gets, who is big and who is small. These ever-present dilemmas of human life appear in both partners at the very moment the therapeutic situation is established. The therapist's art resides in the double ability to discover the dynamic workings of such dilemmas in the therapist's mind before they affect the process, and to do the same with the patient, helping the patient to verbally articulate these workings as carefully as possible. (A treatment always examines the kinds of intentions suspected in the therapist as well as the conscious and unconscious intentions of the patient.) To carry out the task the partners must agree that the patient will try to be truly honest and keep no secrets. The contract is utopian but necessary. To make it real is at the core of the therapeutic work. In their conscious and unconscious efforts to protect themselves from predicted psychic pain, rejection, or humiliation, patients resort to anything at hand. Religion is one of the most subtle refuges from pain in the treatment. The patient may also resort to the consoling and soothing or frightening transcendental powers of religion in an effort to integrate therapeutic gains. In summary, religious themes, practices, and God can be used as a defense in the natural movement of unveiling private experience to a therapist, or as an integration of psychic changes into a system of beliefs. Integration does not mean heightened religiosity but an enhanced articulation of the meaning of spiritual dimensions in the context of preexistent religious belief.

The therapist requires attentiveness and creative imagination to follow the minute-by-minute psychic moves of the patient in what is explicitly said, in what is hinted at, and in what is not said. Unconscious motives and hidden meanings make all human communications fascinating riddles. Such creative attentiveness applies to religious issues as well. The prevailing defensive maneuvers that invoke divine direct or indirect assistance relate to transferential issues, most frequently transferential fears or powerful desires. Some examples will illustrate a few of the many defensive uses of religion.

Regression. A forlorn middle-aged man informed the therapist, a woman, that he had heard a very painful sermon about the love of God. The pain had to do with his wish *to feel* such love. During the service he imagined God, maybe Jesus, saying that he liked children and that people should be like children. Careful attention to the details of his *religious* images and feelings helped him discover that he not only wanted the love of God for him *as a child,* but that he had fantasized *before* going to church about sitting on the lap of the therapist and her telling him she loved him. He had always wanted his mother to do that.

Progression. A woman in treatment for anorexia nervosa attended church most Sundays of her life. She could never say a word about what the service was about, or even recall a portion of the homily. One day during the last therapy hour of the week she felt that she had truly been understood by her psychiatrist. She was amazed that someone could, in fact, want to listen to her. She felt gratitude towards her doctor, a new feeling for her. That Sunday she had another amazing experience, in church. She listened to the sermon, discovered that the pastor made some sense, and was surprised to hear him say that God loves all people, even those who have rejected Him. The therapeutic experience of a dedicated and attentive psychiatrist was transferred onto the minister and God. It was an indicator of a new level in her capacity to trust people as well as God.

Avoidance. A young enraged woman was always suspicious of the malevolent intent of her male therapist. She could not acknowledge her own fury and murderous wishes and persistently accused the therapist of evil aims, while demanding that she be loved and caressed like a small girl. In moments of great frustration she would withdraw into deep silence, punctuated by silent or loud prayer: "God help me." Exploration of her prayer surprisingly revealed that she was also furious with God but she wanted the therapist to feel she had an ally who could make him pay for treating her so badly and not giving her what she wanted. God served as a bodyguard, a menace, to show that she had the power to make the therapist feel rejected. God was a tool, a weapon, in a deeply entrenched transferential sadomasochistic battle. God's presence was her unconscious effort to avoid confronting the therapist directly while achieving her sadistic purpose.

Resistance. A woman in her middle twenties made passing allusions to her prayers, indicating that prayer was very important to her. Any efforts to help her discuss what her prayers were about met with sharp responses. She insisted that she would not reveal her spiritual life to a therapist who did not believe as much as she did. The psychologist said that he would listen respectfully but she insisted it was none of his business while still alluding to her religious life and how important it was to her. If she really meant her religious life to be private, she would not have enticed the therapist's attention with repeated references to it. There had to be an unconscious ulterior motive, and religion had very little to do with it. One of her prevailing character defenses was to veil and to reveal as a way of keeping herself half known. This defense in turn helped her to distract people from finding out that she was "a nothing." If she kept her interlocutor intrigued and confused enough, she would be able to keep him at a distance without his finding out about her and consequently rejecting her. Her prayers were more than transferential tricks, but she used them in the therapeutic situation in a hide-and-seek manner in the service of resistance.

Companionship. An adolescent boy who had lost his mother during the early latency period became very fond of his therapist and found separation from her very painful. At his mother's funeral he had been told she had gone to heaven. He felt he had to be a good boy to be able to reunite with her in the afterlife. The God representation had the mildly stern characteristics of his actual father. He was not too comfortable with either of them, but felt he needed both if he was going to survive. That was at the conscious level. Behind the paternal fatherlike God, there was a maternal God representation, with many traits of his greatly idealized dead mother. When the treatment reawakened the sharp pain of missing his mother, the days between sessions were very painful. He would then go to church and "talk" to God, making explicit his wish that he wanted to see his mother again. He found consolation in the solitude of the protective church and a soothing feeling that God and mother were watching him from above. In this case mother, God, and therapist formed a continuum of needed objects that could be used sequentially or simultaneously in an adaptive unconscious effort to modulate intensely painful affect in treatment. God facilitated the task of mourning the lost mother without losing hope, while at the same time providing a certain continuity to discontinuous sessions.

God as oedipal object. A man found himself bewildered by the intensity of transferential erotic feelings toward his therapist. He felt intensely dejected when he believed she had rejected him by taking a brief vacation. In his usual dramatic mode he thought he had to kill himself (there was no risk of suicide); he rushed to his pastor seeking help. The pastor assured him that God had wanted him since He had created him. The pastor proved his point with scriptural readings. The patient unconsciously experienced the pastor as someone who had given him permission to do what he wanted. When the therapist returned, the patient found himself describing an ego-syntonic fantasy of sexual intercourse with his mother. His mood was greatly improved. The encounter with the pastor provided him with a series of defensive moves to avoid the pain of feeling that the therapist had chosen other things over him, as his mother had done with his father. The pastor provided him with the needed "proof" that he was wanted, and he provided himself with an oedipal victory over his mother and a demonstration to his therapist that he had no erotic need for her because his mother would have sex with him. Creative, complex, and oedipally triumphant in its use of a pastor as an accomplice in oedipal crimes, this scenario helped him tolerate a pain he did not find himself capable of bearing. The moment had to be documented and saved to be analyzed when he could better tolerate the frustration of his intense wishes.

These examples of the psychodynamic processes surrounding religious themes in psychotherapy should underscore the fact that the therapist needs creative imagination and thinking to explore these issues with the patient. The combinations of wishes, defense, beliefs, and human interaction are infinite and each therapeutic pair is so unique that neither prescription nor formula can begin to do justice to their rich patterns. The purpose of this paper is to invite the therapist to discover new ways in which religious issues can appear in treatment and to document them for the benefit of all. When there is enough unbiased documentation of detailed processes involving the appearance of God or religion in treatment we, as professionals and researchers, will be ready to consider larger generalizations as part of our broader theory of psychodynamic processes.

Characteristics of the God Representation

The description the patient makes of her or his God as a psychological being with wishes, intents, motives, and actions can be of great help in understanding several issues. The developmental sources of the God representation appear in those characteristics that resemble traits of a primary or childhood figure. The levels of development and of regression are revealed in the type of God the person presents to the therapist and in the nature of the wishes God seemingly responds to. A God described as a being who loves unconditionally, forgives everything, never gets angry, and watches over you all the time points in the direction of a wish for an idealized parent who would respond to oral and protective demands without requiring a superego response from the believer. A God who is frequently resorted to while constantly feared for his potential for retaliation for wishes and minor crimes may uncover a harsh parent as well as a superego aware of hateful, sadistic wishes or oedipal complexities.

It is always helpful to get some idea at the beginning of the treatment of how the patient represents his God. Often the psychic changes brought about by the treatment may help the patient modify the God representation by means of changes in self-perception as well as changes in the representation, and in the remembering, of the parents in childhood. The God representation may serve as an indicator of subtle psychic changes by providing evidence for the effect of the treatment in transforming deeply settled convictions originating in childhood perceptions.

Attention to detail is also very important. Questions about God's intentions, moods, character traits, and plans may seem a bit strange because we are not used to asking them. On the other hand, patients who believe, think about these issues consciously and quite frequently outside awareness.

Termination

The mutually agreed-upon termination of satisfactory psychotherapy is of great significance for lasting results. Termination as a process is frequently an abbreviated recapitulation of the therapy. Transient regressions to difficult developmental moments are followed by rediscovery of the solutions found during the treatment. The back-and-forth process consolidates the gains and serves as a way of reviewing the events that patient and therapist have gone through together. In mapping out a trip they had embarked on without a map they review their trajectory and recognize that the time for separation is drawing near. The patient has to continue her or his life pilgrimage guided by self-knowledge and by those who share her or his life. Images of departure and the time after the therapy frequently bring with them reflections about larger analogues such as death, afterlife, God the transcending creator, and life as an existential journey. The emergence of such issues, and the patient's need to grapple with them, is a sure indicator that the treatment has helped the patient to face life as it is, a mysterious voyage between birth and death. The therapist in turn has in her or his hands a very special occasion to observe, without the great urgency of earlier transferential moments, the type of representational changes that the patient, the patient's immediate family, and God have undergone as a result of the treatment. The documentation of such changes is invaluable for theorizing about more general issues related to the function of religion in psychic life.

A satisfactorily completed treatment, particularly if the therapist has encouraged the patient to examine all aspects of her or his life including beliefs, is frequently significant for the patient's religious attitude. The changes in self representation, in emotional maturity, in styles of sublimation, in ways of relating to others including the patient's God, do have an impact, however subtle, on the patient's manner of being religious. A woman in her early twenties asked for help because she was failing in school and was frightened by her wild sadistic sexual fantasies and their mild enactment. She was the child of wealthy, highly hedonistic parents who never said a word about religion to their children. The parental behavior towards the children was simultaneously psychologically sadistic and seductive. Constant insistence on her appearance made her withdraw into passive aggressive retaliation through failure and sloppy looks. Prolonged treatment helped her separate from the sadomasochistic attachment to her mother and distance herself from her seductively frustrating father. She was able to define herself, marry, and find a meaningful profession. When these goals were achieved, and during termination time, she looked at the whole world as a universe for the first time. She produced a wish for a religion and a God. She had no religious knowledge and had never set foot in any temple except for social religious ceremonies. After several months of soulsearching she created her own religion by becoming a mild theist. She decided there was a God somewhere whom she was willing to respect. She was not able to say what God was like except that God—unlike her parents—deserved respect. Respect was the deepest feeling that had developed between her and her female therapist. She felt respected and in turn respected the therapist. The feeling was the result of their relation since before it she had not felt respected or respectable. To show her respect for her God she invented her own home rituals. She selected some holidays, read about them, and then celebrated them "in a religious spirit" with special meals and a few candles. She felt quite satisfied with her "religion" and her practices became her tradition.

Religion has nothing to fear from psychotherapy. A person who has made some peace with her or his inner world is well disposed to hear human or divine communications. The worst abuse of religion by the human race has been by believers who have projected their personal hatred onto a cruel and destructive divinity whose vengeful jealousy condones horrifying crimes in the name of God. Human history is a long and painful record that religion without self-examination can be a terrifying justification for the vilest of tortures and destruction. However, religion as an integrated transformation of human predicaments, suffering, and hope into a socially sound faith that allows for sublimation of personal developmental joys and pains may be an essential component of individual and societal health.

Reference

Rizzuto, Ana-Maria. 1979. *The Birth of the Living God: A Psychoanalytic Study.* Chicago: University of Chicago Press.

Countertransference and Transference Aspects of Religious Material in Psychotherapy:

The Isolation or Integration of Religious Material

Tim Kochems

For a psychotherapist to talk, or not to talk, about religion within an intensive psychoanalytic psychotherapy relationship is to assume a position within a complex matrix of countertransference and transference issues. The first part of this paper defines a range of positions frequently taken by therapists and clients. The bipolar extremes of this range are two contrasting forms of what I call the isolation of religious material. One pole is identified by the devaluation of religious material and the other by the specialness of religious material. Points between these poles allow varying degrees of interaction between, or even integration of, a person's religious material and psychological structure and dynamics. The positions that a psychotherapist and a client take along this range have major implications for the process of psychotherapy.

The major part of this paper describes a therapeutic stance that highlights the isolation of religion as it occurs within the treatment and then often leads to integration by understanding a client's personal representations of God, working with this religious material within the transference, and integrating the therapist's awareness of countertransference issues regarding religion. This stance simultaneously illuminates important aspects of the client's personality and the process of the psychotherapy. In response to this stance the client feels invited to interact more with personal religious material with the increased likelihood that it will be better integrated into the client's developing psychological structure and dynamics.

When a person's avoidance of conflict or use of isolation becomes maladaptive in some way, an intensive psychoanalytic psychotherapy with an emphasis on transference interpretation may be helpful. The purpose of such treatment is to facilitate the person's expression of difficult, conflicting feelings within a real relationship while the person's avoidance, interpersonal, and intrapersonal dynamics and psychic structure are gradually understood in the context of the therapeutic relationship and the transference. I hope to illustrate in the case study that the same principles may apply to a person's relationship to God representations. Frequently, there are parallels between a relationship to a God representation and other important relationships. As the transference relationship is worked through and relationships mature, the probability increases that the relationship to God representations will mature also.

The Isolation of Religion in Individuals

I use the word *isolation* descriptively and for heuristic purposes. I know that it invokes associations to isolation as a defense that protects a person's equilibrium from psychic content that could be experienced as disruptive. In the descriptive sense used here, isolation can offer protection in two different and opposing ways. Isolation of religious material can protect one from external as well as internal religious stimulation experienced as threatening to one's psychological structures and dynamics. In addition, isolation can also refer to a structure and dynamic system in which religious material is protected from other, nonreligious, disruptive experiences.

Both poles of the isolation regard religious material as an untouchable aspect of human experience, as if religious material is not able to be—or should not be—integrated into a healthy, developing, fully-human person. At one extreme, religion is felt to be controlling in a repressive, harmful way, or simply a fantasy, a waste of time and energy to consider seriously. This position might be stated as, "Keep it out of my life. It is hurtful or useless." At the other extreme, religion is felt to be so sacred and pure that one's "real life" would only taint it. One might hear, "Keep away from my religion. Anything else is meaningless or dangerous in comparison to something so special." Again, implicit in both positions is the feeling that religious material cannot and should not be integrated into one's entire psychological experience.

One man, when considering the quality or meaning of his life, actively assumed a devaluing position toward religion, spirituality, God, and the question of his own faith. His isolation of religion restricted him from exploring a number of rich philosophical and religious traditions and experiences, including those of his own culture and family. The isolation protected him from feeling the disruptive influence of his family's dynamic interactions with him, which he associated with his family's religion. It also helped to protect him from experiencing a longing for, and anger at, his father. The anger was displaced, directed toward his religion.

A woman held religion to be so special that she did not want to question or diminish it by bringing it into contact with other aspects of her real self and the world—in this case, aspects of her sexuality. Her isolation of religion helped her to maintain an emotionally constricted equilibrium. As long as her religion was treated as so special that it could not be associated with her sexuality, her sexuality as well as her religious material were difficult to integrate fully into her maturing psychological structure and dynamics. In the course of her psychotherapy, a dynamic change occurred to the special, unquestioned, untouched position of religion. It remained important and informative to her but it was no longer as controlling and not her major source of psychic structure. Her sexuality was also experienced differently. At first it began to feel more threatening and out of control but later it became more attractive and capable of integration.

The Isolation of Religion in Interpersonal Systems

This process of isolation functions at the individual level, the interpersonal level (e.g., in a psychotherapy relationship), and even at a cultural level—the cultures of nations, professions, or families. I will identify two broad and contrasting tendencies at the cultural level. One example is the religious culture characteristic of some fundamentalist Christian groups, where religion operates as a special, unquestioned, isolated source of control over (sometimes even replacing) other valid experiences of oneself or relationships. Anger, sexuality, or self-esteem typically cannot approach the special position of religion.

In contrast, other major portions of our contemporary American culture stress utilitarian and expressive individualism (Bellah, Madsen, Sullivan, Swidler, and Tipton 1985). In this example, individuals have difficulty with religion because of its emphasis on, commitment to, and experience of, something outside one's conscious awareness and control; as a result of psychological pressure any religious sentiment is devalued or avoided.

In psychotherapeutic cultures, religion is often isolated or consciously devalued. One reason is Freud's well-documented beliefs about the psychological meaning of religion (Rizzuto 1979; Meissner 1984). He held a reductionistic view of religion as an immature longing for the idealized father to meet security or primary process needs. Today his views are held by many psychoanalytic psychotherapists. A second factor is the pressure felt by social scientists to follow a scientific method that traditionally has emphasized objective measurement (Ragan, Malony, and Beit-Hallahmi 1980). Most of the religious material in psychotherapy is beyond the purview of such empiricism.

That isolation of religion occurs in professional psychological circles has been documented for years. In the first edition of *The Individual and His Religion: A Psychological Interpretation,* Gordon Allport (1950) wrote: "During the past fifty years religion and sex seem to have reversed their positions . . . Today, by contrast [to William James at the turn of the century], psychologists write with the frankness of Freud or Kinsey on the sexual passions of mankind, but blush and grow silent when the religious passions come into view." Even if not blushing or silent, data from 357 experienced psychiatrists, psychologists, and social workers in the greater Boston area (Kochems 1982) suggests the range of positions that isolate religion. The study found that many therapists had either generally positive views about their own broadly defined religiosity and that of their clients, *or* generally negative views. More important, a statistical analysis of the therapists' own self-reports reveals that they managed the religious material of their clients based on how they personally felt about religion (positively or negatively). Imagine the treatment implications of psychotherapists discussing other topics— sex, parental relationships, anger—based on their own positive or negative feelings about these topics.

In other words, both groups of psychotherapists in this study isolated religion. They tended to make general judgments about religious material without taking into account each client's specific material and how it functioned in each client's life. The judgments were held separately, cut off, isolated from the specific data.

While isolation of religion among psychotherapists seems to be common, a subcommittee of the Group for the Advancement of Psychiatry studying religion estimated that as much as 33 percent of randomly selected psychoanalytic material may have religious associations or derivatives (Committee on Psychiatry and Religion 1968). This suggests that religious material has great potential to reflect or amplify the meaning of other clinical material, including its psychological sources and implications. It is remarkable that a topic that arises so frequently is psychotherapy is also so frequently avoided. In the Boston study of psychotherapists, 50 percent tended to agree with the statement "I find that religion in my psychotherapy practice follows the general rule: If you don't ask about it, you don't hear about it." However, it was also clear that few psychotherapists routinely asked about a client's religiosity— with the exception of questions regarding religious denomination. Most seemed to think that a client's religion is important for the psychotherapist to know about only if it is directly related to a client's problems. In the Boston study, 82 percent of the experienced psychotherapists tended to agree with the statement "I initiate exploration of my clients' religious or antireligious values, behavior, or experiences only if they directly influence my clients' problems."

If clients do not explicitly volunteer religious material, how would a therapist know whether a specific client's religiosity directly influences his or her behavior? If one-third of randomly selected analytic material has religious associations or derivatives, how can a therapist miss the opportunity to use such material in exploring aspects of a client's personality structure and dynamics, experiences, and the context of his or her difficulties? Too frequently it seems that when it comes to religious material, psychotherapists either do not ask or do not hear.

If psychotherapists do not ask, hear, or talk about the religious material of their clients, they are not being objective or neutral about religious material. They are colluding with any one of a number of cultural or personal pressures to isolate religion. They are being influenced in antitherapeutic ways by countertransference feelings rather than using those feelings to better understand themselves, their clients, and the psychotherapy process. A psychotherapist's collusion in the isolation of religion sends a clear message to a client that religious material cannot—or should not—interact with (or perhaps be integrated with) the rest of one's psychological structure and dynamics.

Representations of God and the Technique of Psychotherapy

One type of religious material that I identify and utilize in psychotherapy is my client's representations of God. It is hypothesized that everyone affected by Western culture has an intrapsychic representation or image of God (Rizzuto 1979; McDargh 1983; Leavy 1988). Very early in the life of the child, this God representation is formed from a variety of sources. It may function and develop throughout the life cycle as any transitional object may be formed, function, and develop within transitional space (Rizzuto 1979; Meissner 1984). As first described by D. W. Winnicott, transitional objects and space have aspects of both "reality and fantasy" (Winnicott 1951) or, from another perspective, objective reality and subjective psychological reality.

The technique I use in approaching this material *allows for the possibility* that just as a client's parents may possess an objective reality distinct from the client's parental representations, God may possess a reality distinct from the client's representation of God and the representations that contributed to it. An important corollary of this assumption is that the client's representation of God reflects *but is not limited to, or reducible to,* aspects of the client's intrapsychic representations, including those of the client's parents and, later, the psychotherapist. In a less clinically focused context, the Freudian psychoanalyst, Leavy (1988), makes similar points using the word *imago* as roughly equivalent to "representation" as used here:

> The concept [of imago] is strained a little in the form of "God-imago"; nevertheless it is worthwhile to juxtapose the two aspects of the imago dei: on the one hand, the likeness to God that we owe to our creator; on the other hand, the likeness of our creator that we hold, often unbeknownst, in our minds. The latter imago is likely to remain under the sovereignty of parental imagos that are difficult to dispel, and therein lies much of our unbelief. (p. xii)

As a way of exploring a client's religious material in depth, I attempt to understand how a client's representations of God may be related to the client's defenses, identity, intrapsychic structure, sense of self, and interpersonal relationships. I also work with this material within the transference. The emphasis is on interaction and relationship as opposed to isolation.

The Purpose and Limits of the Case Presentation

What follows is an exposition of the therapeutic stance outlined above with a client named John. He viewed and experienced religion very positively but he held it as too special to be experienced with his anger and sexuality. My therapeutic stance did not reinforce John's tendencies or those of his culture.

The exposition focuses on the beginning phase of this twice-weekly psychoanalytic psychotherapy. This phase is particularly important in establishing whether or not, and how, religious aspects of a client will be identified and managed by the therapist. Initial countertransference issues are also very important. The beginning phase of treatment establishes the structure of the treatment and the methods by which transference material will be identified and managed. The subsequent phase of treatment involves the long, slow, repetitive working through of the transference experience, its many meanings, and implications.

To insure confidentiality, only a selected sample of data reflective of the client, his psychotherapy, and his religious material will be related here. The following discussion is not meant to be definitive regarding the meaning of this client's religious material or the meaning of religious material in all psychotherapy.

THE CASE OF JOHN V.

John V. was an only child who had lived his entire life in a mid-Atlantic state. He was in his thirties when he began treatment. At that time he was functioning fairly effectively. He longed for a stable relationship with his father in which he would feel valued, and he needed more psychological distance from his mother. John experienced his mother as overstimulating, and he was overidentified with her. Within the first two sessions, John presented himself as a religiously committed individual to whom spiritual growth was important. Like most clients, however, his spiritual growth was not mentioned as part of his presenting complaints.

I assumed that John's religious material was relevant to other aspects of his life. I obtained more information about John's religious values and life, specifically why he identified himself as someone to whom spiritual growth was important. During this exploration, John said that he was fearful that psychotherapy would interfere with or change his religious values, against his will. He warned me to be careful with these values. I attempted to communicate to John that I had heard his concerns accurately. I said that his spirituality and his concerns about the treatment would be talked about, monitored, and understood better as the treatment progressed. Privately, I wondered to what extent these concerns and warnings signified some attempt on John's part to isolate religion from the rest of his life or from the therapy.

Since psychoanalytic psychotherapy is a very powerful method for helping a client develop and change characteristic approaches to, or experiences of, self and others, a client's faith perspective may also develop or change. John had some cause for concern. Usually a client is aware of, and consciously working toward, the changes that can occur as a result of psychotherapy. However, it is important to note that psychotherapy can have significant unintended effects. These effects are best identified and even shaped by the therapeutic process itself, when the psychotherapist has a consistent, respectful, active, comprehensive, and empathic interest in the client's life, with every aspect understood as meaningful. The client's religious/spiritual life—or the apparent lack of one—should certainly be included in this empathic interest that actively works against the development of a therapist's potential blind spots and countertransference assumptions. It also identifies and allows for the control of any unintended effects of the therapy on the client's religiosity.

John was very perceptive and critical, and he was wary of having his own experience devalued. I believe he would not have entrusted his spirituality to me *to the degree that he did* had I not gradually conveyed to him over the course of the therapy my respect for and personal valuing of belief and ideals. Although the belief and values I expressed were not religious (e.g., the important of the experience of love in one's life), it was clear to John that I had beliefs and values that were important to me and to which I did not adhere just because of psychological principles.

A psychotherapist must know and be in immediate contact with the reality, power, and value of belief and ideals (not necessarily religious ones). From another perspective, I am talking about the reality, power, and value of ideals, transitional objects, and space. These transitional objects, part reality and part illusion, are used and develop throughout one's life and are invested with belief. (I often wonder whether Freud's theory might be usefully described as a kind of transitional object for him.)

The Initial Countertransference Issue: To Explore or Not

Very simply described, the two basic countertransference positions are *to support* or *to react against* the client's spirituality or culture in regard to religion. Either position can undermine the therapist's consistent, active interest in empathically understanding religion as a meaningful part of the client's whole life. According to Kernberg (1965), there are two sources for these countertransference positions: the classical view states that the therapist's own personal or cultural assumptions control or overwhelm his or her more professionally open and reasoned reactions to the client; the totalistic view is that the therapist, reacting to the client perhaps through some projective identification, is enacting an important dynamic in the client's life.

Asking more about John's religious material was the first potential countertransference issue in this treatment. The potentially supportive countertransference position would have been to reinforce the special and isolated position religion held in John's life (e.g., by not asking about religion at all, thereby protecting it, or by promising to consciously leave religion out of the therapy).

The other potential countertransference position, that of reacting against John's spirituality, would have occurred if I had devalued his beliefs by ignoring or rejecting them. Another way of reacting against his position would have been to attack his beliefs disrespectfully, thereby giving him more reason to isolate or protect them. The same might have occurred if I had shared positive views of religion and attempted to focus our time together on talking about religion for my own satisfaction. He could have justifiably experienced such behavior as both an intrusion that broke the contract and boundaries of the therapy and as an attempt to gratify my own needs to have someone to talk to about religion.

At this point in the treatment, there were only subtle hints that John had experienced even my standard respectful inquiries as dangerous, therefore validating his need to isolate and protect his religious material from me. Developments later in the treatment amplified this dynamic and its sources in his past experience. Had John been more conflicted or psychologically impaired, this dynamic would have been much more obvious and powerful, requiring a modification of my usual style in order to be empathically attentive to his needs. The religious area of his life would have been explored much more gradually.

Clearly, continual self-analysis and collegial consultation are important monitors of the therapist's motivations when intervening, as well as of the therapist's understanding of the client and the client's transference. In psychoanalytic psychotherapy, whenever the therapist intervenes, a position is always taken in the complex matrix of transference and countertransference issues.

Religious Material: John's First Representation of God

Throughout John's life and his early treatment, his father reportedly possessed a presence that John often tried to ignore, sometimes despised, frequently disrespected, yet always felt. In a severely obsessive-compulsive manner, Mr. V. anxiously criticized and stopped all initiative within the family to do anything beyond the repetitive routines of everyday life. To the expressed needs of his wife or son for more stimulation and more involvement in their lives, he offered nothing. John's associations revealed that his representation of God paralleled this description of his father. In response to a direct question, John said that God was a distant, judgmental old man who would banish anyone who transgressed his rules. John's father and God modeled isolation as a defense, as so much of life's emotions and activities was devalued, denied, or repressed. This was the earliest representation of God that John was aware of in his life, and it was the first representation of God identified in the treatment.

During the first six months of treatment this representation was also observed in the transference. While demonstrating increased openness and trust with me, John expressed disappointment with me for not giving him the attention and interest he longed for from a father figure. Within the transference, John was actually experiencing and expecting me to be the same as his nonresponsive, judgmental, and controlling father representation and his representation of God. At the same time, these early feelings indicated that John was trusting, testing, and hoping that I was different.

Anger: Transference and Countertransference

About two months into the treatment, for the first time John expressed his anger at my perceived inattention. He felt shaken by this experience since anger was usually split-off or isolated from his sense of self. John then began a discussion of faith. He introduced the concept of faith biblically (Mark 2:22), saying, "You can't put new wine into old wineskins. They'll break." In response to a question about this biblical reference, John explained that he wondered whether or not he could have faith or trust that I would be able to change my therapeutic style (the old wineskin) enough to be helpful to him (the new wine). He wondered whether he should leave the treatment, not wanting to be frustrated as he had been with his father for so many years. This reference might also reflect a wish and longing to have the many experiences of his self—including his anger—contained or held by me (and his father and his God). There was a concomitant fear of being dropped again, not valued, disappointed, and rejected. John's self-idealization in comparing himself to the "new wine" usually associated with Jesus will be addressed later in this discussion. It clearly seemed to be a defensive reaction to the narcissistic injury associated with not feeling attended to.

This was a critical point in the psychotherapy. John was able to risk expressing his anger directly to me. While he thought about leaving therapy because of his anger (which would have reinforced its isolation), he remained in treatment. He did not have to flee from experiencing anger as a part of his self or from any retribution from me. In fact, after this session (from about the third month on), John's anger at his father came alive in the treatment. He then knew through experience that he could risk expressing it. He gave detailed attention to current, frustrating interactions with his father and associated childhood memories. As John felt more capable and freer to express his feelings of anger, he revealed for the first time feelings of humiliation and inadequacy, particularly in comparison to his imposing father. He was expressing powerful feelings associated with an oedipal dilemma: indignation toward his father as well as feelings of being weak and inadequate in comparison. On at least one occasion during this period, John expressed how guilty and fearful he felt about being angry at his father.

In the transference John began working with issues related to his experience of his father. He wondered whether having a relationship with a therapist signified that he was inadequate. He responded to these feelings of inadequacy in the transference with anger and rebellion, or submission and humiliation.

I had to allow John to express his anger at me without becoming defensive or ignoring it, minimizing it, reacting with anger, or deflecting the anger onto John or his father or God. Similarly, I had to allow John to express his anger at God without ignoring it or deflecting it onto himself or his father. For a religious person to express anger at God can be an important, albeit fearful, experience. Obviously, countertransference issues are also relevant here. A therapist's own views of religion or religious issues in treatment could easily short-circuit this important process. Interpretation of John's anger at *God,* too soon or consistently, as also a reflection of his anger at his father—or me—

would have diffused or controlled John's anger. Interpretation of John's anger at *me,* too soon or consistently, as also a reflection of his anger at his father—or God—would also have been an attempt by me to diffuse or control John's anger. Either course would have prevented him from experiencing anger as an aspect of himself that deserves attention and understanding by himself and his therapist and God. On the other hand, if I ignored John's anger, it could have been a message to John that he was insignificant to me or that he could not affect me. If this had happened, John and I (in my countertransference) clearly would have been reenacting frustrating and hurtful aspects of his relationship with his father.

The Second Representation of God

During the first six months, one of the ways in which John thought about leaving the treatment was to wonder whether he needed pastoral counseling or spiritual guidance with a religious professional, instead of psychotherapy. Pastoral counseling was associated with several important elements of John's transference and psychic functioning: it served as a resistance to the further development of the transference and it was another expression of his rejecting, belittling anger toward me. It also introduced a triangulation that seemed to parallel his relationship to his parents. John talked about a pastoral counselor as an alternative to the therapist especially at those times when he perceived the therapist as too frustrating. John often talked about his mother as a saving alternative to his father. As the therapist reflected a representation of God that was similar to John's experience of his father, the pastoral counselor was related to a different, alternative representation of God that was similar to John's experience of his mother. With this, a second representation of God was beginning to be observed in the treatment.

In contrast to John's unresponsive, frustrating father, John's mother was very supportive. John's transference feelings toward me were that I was as frustrating to him as his father. John felt that perhaps a pastoral counselor would be as supportive as his mother. Throughout his early life, at least until adolescence, he consciously wanted to be like her rather than his father. He often felt that she was the stable ground on which he stood. Strongly traditionally religious, she consistently seemed to be the source of all things positive in John's life. However, she was not only supportive, she was also overly stimulating. He remembered several occasions during his early years when she was sexually provocative. She would often tell him that she found him more enjoyable and involved than his father, and she would help him avoid his father's strictures. Her behavior fueled an idealized image John had of himself that could have been associated with his earlier image of himself in the treatment as "the new wine."

The second, alternative, representation of God explicitly appeared about six months into the therapy. This was God represented as an image of a steady wall of concrete that John would stand on or hold onto when everything seemed chaotic around him. This representation of God was always described as existing in the midst of a chaos that felt simultaneously exciting and overwhelming. For John, one of the best qualities of this representation of God was that it was not "sterile," a word he had used more than once to describe his father. In contrast, this second representation of God was stimulating. It was clearly associated to his mother as a responsive, stable, exciting, and confusing alternative to his father. She often appeared in John's dreams in a role that was similar to this stable God amidst exciting chaos.

Another possible interpretation of some of the images during this period came from John's association of a strong male (e.g., an upright steel girder) amid the excitement and confusion associated with his mother. This association seemed to reflect a wish for his father or God to give him the strength and distance he needed to manage his mother better, and an experience of the stability of the therapy.

Countertransference Issues with Sexuality, Religion, and Mother

Periodically, John would mention that he did not know my personal religious beliefs, if any. Since he did not directly ask, I did not share my beliefs, although I felt countertransference impulses to do so. Sharing my personal beliefs might have trespassed important boundaries, paralleling the behavior of John's mother and creating a countertransferential reenactment. For the gratification of her own needs, John's mother contributed to the compromised boundaries in their idealized, protected relationship. If I had initiated sharing my beliefs to have a special relationship with John for my gratification—thus compromising boundaries—I would have been inviting John into another idealized relationship that could not be fulfilled and would obstruct his continued self-knowledge, self-acceptance, and growth. He might, for example, have felt even more pressure not to express anger with me.

John had some sense of this. Several times during the course of the treatment he said that while he had desires to know more about me, he did not want to know about me personally, or about my beliefs. Much later, as termination approached, John revealed that in the beginning of the treatment he had felt that even my questions about religion were for my personal gratification. Looking back on the beginning of the treatment, John revealed that he had angrily thought about withholding religious information. This impulse demonstrated again his defensiveness and isolation of religion—his protection of the special position religion and his mother had in his life. It also suggested a preconscious awareness that boundaries are important to maintain, that no one else should be allowed to trespass in the uncontrolled manner of his mother.

I believe my own questions were appropriate, reasonable interventions with the growth of the client as the primary goal. They definitely tested limits and boundaries, but did so openly and in a way that could be talked about, monitored, and understood. Within a transference-countertransference matrix, my questions paralleled the behavior of John's mother. They were experienced as selfishly intrusive. Of course, his experience also indicated an ongoing maternal transference. The maternal transference, in fact, was addressed directly later in the treatment, after the period covered in this discussion.

Sexuality and the Second Representation of God

As a result of his mother's stimulation and sexual provocation, John's second representation of God amidst exciting chaos was also associated with sexuality. John described a number of events when he was in his late twenties as "psychic rape." His first, major, religious conversion experience was also associated with this phrase. These events occurred in work situations in which he thought he would be able to follow his religious values and help people who were impoverished in a variety of ways. He was consciously overstimulated by and emotionally drawn to the neglect, neediness, impulsive sex, and violence experienced by the people whom he was trying to help. Each time he explicated these experiences, he associated his experience of psychotherapy to them.

In these situations, John could not rely on the obsessive formal strictures of life—learned from his father—to protect him from the associated anxiety. He was buffeted between overstimulation and rigid defensiveness, between his competing identifications with his mother and father. As John was able to report these experiences and the feelings associated with them, he shared new feelings of guilt and shame associated with other past personal experiences of illicit sexual contact and the disruption of interpersonal boundaries.

The Expression of Sex and Anger
Within the Father Transference

As this impulsive, previously split-off material was revealed (six to eight months into the treatment), John often talked about my eyes looking at him like an intense, piercing laser *and* as the all-seeing, judgmental eyes of God—associated with his father as well. Within the transference, he actively worried whether I (God, his father) would judge and reject him—banish him from treatment. These feelings were reflected in some of John's fantasies: I might hospitalize him or send him to prison because he felt his feelings were so overwhelming and uncontained. These uncontained feelings were depicted in sexual fantasies with women and aggressive fantasies in which he violently exercised power over me.

In one session eight months into the treatment, he continued to share the fantasy of demonstrating some physical power or capability over me. He also reported the words of a song that he associated with me: "Does he really love me?" as well as a very intense, graphic image that combined religion, orality, and male sexual aggression directed at me. These were very difficult internal events for John to share. They illustrated the interconnectedness of John's religiosity, sexuality, anger, and longing to be accepted (taken) into (or sadistically forcing his way into) my life. The specific religious aspect of the image echoed the "new wine" image and John's idealized self. John feared the sexual and aggressive impulses so graphically depicted in the image. The feelings of longing reflected in the events he reported also frightened him. He felt it was humiliating and shameful to have such impulses and to share them with me. He also thought that he might be rejected by me for having such impulses. He wondered if he might be psychotic because the image was so disorienting and confusing. He did not know how to integrate it into his sense of self.

These images, reflecting previously unconscious feelings and aspects of John's self, were touched in the therapy because the transference was allowed to fully develop. Sexual and aggressive feelings were simultaneously held with feelings about his mother, father, God, and therapist. John was frightened at what had been uncovered in him by the transference. He was also thankful that the therapy allowed and helped him to touch extremely sensitive, powerful core material in his personality. In addition to making this depth of treatment possible, the therapeutic relationship, of which the transference was a major part, made this material safe and useful. He experienced this material within a relationship that contained and held it—a relationship that gave him a context not only to feel this material, but within which it could mature and gradually be integrated.

At this early point, eight to nine months into the treatment, I did not interpret this material deeply. Since John felt it to be so potentially disorganizing, humiliating, and provocative my comments were directed at making it clear to him that I respected its expression, that it was possible to contain it, and that we would gradually view it as meaningful in many ways. We had already begun to talk about his longing for a loving father, his reactive anger and grandiosity at feeling devalued and controlled by his father and other men, and the consolidation of his masculine identity.

Signs of Integration and Relationship: A Third Representation of God

By the tenth month of treatment, psychotherapy and I had become a central part of John's conscious daily life. He looked forward to sessions and continued to explore and associate to the material that he uncovered. In addition to the transference feelings related to his father and a particular representation of God, John talked about my recognizing him and affirming him. He appreciated me for being able to maintain my own boundaries—unlike his mother—even while holding intensely emotional material—unlike his father, whose rigid, obsessive defenses would not permit such material to be recognized. John felt he was making progress in acknowledging aspects of his life—anger, sexuality, and his desire to be valued by his father—and feeling comfortable with them for the first time.

Ten to twelve months into the treatment, John began to talk to me about a new way that he was praying. He had changed from cognitive, discursive, conversational prayer to contemplative, quiet, repetitive prayer. He experienced this as a more calming way to pray, more accepting of his true self. He felt it allowed him to be more open, rather than obsessive like his father, or hysterical like his mother. It was clearly less structured and effortful on his part and at the same time less emotionally stimulating and intense. Since it was still well grounded in his religious tradition, it was clear that as he grew personally he did not have to abandon his religious values. In fact, he was experiencing aspects of his tradition that actually reinforced his new growth.

During the next year of treatment, the feelings and transference material that have been described continued to be worked through gradually and on deeper levels. John shared murderous feelings toward me, and his mother was shown to be a major factor in his sexuality. These images and feelings stirred anxiety, but he was gradually becoming more critical of, and differentiated from, his mother. He was also feeling more appreciative of his father, and related more consistently and maturely to other people. As he was increasingly able to know and hold more aspects of himself in his relationship with me, he developed more differentiated views of his parents and others, including God.

About two years into the treatment, John reported a powerful, positive religious experience. He saw God collect in God's arms fragments of John that were scattered throughout the universe, and then pour these parts into John. This was the first time that John talked explicitly about what became a third representation of God that seemed to reflect some of his experiences in psychotherapy. It also reflected his experience of, and transference to, me. This was a God who could recognize, collect, and hold the many aspects of John that had often felt unintegrated and make him feel they were valuable and available to him. This representation of God seemed very much associated to the new way of prayer that he had been practicing for about a year. As the therapy progressed, John continued to rework the same feelings and themes, each time with more depth, understanding, and integration. While John's first two representations of God still characterized some of his experiences, his third representation of God became more stable and available to him, more supportive of his continued growth.

John is an example of a person having two distinct representations of God which coexisted for much of his life. The first representation was of a nonresponsive, judgmental God associated with John's father. The second representation of God amidst exciting chaos was related to his experience of his mother as both responsive and overstimulating. This case illustrates how, facilitated by psychotherapy, a new representation of God can develop. This new representation existed along with the other two and was clearly related to the experience of the therapy.

This therapy experience was intense and emotionally demanding of John. It required him to become aware of, share, and then hold within a relationship, aspects of himself that he had previously shared with no one else—aspects that were previously repressed, split-off, or isolated. He had to tolerate ambivalent and conflicting feelings. Within the therapy, these aspects of John were gradually identified, attended to, valued, and integrated.

In addition, he had a closely related, very moving, and powerful experience of God as seeing, attending to, and integrating his entire person. This experience came at a time when John felt murderous feelings toward me, and was perceived by John as both independent of the therapist and yet supportive of the therapist and psychotherapy.

One may speculate that if John's religious material had not been integrated into this psychotherapy, John's God representations might have been isolated from the benefits and development of the transference as well as the concomitant maturing of his object relations generally. John might have been able to continue to isolate his religion from the rest of his life. There is also the possibility that John's religion would have gradually become less vital to his life as he—and his religion—became more differentiated from his parents, and he continued to think that religion could not be integrated with feelings of sexuality and anger. Isolation of religious material within the psychotherapy would have supported its isolation by John in his psychological structure and dynamics, impeding the development of more mature, differentiated object relations.

References

Allport, G. W. 1950. *The Individual and His Religion: A Psychological Interpretation.* New York: Macmillan.

Bellah, R., R. Madsen, W. Sullivan, A. Swidler, and S. Tipton. 1985. *Habits of the Heart: Individualism and Commitment in American Life*. Berkeley: University of California Press.

Committee on Psychiatry and Religion. 1968. The psychic function of religion in mental illness and mental health. *Group for the Advancement of Psychiatry* 6(7).

Kernberg, O. 1965. Notes on countertransference. *Journal of the American Psychoanalytic Association* 13: 38–56.

Kochems, T. P. 1983. The relationship of background variables to the experiences and values of psychotherapist in managing religious material. (Ph.D. dissertation, George Washington University, 1982). *Dissertation Abstracts International* (order no. 83111196).

Leavy, Stanley A. 1988. *In the Image of God: A Psychoanalyst's View*. New Haven: Yale University Press.

McDargh, John. 1983. *Psychoanalytic Object Relations Theory and the Study of Religion: On Faith and the Imaging of God*. Lanham, Md.: University Press of America.

Meissner, William W. 1984. *Psychoanalysis and Religious Experience*. New Haven: Yale University Press.

Ragan, C., N. H. Malony, and B. Beit-Hallahmi. 1980. Psychologists and religion: Professional factors associated with personal belief. Unpublished manuscript.

Rizzuto A. 1979. *The Birth of the Living God: A Psychoanalytic Study*. Chicago: University of Chicago Press.

Winnicott, D. W. 1951. Transitional objects and transitional phenomena. Printed 1958 in *Collected Papers: Through Pediatrics to Psychoanalysis*, pp. 229–42. London: Tavistock.

Ministry or Therapy:

The Role of Transference and Countertransference in a Religious Therapist

NANCY C. KEHOE
THOMAS G. GUTHEIL

All therapists have more than one identity: in addition to their clinical roles, therapists have sexual, national, and ethnic identities, are married or unmarried, parents or childless. A client's selection of a therapist is frequently based on the therapist's identities and represents an attempt to "match" the client's identity with that of the therapist; i.e., a woman client chooses a woman therapist, a Jewish client chooses a Jewish therapist, or a gay client chooses a gay therapist.

In this essay we discuss a particular dual identity—that of clinical psychologist and Roman Catholic nun. None of the other dual identities noted above are so explicitly revealed by the therapist's actually being called by a different title ("Sister" versus "Doctor"). The senior author, a psychologist-nun, served as the therapist in the case to be presented. The second author is a psychiatrist who consulted on the case.

Thirty-three years in religious life and twenty years of education and practice as a clinical psychologist have shaped the dual identity of the senior author, making available two distinct formations from which to draw in working with clients. The senior author chooses to wear neither a habit nor any identifying symbol of her religious commitment. This option is in keeping with a national trend among members of religious orders to wear secular dress and with the author's own wish to confer maximum freedom upon the therapeutic encounter. However, the following case history and discussion will indicate that for clients who know that the therapist is both a psychologist and a nun, and chose her for that reason, she always wears a "veil."

THE CASE OF J

Background

All identifying data in this case have been altered to protect the client's anonymity.

When she entered into therapy J was twenty-nine. Caucasian, Catholic, and unmarried, J was on a medical leave of absence from work due to debilitating headaches. Her feelings of guilt, her anger toward her parents, and her inability to forgive them were the presenting problems that caused her to seek therapy. She also felt guilty because she had left the church as an adolescent and had only recently returned to regular church attendance.

J is an only child who, since graduating from college, had alternated between living at home with her parents and living on her own. When she began therapy, she was living alone in an apartment not far from her parents. J had earned an MSW; at the time of her medical leave she was working in a mental health clinic with child abuse cases. Her choice of this particular area of social work was related to her own history of emotional and physical abuse.

J described her mother as self-centered, cold, distant, unpredictable and for the most part unavailable. She could fly into a rage if J licked the spoon and put it back into the peanut butter jar or she could dismiss J's running away with a laugh. J remembers a few occasions when she was somewhat warm and caring, i.e., giving her a hug or holding her hand as they walked.

J's father was a general practitioner who enjoyed a significant reputation in the community. Although he was the senior member of a group practice, he also saw patients in his home office. Thus J was able to observe his interactions with patients as they came and went. Although J's father could be attentive to the poor, he was emotionally as well as physically abusive toward J. When he was in a rage, he would use his belt on her.

As with her mother her father's rages were unpredictable. Occasionally when she was sick he would be attentive; at other times he would accuse her of faking the illness. J vividly recalled that when she had her tonsils removed both parents were very caring; they brought her ice cream and presents and were kind to her. In contrast, both when J had an infected tooth and when she had a kidney infection, J's father said that she wanted attention and did not get her medical treatment for several days. These attributes of her parents had ramifications for the transference in the course of the therapy.

On several occasions when J was a young child, her mother threw her out of bed in the morning when it was time to go to school. She was made to lie down on the floor of the car "so no one can see you and know that you are my daughter." J felt rejected by such actions and thus internalized a rejected self (Winnicott 1971). J remembers the physical abuse beginning when she was about five and continuing into her high school years. J never knew what would merit the slaps or the verbal abuse. A "B" on a report card might mean that she would be slapped or that nothing would be said. Minor mishaps, such as breaking something, could merit a beating or could be ignored or laughed at. As J approached puberty, her mother mocked her developing breasts and pulled at her nightgown in a taunting way when J's father was present. Once after J ran away to spend several days at her girlfriend's house, her parents were so enraged at her letting people know about family matters that they locked her in her room for several hours and then threatened to put her in a mental hospital if she ever did that again. Such threats have dire consequences in a child's mind for they play into his or her worst fears of being isolated and abandoned (Bowlby 1973).

J remembered being touched inappropriately by her grandfather on a few occasions. Although J was rarely left alone by her parents, she felt emotionally abandoned by them because of their lack of responsiveness and unavailability. This emotional deprivation resulted in an anxious attachment to both parents and a terror of being abandoned that manifested itself in panic attacks, a dramatic manifestation of separation anxiety (Bowlby 1973).

Her parents espoused conflicting values. J's mother was socially ambitious and materialistic. Her father was concerned about his service to the community and to his patients and volunteered several hours each week to caring for children in various housing projects in the city. When his choice to do so conflicted with a social event that his wife wanted to attend, she would scream in an uncontrolled way. J frequently witnessed these scenes. These outbursts added to J's anxiety and fear of being left by one or the other parent in the event of a separation. J's father was generous with monetary gifts to poor families at holiday times, which also made J's mother furious. To retaliate she would spend large amounts of money on herself and on clothes for J.

J attended Catholic grammar school and high school, less for religious reasons than for educational ones. In kindergarten and first grade, J experienced school phobia. As Bowlby notes, a resistance to going to school is actually a fear of leaving home because the child does not know what will happen in her absence (Bowlby 1973). In school J hid under the desk or tried to run away. In retrospect J saw this as a plea for people to notice that she was in pain. But she felt instead that she was dubbed a difficult, uncooperative child.

She thought many of the nuns who taught her lacked in understanding and were cold, rigid, and indifferent. Their unresponsiveness to her was similar to her mother's and confirmed her sense of badness. Since there were a few nuns who J felt cared for her and nurtured her, that meant she couldn't be all bad. In relating to the nuns she had additional "good objects" and "bad objects" that she internalized. Only late in the therapy did J acknowledge that her grammar school teachers were members of the same religious order as the therapist.

Although she disobeyed the rules in school, she also felt contained by them. The strict rules were at least clear and predictable, in contrast to the unpredictableness of her home, where J was never sure whether her behavior would be rewarded or punished. After high school she entered the convent for a brief period; there she felt nurtured and cared for. The experience of being cared for and supported by some nuns and feeling coldness and indifference from others reminded her of her parents' uneven support.

In order to understand some of the content of the therapy as well as aspects of the transference it is necessary to explain some of the church's teaching that J was exposed to in her early grammar school years—a teaching that has changed significantly since then but that left its mark on this impressionable child. Most, if not all, of J's teachers were nuns. Children in parochial schools learned a prayer that stated, "I have sinned exceedingly in thought, word, and deed"—an all-encompassing concept of sin that was understood by the "faithful" to include feelings, fantasies, and desires, as well as actions and omissions. Feelings and fantasies were treated as equivalent to action. A scrupulous child might experience most of her thoughts, feelings, and wishes (e.g., anger at her parents, sexual desires and feelings, disobedience in school) as sinful. Not just the feelings become identified as sinful; the child herself is bad. Weekly confession to a priest meant a careful examination of one's conscience and an acknowledgment of the number and kind of one's offenses. Sinful actions were categorized as venial, or minor, offenses and mortal, or major, offenses with eternal damnation the punishment for mortal sins. Masturbation was in the category of mortal sins.

One of the sins J felt chronically guilty about was her habit of masturbating as a child and teenager. Although she could eventually say that masturbating was due to her extreme anxiety, her sense of deprivation, and the experience of being trapped, she had learned that it was sinful, and her early education reinforced that idea. For her, guilt was not just an expression of an internal conflict but a result of actual behavior (or thought or feeling) interpreted as sinful by the Church. Although masturbating was a substitutive satisfaction that she resorted to in default of a satisfactory relationship with her parents (Fairbairn 1952), it was deemed sinful. The feelings of guilt, as J talked about them in therapy, were both real in themselves, related to church teaching as learned in school, and a defense against other feelings.

Another element of her experience in Catholic schools that influenced the therapy was the manner in which nuns were moved from one place to another. In taking a vow of obedience, nuns and priests, with no opportunity for discussion, were subject to being moved at the discretion and will of their superiors. In the past twenty years, the understanding of the vow of obedience has changed and now includes more dialogue between a superior and an individual. J was unaware of this. During her school years, such abrupt changes meant that J "lost" some nuns that she had grown close to—as well as some priests, "Fathers", who had become caring figures in her life. J carried a persistent fear that this would happen in the therapy, though it was not discussed until midway through the therapy. As the Bloom-Feshbachs (1987) have noted, we experience loss, symbolically and actually, in many ways. By her parents' rejection and cruelty, J suffered a loss. When cared-for nuns and priests were transferred, she *actually* lost important persons she had come to depend upon. This fear of abandonment was to be central to the termination.

The Course of the Therapy

In the eighteen months prior to beginning therapy with the psychologist-nun, J made three attempts to deal with her guilt and her feelings of being a "bad" person. While on a parish retreat, J spoke to a nun who wore the traditional religious garb. "Sister" told J that she should rejoice in her suffering, for that was a way of being like Christ, who suffered for us. The second attempt, about six months later, involved one meeting with a psychologist who had a fundamentalist religious background; he told her that if she would forgive her parents she would stop feeling angry and guilty. Although this man had both a religious and a psychological background, J felt that he addressed only the religious part of her dilemma. About three months later she spoke to a priest who quoted scripture to her: "If, when you are bringing your gift to the altar, you suddenly remember that your brother [mother-father] has a grievance against you, leave your gift where it is before the altar. First go and make your peace with your brother [father-mother] and only then come back and offer your gift." (Matthew 5:23–24)

These attempts left J feeling hopeless and depressed. All three professionals had addressed themselves to the issue of guilt solely in religious terms without considering any underlying psychological issues. By addressing the guilt, but holding her responsible for it as having committed sin, they seemed to J to be accepting her belief that she had done wrong. None of the spiritual directors or therapist could convince her that God would forgive her. We suggest that her attempt to seek therapy with a person who was a therapist as well as religious reflected her knowledge at some level that her problem had psychological components as well as religious ones. J felt no significant sense of improvement as a result of these meetings because she was insecure in her self representation (McDonald 1981).

J is a tall, slender, attractive woman who generally wears very bright, colorful, slightly flamboyant clothes. When she arrived for her first session, she immediately described her referral sources and her three unsuccessful attempts to deal with guilt. She focused on the guilt as *the* problem and mentioned, in a somewhat detached way, that she had been abused as a child by both parents.

J's sensitivity to the therapist's dual roles was present from the beginning. Would the "Sister," the representative of God, assure her that she was not a bad person, that God loved her and would forgive her? Would the "Doctor" diagnose her correctly, understand the panic attacks, support her taking medication for them, and assure her that she was not losing her mind and that she would not end up in a hospital? (J's family doctor had prescribed medication for her anxiety attacks. In the course of therapy, the doctor retired and moved to another part of the country. At that time, the therapist referred J to a psychiatric colleague of hers so he could follow J's medication. When J decided to end therapy with the psychologist-nun she chose to see this doctor for medication and therapy.)

J was not seeking to understand the sources of the guilt or the anxiety attacks; she merely wanted to be rid of the bad feelings. Forgiveness and freedom from guilt and anxiety were anticipated benefits for confessing one's sins and receiving absolution. She wanted the "authorities" to make the difference—the church figure to offer forgiveness and the doctor to support her need for medication. One might conclude that at this point she was resisting treatment by choosing a psychologist-nun who could neither give her absolution nor prescribe medication.

During the first six months of therapy, J very persistently prodded the psychologist-nun to address her guilt, to reassure her that she was not a bad person. When the therapist tried to explore with J the origins of the guilt and the family abuse that might have caused the sense of "badness," J countered this by seeking out a priest for confession or buying Catholic books of a fairly conservative nature which confirmed her sense of sin. As a child and adolescent, her guilt feelings were frequently associated with masturbation. As an adult, her sense of guilt was related to her sexual behavior or fantasies regarding men she was dating. By focusing on the guilt and grounding herself in Catholic literature that reinforced this feeling, J was able to maintain a resistant stance toward the work of therapy, warding off painful affects like anger, depression, and anxiety related to loss (Greenson 1967).

After the subject of the parental abuse was discussed, she described panic attacks and wanted the Doctor—the psychiatrist who was monitoring her medication for the panic attacks—to deal with them. Any effort to explore the origins of the panic attacks was met with resistance, because J thought that this meant that the Doctor was going to hospitalize her. The therapist's reference on one occasion to J's using an emergency room as coverage over a weekend if J felt she could not cope, resulted in anger at the therapist—anger that periodically resurfaced throughout the therapy. J's friend had been in a mental hospital intermittently for two years, and J was terrified that she might also end up in a hospital—the ultimate form of being trapped. J wanted the "Sister" to be the accessible figure who would protect her, not the "Doctor" who could hospitalize her. This transference reaction was related to her fear of being abandoned and the power of threats (Bowlby 1973). Much later in the therapy J acknowledged that her father had threatened to have her hospitalized when she was a teenager, after she had run away from home and had stayed with a friend for several days.

It slowly became evident that the client's sense of guilt, her scrupulous conscience, and her frequent confessions as a young woman, though based on her religious formation, also represented attempts to devalue herself and to reinforce her negative self-image. J was able to verbalize that masturbating was due to her extreme anxiety, yet she continued to feel guilt and continued to confess. Faith in God had been a support to her as a child, but had also provided a socially-condoned belief system that enabled her to frame issues of punishment, blame, self-doubt, abuse, and suffering as appropriate responses to her bad self. One confessed according to the requirements of faith, thus letting the child take an active position, yet the feelings of guilt remained. Exploratory questions met with resistance because the psychologist-nun was not being the "right kind of Sister." The right kind of sister would have assured her that God understood and forgive her and that God did not think she was a bad person. For J guilt feelings were related to masturbation, which was sinful; this was conscious. But J kept at a more preconscious level the fact that masturbating was related to anxiety and the anxiety was related to anger and a sense of loss. As with so many abuse victims, guilt may be disabling; this psychological position is often preferable to the intolerable realization that the abuse is senseless, without justification or explanation. Responsibility and guilt seem to supply a painful order as an alternative to the dizziness of incoherence.

Soon after recognizing the power of the parental abuse, J confronted her parents with this fact. They acknowledged their abuse of her and apologized. They also told her they had themselves been abused as children. All this was minimized in their statement that "We all have to let the past go." But J continued to confront her parents with her anger over their treatment of her, while in therapy she tried to understand what their behavior meant. "I was not bad. I did not deserve that." Yet it seemed easier for her to struggle with her own badness and be angry at them rather than look at the emotional ramifications of what she had heard once from her mother: that they had not wanted to have her, that she was a mistake and had interfered with their lifestyle. Being unwanted, for her, was worse than being abused. J began to recognize that by focusing on guilt, which she generally related to masturbating, she could defend herself from feeling anger at her parents and anxiety about losing them. By seeing herself as bad, J attempted to make her mother and father good, which in turn would make her environment more tolerable (Fairbairn 1952).

As the therapy progressed, it slowly became evident to J that talking about guilt was a defense against her own anxiety and fear of loss but she continued to deny her own feelings of rage. J's resistance can be explained as a "defensive reaction against internalized objects which appeared intolerably bad to the ego" (Fairbairn 1952: 164). But this maneuver furthered the expectation that she would be abandoned because she was not the kind of person someone would want to stay with (Bowlby 1973).

Eight months into the therapy, J said that she wished to change the contract from therapy to spiritual direction, a separate process aimed at helping a person deal with his or her spiritual life. This request came one month after J had talked about terminating. She claimed that she had planned terminating and then changed the request to spiritual direction because she thought she understood her guilt and the effect her parents had had on her. As she understood it, her focus on guilt was a way of avoiding other feelings toward her parents—her anger at them and her anxiety about losing them. J ostensibly hoped to focus on what she wanted to do with her life; she wondered if she should consider re-entering a religious order.

Although the therapist thought this a defensive move aimed at the avoidance of painful issues, she agreed to it. She saw the use of her dual identity at this point as a means of maintaining some alliance. She hoped that J's nonsexual positive transference to the *nun*-psychologist would help J to look at what was otherwise considered too threatening. Relating to the nun would in the client's mind be relating to a desexualized person (Greenson 1967). The therapist was very consciously using her dual identity with the hope that, by making the "Sister" available, J would decide that she really needed the "Doctor" to work through her feelings of anger related to the emotional and physical abuse and her anxiety related to separation and loss. The therapeutic risk in agreeing to this change proved useful. J might have decided to continue with the spiritual direction as a way of resisting the therapeutic work she needed to do. But the therapist knew that if this happened, she would reintroduce the idea of therapy.

After only two months and a mere two sessions of spiritual direction, J came in and said, "Hello, Sister. I have decided that I really need to do therapy, rather than spiritual direction. I'm feeling overwhelmed with the sense of loss and fear of my parents dying." She and the therapist agreed to resume therapy.

With this decision, J's commitment to doing the work of therapy became more evident. J began to discuss her fear of growing up and her sense that being sick was a way of getting something. She realized that "feeling guilty" was the spiritual equivalent of being physically sick. Along with this awareness, J was able to identify that she wanted "the nun" to take care of her more often than she wanted "the psychologist" to treat her as an adult. This became apparent in J's fury at the therapist when she was billed for a balance after her insurance ran out.

> J: I was angry that you sent me a bill for the balance after the insurance ran out.
> THERAPIST: What made you angry about that?
> J: It's a sign that you're just in business; you're supposed to be a minister.
> T: What do those two roles mean to you?
> J: A minister is supposed to be available, like when I call you on the phone. But if you are in business, that means that you don't care, that you can keep your distance, that I am just a fee. If I were to cross the street and get hit, you probably would not even come out to see what happened, but just go on seeing your next client.

T: Are you looking to me for the nurturance you did not receive from your mother or are we trying to understand your life and what you want to do at this point, given all you have experienced?

J: I don't want to grow up.

This last interaction indicates where the therapist's own countertransference regarding her two roles inhibited a more empathic response toward J's understandable wish that she be cared for and be able to depend on someone. It is also an example how J's use of the name *Sister* was a resistance to working on the transference related to her mother.

In this middle phase of therapy J began more directly to express her dependency needs by a shift away from the constant focus on guilt so evident at the beginning. Now she only talked about guilt after some major life event such as the suicide of a close friend or J's decision to return to work after her medical leave. Again, after a visit with her parents, if the interaction had been explosive, she described feeling very guilty. But she recognized more quickly that she used guilt to defend against other feelings that she considered unacceptable, such as anger, dependency, or fear of loss.

As J became more willing to consider a possible unconscious element in what she did, she decided to stop going to confession. Although going to confession was related to her guilt connected with masturbation and sexual fantasies, it was also a form of acting out in relation to the therapy. She was more willing to deal with interpretations introspectively, searching for further self-understanding in the light of the therapist's comments (Kernberg 1980). She also wanted to taperecord the sessions, apparently so she could have a transitional object that she could hold onto as she began to explore more difficult inner territory. Spiritual direction had been one form of maintaining a bond with the psychologist while she made use of the nun. Now the taperecorder represented a form of holding on to the psychologist.

She also began to deal with her anger toward the church, the authority figures in the church, and the messages learned early that so problematically reinforced her familial experience: if she committed mortal sin she would go to hell—ultimate abandonment; if she ran away she would be sent to a mental hospital—abandonment by family. She also began exploring how those messages had served as a protection for her because right and wrong were clearly delineated and she could therefore avoid assuming responsibility for her own life and choices.

Despite the inconsistencies of some clerical figures the church had been a stable force for her as a child. The rules and regulations were clear. Rewards and punishments were clear. A faithful follower did not examine beliefs and take responsibility for one's own life but rather complied with the authority figures and was thus assured of salvation. With this exploration J began to develop an adult relationship to the church. While the "Sister" part of the dual identity was necessary to bring J into treatment and to elicit transference that could then be analyzed, her relationship to the psychologist part of this dual identity enabled her to form a working alliance (Greenson 1967).

Although J was now working on therapy issues, the duality of the therapist's role continued as an enduring presence. Two years into the therapy, J said: "You didn't tell me you were the head nun. I have been sweating out all this time that you could just leave at any time and now I find out that you are in charge." This revealed how everpresent was the fear that the therapist could leave abruptly, a fear based on her insecure and ambivalent attachment to her parents, compounded by earlier experiences of nuns and priests leaving suddenly for other assignments at their superior's behest. Yet as the therapist and J explored the significance of these fears, a deeper theme emerged. J was becoming more invested in the therapy, and her perception that the therapist, being senior, might have choice with regard to her own life circumstances was reassuring.

Ironically the termination of the therapy was precipitated by the therapist's decision to do some work for her order which necessitated a three-month summer absence from her clients.

Five months prior to the leave, when the therapist made reference to "nothing being predictable," J wondered if that indicated that the therapist was preparing her for something. Although that had not been the therapist's intention, she used the opportunity to tell J of the forthcoming extended absence in the summer.

A few weeks after this revelation, J announced that she had to terminate because she could not tolerate the extended absence or the extended time in which to talk about it. J would consider only two more sessions to discuss the termination. The therapist's absence and implied rejection of her were too painful to bear as they re-evoked her experience of parents who had not been available to her when she wanted and needed them, and nuns and priests, who she thought she could count on, leaving her. She was being abandoned once again. Because she had not worked through these previous losses and all that they meant to her, she was unable to tolerate all of the feelings that arose with the therapist's departure.

Because of the abrupt end of therapy, J and the therapist were unable to work through the transference. However J expressed a willingness to continue the work with the male psychiatrist who prescribed her medication for panic attacks. J made the transition successfully and, to the author's knowledge, has continued in that therapy.

Transference

The question of how a therapist is addressed occurs frequently in therapy (Senger 1984). In this case the choice of names served as a critical metaphor in the transference, reflecting J's relation to her parents and to church figures. The client identified three related wishes: (1) to work with a psychologist, a "Doctor," to do therapy; (2) to work with a "Sister," seen as a representative of God (a connotation that the client herself affirmed); and (3) to call the psychologist-nun by her first name, thus attempting to place the work on a more personal level, to transgress whatever boundaries would be set by the use of the other two titles, and to avoid selecting one or the other. (In religious settings today it is common practice to address nuns, priests, and ministers by their first names; thus, in a purely religious context, J's wish was not unusual.)

Interestingly, when paying her bills, the client always addressed her checks and her envelopes to "Sister" or to the therapist's name followed only by those letters that identified the therapist's religious order. This could be interpreted to mean that the client was consistently resisting the work of doing therapy with the "Doctor" or that, in her own mind, J was addressing the "Sister" and thus was paying for ministry, not the "business" of therapy. The client's choice of names in relation to payment was also a sign of her ambivalence about the work; she had accused the "Sister" of being in business and not caring about her, yet she was paying the "Sister," not the "Doctor," for the work of therapy. Although the client was not neglecting to pay (a form of resistance noted by Greenson 1967), she was unconsciously attempting to deny her relationship to the therapist. The therapist's countertransference inhibited her from dealing more directly with the name on the check.

Because the therapist was conscious that her primary role was that of psychologist and not that of nun, she had initially introduced herself as "Doctor," addressing J in turn by her last name. J, however, wanted to be called by her first name and said, "It's your right to be called what you want, so if you want to be called 'Doctor,' that is your right, but I want to be called 'J.'" At a later point in therapy she said, "I will never call you 'Doctor'; that is too cold and professional." At another time an exploratory question was greeted with, "You 'shrinks' are all the same." At times J would provocatively say "Sister," as a way, she confessed, "to see how you'd react."

For J to call the therapist "Doctor" conjured up the image of two rejecting parents—a cold, aloof mother and a father, the Doctor who cared for his patients more than he seemed to care for her. Because J's father had an office in his home, J overheard many patients call him by his first name; hence even "real" doctors were called by their first names. So there was not even a professional reason for calling the psychologist-nun "Doctor."

For J to call the therapist "Sister" conjured up both her positive and negative experiences with nuns; this title was usually employed when J sought the minister to care for her, not the therapist to work with her. For J to call the therapist by her first name was to try to establish a warm, personal relationship but perhaps also to circumvent the hard work and implied limitations of a therapeutic relationship.

Shortly after the therapist told J of the extended summer absence, J stated that she wanted to call the therapist by her first name. In the course of therapy this had never been settled: usually both avoided the use of any direct address except for the incidents cited. In this same session J told the therapist that her father was receiving a major community award. The "Sister" and the Doctor were both being recognized by their respective communities, which J could narcissistically vicariously enjoy because of her identification with both. J asked to see a photograph of the psychologist-nun in her religious garb yet stated that she never felt that she could talk about prayer in their sessions because "you aren't a nun here."

Calling the therapist by her first name was also related to J's desire for a warm relationship with the therapist to compensate for the poor relationship she had had with her mother. Because J perceived her mother as a woman who was cool and detached, she was always in search of a person who would be emotionally responsive and available. In the beginning of therapy the therapist was perceived as the good mother/good nun who tried to understand J and was available and predictable. Inevitably as the transference shifted in the course of therapy, she also "became" the bad mother/bad nun who was unavailable, who did not hear J's pain, and who refused to tell her that God loved her, accepted her, and forgave her. J's negative transference to the therapist was evident in such comments as, "If I was hit by a car when I left here, you would not even come out. You would just go on and see your next person."

Instead of working with this transference reaction, with her feelings of anger and sense of loss that stemmed from her experience of an unavailable mother, J would accuse the therapist of being a cold professional, of not being the right kind of minister: "A minister is supposed to be available," code words for her implied accusation that the therapist was failing to be a good mother. J had organized her experience with previous nuns (and now with this psychologist-nun) by classifying them as "good" or "bad." The "good nuns" were those who were more available attachment figures who allayed her anxious, angry feeling; the "bad nuns" were those who made her feel her own badness by not being there for her. Although she would blame them, J internally concluded that she caused their absence by her own badness. Bowlby notes that one variable in an attachment figure's unresponsiveness turns on whether the self is judged to be the kind of person to whom another would respond (Bowlby 1973). For J a nonempathic response was a confirmation of her badness. J's ability to understand these transference-based feelings was rendered more difficult because J kept insisting that the minister-therapist be more "Christian." In other words, J's fixed and narrow concept of a "good Christian" (especially a minister) made it difficult to see the therapist as other than a compensator for the mother's deprivation. Rather than experience her sense of deprivation and loss, she could accuse the minister of failing to be "Christian": caring, available, and nurturing. Using religious ideology, she maintained her way of being with a rejecting object, while struggling for an idealized object. Religion was thus used as a resistance to therapy (Kehoe and Gutheil 1984).

The father transference was also intensified by the therapist's dual roles. The therapist's vocation made her resemble J's compassionate father who cared for the poor. Yet the therapist was also the bad father who cared more about reputation than about "family", i.e., her clients. As a doctor, her father commanded respect; J looked up to him because of his renown, yet she feared his physical abuse. He was someone who took care of others but not of her. As a result the title of "Doctor" connoted not just a professional identity as caretaker but a focus for many conflictual feelings about a primary figure. The therapist was "the head nun," a position that J valued because she hoped it would protect her from separation; but this respect was clouded by the fact that she did not feel "cared for" and secretly anticipated being abandoned. Just as she had experienced a conflict between her father's assigned importance in the community and his neglect of her, so she felt torn by the planned leave. The fact that the therapist had been asked to do this work by her order was a sign of her importance and renown, so J could take satisfaction in the nun's importance; but the consequence of this importance was neglect of J. Here is an example of this ambivalence:

> That was my worst fear. I hate nuns. I hate the church. I knew this would happen. You don't care. If you cared, you wouldn't leave me. Last week I felt you cared and today you tell me you are going away for three months. I don't think you'll ever be coming back. They will ask you to stay in Rome and do some high-powered work . . . You could become the president of the order and at least then I would know that I had a famous therapist.

Another aspect of the father transference involved sickness and guilt. J recognized midway through therapy that being sick was a way of being cared for by her father. An episode of illness was one of the few times when he was sensitive to her needs; at other times, such as when he threatened her with hospitalization, she experienced only the powerful negative aspects of his being a doctor. Thus, when the therapist offered J the use of an emergency room, she was being the insensitive, hospitalizing father who had power. Moreover, coming to a religious professional with guilt was the equivalent of presenting "sickness." J thus received care when she was sick or when she was spiritually sick, i.e., feeling guilty.

By probing for other feelings that might be defended against by the guilt, rather than responding caringly to the "sickness," the therapist was failing to be the "right kind of minister" who should assure her of God's forgiveness. Once again, J used God and guilt, two powerful allies, to defend herself from feelings of anxiety, loss, and betrayal. As discussed earlier, many religious interpretations lend themselves too readily to the use of guilt as a defense and as a way of avoiding the real meaning of one's deepest feelings.

Any three-month leave by a therapist is bound to evoke understandable anger on the part of clients. Such an unexpected and prolonged absence is a hardship for clients, even with adequate coverage and advance knowledge of the absence. The particular nature of the therapist's dual role was evident in the way this client (and others) experienced the anticipated absence. The therapist explored whether the three-month hiatus felt different from a maternity leave or a change required by a spouse's work relocation; in every case, clients responded affirmatively. Apparently the psychologist-nun was not entitled to her own life; she had "given over" that life to God and to the service of others. Clients expected constant availability. For the therapist to choose to be absent for religious work, then, was experienced by the clients as a "conflict of interest" somehow different from comparable conflicts that other therapists might have. The psychologist-nun was expected to be the perfect mother.

J chose to leave therapy at this point, rather than endure the break and work on the issues involved. Other clients did not terminate abruptly because of the planned absence. Some used it as an opportunity to work toward a genuine termination; others waited for the therapist's return and used the coverage she provided; still others experienced the absence as a trial period in which to work on some issues without therapy.

J's decision to leave therapy was based in part on her fear that the psychologist-nun would not return to work, but would instead be elected to a more responsible position in the order. She chose to "abandon" the psychologist-nun by terminating first rather than experience the more painful alternative of being abandoned. Most clients fear that the therapist will not return after a holiday or some unexpected absence (Bowlby 1973). In addition, J feared that if the therapist *did* return, she could leave her again.

J's words—"That was my worst fear. I hate nuns. I hate the church. I knew this would happen. You don't care. If you cared, you wouldn't leave me"—capture the transference to the psychologist-nun.

Countertransference

The therapist had spent more years in religious life than as a psychologist, but this offered no immunity from having to deal with her own countertransference issues. As frequently happens, clients can intuitively identify areas of vulnerability in a therapist that are not fully integrated or that continue to be problematic. Despite many years of working on being "Doctor" rather than "Sister," the therapist had not yet fully resolved what those two roles meant for her. Legitimate therapeutic restraints such as not responding to whatever clients said they needed, being unavailable for "extra" phone calls, and not giving simple reassurance felt at times cold, hard, and "unChristian."

The call to the ministry or religious life is a call to serve God's people. The training is directed at the formation of both the person and the service, i.e., preaching, leading worship, teaching, visiting the sick, pastoral care, and counseling. Love is the great command: love for the neighbor should usually outweigh love for oneself. In other words, the identity formation of the nun is directed toward the other. The explicit and implicit message of loving the neighbor means that one is always available, giving of oneself for the sake of the other, responding to the suffering of the other. Caring feelings are to be fostered while noncaring feelings (such as anger) are to be controlled. Nonjudgmental, supportive, concerned, kind, and generous attitudes towards others are nurtured; demanding, self-critical, perfectionistic, and harsh attitudes towards oneself are comparably encouraged. Setting limits, expressing or feeling anger, saying no—all are seen as contrary to the underlying principles of religious teaching (Kehoe and Gutheil, manuscript in preparation).

As a consequence, training that emphasizes "turning the other cheek," "going the extra mile," and being completely available can seem to be in contradiction to the therapeutic values of setting limits, maintaining boundaries, and focusing on the work of therapy rather than on the caring by the therapist. The therapist's interaction with J coincided with a time in which she herself was coming to terms with ministry "versus" therapy. When the client addressed the therapist as "Sister," she impinged on this struggle. At times when the client accused the therapist of not "caring," the therapist reacted defensively and wondered privately if that were true. Indeed, the therapist's ambivalence may have impeded her from addressing more directly all the transference manifestations elicited by her dual identity.

For example, the issue of names surfaced periodically throughout the course of therapy but was never resolved, partly due to countertransference inhibition on the part of the therapist. This inhibition hindered the therapist's ability to work through the transference. In retrospect, had the name issue been addressed earlier and pursued more consistently, the course of the therapy might have been different.

Forty percent of the therapist's clients are current or former nuns or priests. Another forty percent are laypersons who select the therapist because they believe she will deal respectfully with the religious aspect of their lives. The remaining twenty percent are referred to the therapist as a clinical psychologist with no direct reference to religious issues. Some clients learn in the course of therapy that the therapist is also a nun; others apparently do not. In only two instances did clients terminate because they learned the therapist was a nun. (Note that all checks received in payment for therapy fees are endorsed by the financial office of the religious order, a fact that might provide a monthly revelation or reminder of the therapist's identity.) With few exceptions, clients' expressed reasons for seeking therapy are not explicitly related to religious issues.

Most clients harbor fantasies that the therapist will magically heal them. This fantasy is an important part of the therapeutic process. In the case of this therapist's dual identity, a minister offers forgiveness, hope of healing, and a presence outside the restraints of time or finances. The dual roles of minister and psychologist, in the fantasies of some patients, provide everything they could wish for: self-understanding, healing, forgiveness, psychological wholeness, spiritual salvation—ministry *and* therapy. This dual identity may thus hold out the promise of magical healing to a greater extent than other dual identities.

Other dual roles (a therapist who is married, a therapist who is black, or a therapist who is gay) convey no expectation that the therapist's "other" role should *do* something. Those identities are not associated with a "ritual aura" and the accompanying expectations of the minister.

Being "ministered to" conjures up an image different from doing therapy. Being ministered to suggests the passage from the prophet Isaiah (61:1–2), "to bind up the broken hearted, to proclaim liberty to captives, and release to those in prison; to comfort all who mourn." All of these images assign activity to the minister and passivity to the one who is wounded. In contrast, doing therapy is active and involves both therapist and client as participants fully engaged in the process.

The case of J was chosen because it highlights the complexity of the therapist's dual roles; it also reveals how the manner in which the client and the therapist understood and enacted those two roles became a recurring issue and tension in the treatment. But the case of J is not unique in the therapist's experience. For clients who know that she is both a religious woman and a psychologist, that reality is ever-present in the therapy. Clients have acknowledged that they never forget the therapist is also a nun, even when the therapist is more aware of herself as a therapist. One effect of this is significant delay and inhibition in clients' introducing subjects such as sexuality or money.

Clients also appear to hold a split image of the nun, with multiple expectations: that she be the minister, always available, with no limits; that she be unworldly, and not "well dressed in contemporary fashion"; that she be willing to be the target of anger toward more traditional church figures; that she be cared for by her order, not dependent on client fees (and thereby not raise her fee); that she be exempt from ordinary struggles, i.e., rent increases, housing problems, or problems in relationships; and that she be unable to "really understand." They also expect that the tradition of availability and self-sacrifice should mean that some of her own needs do not need to be satisfied, for example, by taking time off.

Clients strongly resist expressing anger at the church or at church professionals because the therapist is seen as a church person. They also may harbor resentments for what nuns or other authority figures did to them in school. This response is no different from other therapy situations in which the therapist is perceived as allied with "the others," be they "male chauvinists," "feminists," "racists," etc.

Seeing a psychologist-nun evokes the longing to have all one's needs met in a caring, ministerial fashion, the best of all possible worlds. Peteet (1984) and Smith (1977) describe a similar idea when they write about the "patient's golden fantasy," the wish that therapy meet all needs, not just therapeutic ones. The therapist's commitment to working seriously in therapy may at times be experienced as her being "cold and withholding, not caring and supportive," which may result in anger, struggle, and in a few cases, termination (Kahn 1984).

We suggest that the transferential response to a dual identity is a variation on defensive splitting that utilizes the two identities of the therapist to facilitate the split. Rather than treating "this week's therapist" as bad and "last week's therapist" as good, the client sees the nun as good and the psychologist as bad or vice versa, as her dynamics may require. What is maintained, however, is a splitting off from the central ego of all those exciting and overrejecting elements that are bound up with compensatory internal relations. Lost, of course, is the integrity and wholeness of the ego and the ability for real object relations (Fairbairn 1952).

Since the psychologist-nun is an enduring "split," it is easier to maintain. In fact, the split is supported by a whole set of professional assumptions from both identities. As in the case of J, this can prevent someone from integrating good and bad aspects of herself.

A few vignettes will illustrate how the dual identity applied to other cases and how it raised issues of transference and resistance.

In one case, the senior author worked with a woman who in the course of therapy decided to leave her religious order. After she left religious life, she wanted to begin dating but resisted talking to the therapist about sex because "she knew what nuns thought about sex." In fact she ended therapy at that point. Without in any way testing her belief, she felt that the therapist-nun could not help her adequately deal with this area. It is worth noting that the client assumed the therapist as nun was prepared to work with her regarding her decision to leave the sisterhood but was too *much* the "nun" to work with her on other issues.

Some clients appeared to select the therapist in part for her presumed ability to take seriously the religious as well as psychological significance of guilt and sin. Other clients sought the therapist's implicit "understanding" and conveyed their hope that the religious issues would be simply accepted without exploration, a clear form of resistance. The following phone conversation illustrates this point:

T: Hello, this is Dr. Kehoe.
C: Hello, my name is Sarah Lawrence. I got your name from the MPA; they said you were a Christian therapist and that is what I am looking for.

T: I wonder if you could tell me what makes that important?

C: I want to work with someone who is religious so I don't have to explain about my beliefs.

T: I think it is important in doing therapy not to presume that the other person knows your experience even if you think they profess the same beliefs you have. I would be glad to see you for an evaluation, but it will be necessary for us to try to understand that part of your life, not to take for granted that I do.

C: I am surprised that you are asking so many questions. I'm not sure that I want to go into all of that with you or any therapist.

The choice of a therapist within the faith may thus contain several contradictory wishes: the wish to be understood and to use that understanding as a basis for exploration; the wish to be understood as a resistance to detailed exploration; and the wish to avoid or obscure certain sensitive matters.

Although it adds complexity to the therapeutic relationship, the dual role has beneficial aspects as well. For example, clients may be able to express conflictual feelings such as their anger at the psychologist-nun and because of her dual identity to experience acceptance of those feelings by two important sources, one psychological and the other spiritual. Religiously committed patients may fear that therapy will succeed in "curing them of their faith," as though faith itself were an undesirable symptom and that to question and explore faith is to destroy it. Choosing a therapist from within the faith may be an attempt to dispel this fear. The therapist in her dual identity communicates nonverbally that it is possible to question and to believe. For other clients the choice of a therapist from within the faith may occur at the cost of creating a resistance described elsewhere (Kehoe and Gutheil 1984). In working with more disturbed patients in inpatient settings and day treatment programs, the dual role may be used even more purposefully in order to convey to patients that their faith need not be distorted by their illness (Fath 1979; Kehoe, work in progress).

Whenever a client chooses a therapist explicitly because of the therapist's dual roles, much useful therapeutic material may become available by using those dual roles actively, freely, and directly. Such an open exploration tends to neutralize possible sources of resistance at their earliest, most manageable levels. In general, the dual role of the therapist as psychologist and as nun can be useful as a statement that all dimensions of a person's life can be candidly explored, including the religious one, without labelling the religious concerns immature, unhealthy, pathogenic, or conflictual, and thus in need of resolution. The dual role also allows a person to explore sexual orientation, sexual behavior, thoughts and fantasies, suicidal ideation, anger at God or church, without being judged by a church person as sinful or wrong. Such exploration conveys the idea that a person may arrive at a less judgmental awareness, both religiously and psychologically.

Because J's presenting problem—the questions of guilt, sin, and forgiveness—was framed in religious language, the dual identity of the therapist was of particular significance. One might speculate as to how this client might have worked with another therapist who did not combine these roles in such an overt manner.

In all cases a dual identity potentially evokes complex transference and countertransference reactions. Because of this complexity, and the power and significance of the feelings that a dual identity arouses, it also offers an invaluable therapeutic opportunity. If explored and worked through, the transference and countertransference associated with a dual identity can greatly assist the course of therapy.

References

Bloom-Feshbach, J. and S. Bloom-Feshbach. 1987. *The Psychology of Separation and Loss*. San Francisco: Jossey-Bass.

Bowlby, J. 1973. *Attachment and Loss*. 3 vols. Vol. 2, *Separation*. New York: Basic Books.

Fairbairn, W. R. D. 1952. *Psychoanalytic Studies of the Personality*. London: Routledge and Kegan Paul.

Fath, G. 1979. A special ministry in long-term care. *Hospital Progress* 60: 64–65.

Greenberg, J. A. and S. A. Mitchell. 1983. *Object Relations in Psychoanalytic Theory*. Cambridge: Harvard University Press.

Greenson, R. 1967. *The Technique and Practice of Psychoanalysis*. New York: International University Press.

Horowitz, M. 1977. Cognitive and interactive aspects of splitting. *American Journal of Psychiatry* 134: 549–53.

Jones, A. 1966. *The Jerusalem Bible*. New York: Doubleday.

Kahn, P. 1984. Religious values and the therapeutic alliance, or, "Help me Psychologist, I hate you, Rabbi." In M. Spero, ed., *The Psychotherapy of the Religious Patient*. Springfield, Ill.: C. C. Thomas.

Kehoe, N. and T. Gutheil. Religious issues groups: A nine-year experience in day treatment programs. Manuscript in progress.

——. 1984. Shared religious belief as resistance in psychotherapy. *American Journal of Psychotherapy* 38: 579–85.

Kernberg, O. 1976. *Object Relations Theory and Clinical Psychoanalysis*. New York: Jason Aronson.

——. 1980. *Internal World and External Reality*. New York: Jason Aronson.

McDonald. M. 1981. The psychoanalytic concept of the self. In K. Robson, ed., *The Psychiatric Clinics of North America*. 4(3).

Peteet, J. R. 1981. Issues in the treatment of religious patients. *American Journal of Psychotherapy* 35: 559–64.

Rayburn, C. 1985. The religious patient's initial encounter with psychotherapy. In E. Mark Stern, ed., *Psychotherapy and the Religiously Committed Patient*. New York: Haworth Press.

Rizzuto, A-M. 1979. *The Birth of the Living God*. Chicago: University of Chicago Press.

Senger, H. 1984. First name or last? Addressing the patient in psychotherapy. *Comprehensive Psychiatry* 25, no. 1 (January–February): 38–43.

Smith, S. 1977. The golden fantasy: A regressive reaction to separation anxiety. *International Journal of Psychoanalysis* 58: 311–24.

The Use of Religious Imagery for Psychological Structuralization

Martha Robbins

In her seminal work on the formation, function, and transformations of a person's God representations throughout the life cycle, Rizutto (1979) shows how God representations, once formed, may facilitate or impede psychological growth and equilibrium. She contends that the characteristic uses and changes of the God representation, especially during times of crisis, provide an excellent tool for investigating the vicissitudes and transformations of the representation of significant persons (objects) with corresponding changes in the self representation. While pointing out that the therapeutic process helps persons to analyze the sources of childhood imagos and corresponding self representations and to transform them into a more mature psychological structure, Rizutto notes that a patient's "silent communication with transitional objects, God or others, will continue parallel to the analytic process" (205). However, she does not explore how the use of implicit or explicit religious imagery *during the course of therapeutic treatment* may enhance or inhibit psychological structuralization or transformation.

In my clinical work, I have found that hypnosis in conjunction with dynamic psychotherapy offers both sound theoretical foundations and clinical tools by which to understand and facilitate the process of psychological structuralization through the constructive use of religious imagery. In this paper I illustrate this process of structuralization through the use of religious imagery by presenting the case of Bob. First I will define what I mean by psychological structuralization and religious imagery. I will also describe several elements in dynamic hypnotherapy that permit the clinician to use the patient's imagery (religious or otherwise) to facilitate psychological structuralization.

Psychological Structuralization and Religious Imagery

Atwood and Stolorow (1984) define personality structure from the perspective of psychoanalytic phenomenology as "the *structure of a person's experiencing*." Accordingly, the basic units of personality analysis are "*structures of experience*—the distinctive configurations of self and object that shape and organize a person's subjective world" (33). Structures can be thought of as "organizing principles [Piaget 1970]—cognitive-affective schemata [Klein 1976; Slap and Saykin 1980] through which a person's experiences of self and other assume their characteristic forms and meanings" (Atwood and Stolorow 1984:34). While such structures or enduring organizations of self and other are disclosed in the thematic patterning of a person's subjective life, these structures are "prereflectively unconscious" (Atwood and Stolorow 1984:36).

Personality development—the process of structuralization of personal experience—involves the differentiation and integration of self and other representations. This process begins with the establishment of a rudimentary sense of self-object (body) boundaries (Mahler, Pine, and Bergman 1975) and moves through a phase of relying on significant others as "self-objects" (Kohut 1971, 1977) whose idealized attributes and mirror functions provide a sense of self-cohesion and stability. Progressive internalization of the functions provided by these "self-objects" allows a person to stabilize and consolidate an internal self-structure that eventually can tolerate and integrate diverse or contrasting affective experiences. The self then becomes able to recognize both the positive and the negative qualities of the other, whose unique feelings and needs are distinct from one's self (Kernberg 1976).

Optimal structuralization allows the person to assimilate new experiences without fearing that his or her subjective world will disintegrate or dissolve. Similarly, the personality is flexible enough that the person can accommodate new configurations of experience of self and other. One's organization of subjective life continues to expand in complexity, fluidity, choice, and articulateness (Piaget 1970; Atwood and Stolorow 1984; Robbins 1990; Surrey 1985).

Failure to achieve this balance may result in two types of psychological disturbance that require different kinds of therapeutic intervention (Atwood and Stolorow 1984; Stolorow and Lachmann 1980). Psychological disturbances that reflect rigid consolidated pathological structures (constricting one's subjective world by warding off emotional conflict) benefit from therapeutic interventions that focus primarily upon interpretations pertaining to the nature and patterns of psychological conflict. Disturbances that reflect a structural vulnerability of insufficient self/object differentiation require therapeutic interventions focused primarily on the structuralization and consolidation of a cohesive self-experience. Any patient may experience both conflict and structural deficits, and the clinician must ascertain which is salient at any given point.

The patient may utilize "transitional objects" (Winnicott 1953) to facilitate the process of psychological structuralization or transformation of rigid psychological structures. Transitional objects may take the form of material objects, specific images, or rituals; or they may be highly symbolized abstract conceptualizations. They perform psychological functions similar to those attributed to self-objects: soothing, mirroring, admiring, encouraging, challenging, etc. (Adler 1985).

From the perspective of psychoanalytic phenomenology, God as symbolic other (or other religious objects, images, and rituals) functions as a transitional object. Religious imagery may be visual, auditory, tactile, olfactory, gustatory, kinesthetic, or conceptual images that evoke a sense of positive or negative connection to what one holds to be of ultimate worth and value. Religious imagery may be evoked not only in relation to formal religious beliefs, symbols, and rituals, but also in the very activity of making meaning of internal and external life experience (Kegan 1982; Parks 1986). Underlying a patient's search for meaning (inherent in structuring or resymbolizing one's subjective world) is an implicit yearning for connection or reconnection with a self grounded in something larger than one's self (Robbins 1990). One patient may need to order or reorder one's subjective world as a response to the presence and activity of God in the particularities of his or her life—a representation of God which calls the person into a more complex and truthful way of being in relation to self, others, and the world (Niebuhr 1963). Other patients, however, may experience the disruptions or disturbances within their subjective world not as invitations to grow but as punishment from a punitive, hostile God representation. Consequently, when patients bring religious imagery into therapy, it is important to investigate not only the symbolic meanings embedded in the imagery, but also how these meanings may be related to conflicts or structural vulnerabilities (Lachmann, Beebe, and Stolorow 1988).

Dynamic Hypnotherapy

Hypnosis in conjunction with dynamic psychotherapy provides a rich opportunity to observe the ingenuity and creative symbolic ability of the human mind in making and transforming images of self in relation to others. In hypnosis, a patient enters into an altered state of consciousness or "a trance state" through relaxation or various induction techniques (Brown and Fromm 1986). One's awareness of surroundings fades; perceptions and thought patterns associated with secondary process thinking change (Brown and Fromm 1986; Fromm 1977; Hilgard 1973; Shor 1959). These changes enable the patient to more deeply absorb and attend to internal experience characteristic of primary process thinking, with its flow of images, memories, and associated feeling states (Bowers and Bowers 1972; Brown and Fromm 1986; Fromm 1977).

By observing the patient's characteristic patterns of response to the spontaneously produced images with their associated affects the therapist may more readily understand the patient's personality structure and underlying developmental arrests or conflicts (Brown and Fromm 1986; Horowitz 1970; Reyher 1963; Silberer 1951). Changes in emotion may signal significant shifts in the patient's representational world, indicating the activation of a particular image of self and other (including God as symbolic other) in that moment of the imagery experience. Through the unfolding imagery the patient may discover and rehearse more constructive ways of dealing with problem areas. The patient provides "the building blocks for therapy" (Brown and Fromm 1986:166) by indicating his or her readiness for the next incremental step in the structuralization process (Lachmann, Beebe, and Stolorow 1988).

The spontaneous use of religious imagery by patients with structural deficits, therefore, can provide a key to understanding the nature of the structural weakness and can suggest an approach to developing a more cohesive self. Self-experience becomes more cohesively structured as the patient integrates affects with memories, fantasies, and self and object representations. Some patients may become aware of the symbolic meanings of their images during trance. However, the gradual integration of those meanings and affects takes place in psychotherapy in the waking state.

Here I turn to a detailed description of this process of structuralization through the use of religious imagery in dynamic hypnotherapy. In the case of Bob, religious imagery played a significant role in this process of structuralization; indeed, "the psychic process of creating and finding God—this personalized representational transitional object" (Rizutto 1979:179) was intimately related to creating and finding his self and the other. We will observe how religious imagery as transitional space and God as transitional object facilitated Bob's transformation of his childhood parental imagos and corresponding self-representations into a more mature psychological structure. Bob's initial imagery of the masked/unmasked man revealed the core issues to be dealt with in two years of therapy. We will trace the therapeutic process of structuralization through Bob's selection and use of four predominant religious images: the Christ light; the Madonna and Child; the prodigal son; and Jacob wrestling with the angel.

THE CASE OF BOB

"Lost in a Tumultuous Sea"

Bob entered therapy because intense episodes of anxiety and depression threatened to overwhelm him. Stating that he felt "lost in a tumultuous sea," Bob described a disintegrating anxiety that seemed to result from his decision to leave his career at age forty-three and enter seminary. This major change in vocation began when he served a term on the board of governors of a Unitarian Universal church on the west coast. Bob's "increasing awareness of religious feelings and experience" prompted him to explore the ministry as a "calling."

I met Bob as he was completing his first year of studies in seminary. Bob contacted me after hearing me lecture on psychological and spiritual transformation during midlife. He felt that I could help him work through his "spiritual crisis." In two previous therapies, Bob had been reticent to speak about his religious experience because he felt "they were interpreted away" by both therapists.

While exacerbated by his recent change in vocation and life-style, Bob's internal experience of "being in turmoil and confusion" was not new. As the oldest of three children in an upper-middle-class family, Bob recalled being very lonely as a child. He reported that he never developed close relationships with his siblings. His first asthma attack occurred at age three, shortly after his brother was born. Bob longed to have more contact with his father, whom he described as a successful architect and businessman, but quiet and distant. Bob described his mother, a homemaker, as "depressed, sad, lonely, very, very controlling, and intrusively demanding." When she was sad, Bob felt close to her. Likewise, his mother would comfort him when he was scared or sad, but she would not tolerate expressions of frustration or anger. "She wanted me to be perfect and everything to be orderly." Both parents were political conservatives who actively participated in a large Presbyterian church. Evangelical religious beliefs and practices pervaded the family ethos and rituals, and were an important part of Bob's life until he went to college.

In college, Bob rejected his religious beliefs and practices. "In my search for truth, I became more and more agnostic and then atheistic." His search for truth combined with his longstanding curiosity about "how things worked" led him to major in science and then pursue doctoral studies at a prestigious university "as far away as possible from my family."

As a doctoral student, Bob met and married Sarah, also a doctoral student. A year after his marriage and before completing his dissertation, Bob took a faculty position at a prestigious university on the west coast. He resigned after three years of teaching because of "feelings of restlessness" and a "certain growing alienation from myself." This also created much tension in his marriage and family (two daughters were born within the first three years of marriage). The following year Bob and Sarah divorced. To give himself "some time to think and sort things through" in therapy, he became a construction manager for a real estate developer. Bob joined the Unitarian Universalist church at this time.

Two years later Bob married Joan, "an Episcopalian with a

strong sense of religious roots as well as a strong sense of family lineage." They had two daughters. Through Joan, Bob tried to regain aspects of his life that he had rejected. Bob became a consultant with a small firm, a position he held for six years until becoming a fulltime seminarian.

Each major career and lifestyle change intensified Bob's inner turmoil and confusion until these feelings threatened to overwhelm him. In his initial visit, Bob expressed a profound shifting in his internal structures of experience:

> I sold our home and made this move with my family and I'm not sure why I've done so. I mean I know that I wanted to pursue studies for the ministry, but I haven't been able to feel any real meaning and purpose in all this. Umm, well, I mean that I'm not sure who God is anymore or what it means to be a minister. I thought that after a year of study, I would have gotten more bearings. I am very confused and can't get a handle on my confusion. I feel like I might drown in this sea of turmoil and confusion. My asthma has gotten worse.

Bob's statement of "not knowing how God is anymore or what it means to be a minister" indicated a shifting in his self and other representations. Intense anxiety accompanied this shift. This suggested fear of a fragmentation of a self so fragile that it relied upon external structures to provide the missing internalized structures. Bob could not "get a handle on his confusion." His intensive affective state was vague and diffuse. This vagueness could be: (1) a produce of defensive separation of emotional experience into affective and cognitive fragments; or (2) the result of developmental arrest at, or regression to, the inchoate, undifferentiated, overwhelming, inexpressible, and somaticized affective states experienced before the structuralization of self and object representation (Krystal 1974, 1975; Lachmann and Stolorow 1980). Initially I suspected a developmental deficit as Bob reported that his asthma (a possible somatization) had worsened. It was vital to clarify the nature of Bob's disturbance. The core issues and themes that arose from Bob's imagery of a masked/unmasked man during the initial sessions confirmed my hypothesis that Bob's treatment needed to focus upon the structuralization of his self and object world.

The Masked/Unmasked Man

In our second meeting, Bob recounted a dream he had after our initial session:

> I was lost in the woods, which felt both strangely familiar to me and thus comforting, yet felt very apprehensive. The sun had set and night was near. As I walked along searching for the path, I met a strange man who had a mask on his face—an African-like mask. Terrified, I awakened immediately in a sweat.

As Bob recalled this dream, I noticed that he became deeply absorbed in the images with their associated affects. I suspected that Bob's dream images contained valuable diagnostic information. Moreover, his absorption in the images indicated an ability to use imagery in an altered state of consciousness or hypnotic trance.

I asked him if he wanted to explore these images further. He did. I explained that I would not guide the flow of images in terms of content suggestions but would assist him in regulating the affective impact of his images as he described what came to his awareness (Brown and Fromm 1986). Bob spontaneously reentered the dream scene, vividly describing his sensory sensations (smells, sights, sounds, etc.) of the woods. He saw the African-masked man behind a distant tree. He walked toward the man and stopped, feeling "both frightened and some anticipation because I want to know who that man is." After I suggested that he would find a way to protect himself, Bob imaged a glasslike bubble surrounding him. Thus contained and protected, Bob asked the man for his name. There was no response, but the man moved from behind the tree and stood in full view, still at a distance. Bob asked the man if he would take off his mask. After a long pause, Bob gasped and reported that the man had removed it. "The man is somehow like my father and somehow like myself but the face is only an outline of a face." Bob described the man as having a numinous quality that evoked Bob's fascination and dread. "There are no features . . . I can't make out any features on his face. I feel this weird attraction and repulsion at the same time. Somehow, I feel that he wants me to know him—that in time, I will know who he is and see the features of his face—that I am meant to know and have a relationship with this man." At this point, the images faded. Before Bob returned to full waking consciousness, I gave the posthypnotic suggestion that he would understand more fully the meaning of this encounter with the masked/unmasked man according to his readiness to understand and integrate it.

Upon returning to full waking consciousness, Bob made some associative comments. "The awesome quality of that man . . . yea, it's true, I don't know who God is anymore . . . Wow, it's just like me, a picture of me. I don't know who I am or what my features are either." Bob immediately connected the "awesome quality" of the masked/unmasked man to "God," whose representation he did not know, and then quickly attributed the featureless face to his sense of self. Surprisingly, Bob did not mention his first association to the unmasked man *during trance:* "The man is somehow like my father and somehow like myself." After Bob attributed the featureless face to his father during trance, he attributed a numinous quality to the man that evoked fear and fascination. I suspected that Bob needed to idealize his father representation and transform it into a representation of God to maintain the stability of his inner world. This representation of God contained elements of the wished-for and dreaded father image activated during trance. The absence of defined, recognizable features on the man's face indicated an undifferentiated sense of self and other, including God as symbolic other.

The ingenuity of Bob's symbolizing activity indicated his essential developmental task during therapy: to develop the capacity to "distinguish the features of the man's face in order to have a relationship with him." I encouraged Bob to elaborate on the connections between the dream/trance images and his present feelings of anxiety and being lost. By so doing, Bob clarified his motivation for entering into therapy. He wanted to develop more differentiated features of his self and object world; he wanted "to know who that man is . . . his name and identity." Bob yearned to discover and become his "true self" in order to relate to more fully differentiated "real" others whose unique features he could recognize and accept.

Although developmental deficits in self and object representations (and their associated affects) can be assessed only by evaluating the ongoing therapeutic relationship (Brown and Fromm 1986; Kohut 1971; Ornstein 1980–81), the initial interviews with patients may present sufficient data for hypothesizing about appropriate intervention strategies. In stating that he did not know the features of his face (self), his father (other), or God (symbolic other), Bob acknowledged that his "true self" had not developed. He could only relate to others from behind the mask of a "false self" (Winnicott 1965; Modell 1986). The African-like mask and the featureless face could be mirror reflections of Bob's more archaic, primitive self-other structure. Indeed, it seemed that Bob was prevented from involvement in living because he was developmentally stuck between "the mirror and the mask"—a reflected appraisal of himself, or a disguised search for one, through which the self finds or seeks affirmation of its own significance. Living had become a process of controlling the environment and other people from behind a mask (Bromberg 1986:439–40). How seriously fragmentation threatened his personality structure remained to be seen. The bubblelike image that contained and protected him during the trance experience suggested an activation of the archaic formations of his grandiose self and the idealized parental imago. This activation threatened the loss of self-cohesion and possibly indicated an underlying threat of an annihilation of the self (Adler 1985; Brown and Fromm 1986; Meissner 1986). The bubblelike enclosure also indicated Bob's need for a firm yet empathic matrix within which to soothe his fear and anxiety before he could systematically differentiate and integrate his representational world (Adler 1985; Bromberg 1986).

Since Bob easily entered into the trance state and readily expanded his awareness of the flow of images and affect, my task was to help him modulate the intensity of affect aroused, especially that of anxiety. Bob needed to develop an internal capacity for soothing before he could endure and integrate anxiety and, later, tolerate the emptiness, frustration, and rage behind the mask of a "false self" protecting the nuclear structure of a "grandiose self" (Kernberg 1975; Kohut 1971, 1972, 1977). Bob's growing ability to tolerate anxiety went hand in hand with his developing and structuring of his self (Bromberg 1986).

The Christ Light

The first month of therapy coincided with the beginning of Bob's second year of studies in ministry. Bob was learning different methods of meditation and prayer from a Catholic male professor whom Bob greatly admired. Stating that he needed "a safe place" to explore various types of meditation, Bob spent a weekend at a nearby monastery. Bob realized that he stood outside the religious tradition of the monks, and this awareness triggered "great grief and sadness" since "their spirituality is appropriate there for them, but it's not my tradition." Similarly, while reading the works of a Catholic theologian, Bob felt frustrated that he "would never really know" or understand them because they were written "outside my tradition." After Bob returned from the monastery, an elder from his own church contacted him. Bob felt validated and affirmed by someone within his own tradition. "I felt his respect for me even over the phone. I never had that before. When I hung up I cried and cried. I haven't plumbed the depths of that. I feel like I can begin to affirm my own spirit, which is precious—my very self."

Bob knew before he contacted me for therapy that I was raised in the Catholic tradition. In sharing his retreat experience, Bob conveyed to me his fear that I would never really know or understand him because I, too, stood "outside his tradition." I understood that it was important to validate his feelings of sadness (which his mother could affirm). But it was even more important to allow him to express his fear and frustration for being different from me (the expressions of which his mother inhibited).

During the first month of therapy, Bob vacillated between

91

feeling elated and good about himself when he received affirmation from admired others to feeling depressed and empty when he felt he could not "make contact" with them. Bob experienced frustration at being unable to make contact with admired (idealized) others as "ego depletion" (Bromberg 1986). Attributing power and strength to an idealized self-object, Bob felt empty and powerless when separated from it (Meissner 1986). During this time I functioned much like a parent who mirrored and affirmed Bob's vague affective states, helping him to perceive, differentiate, interpret, and verbalize his feelings as they were triggered by idealized self-object configurations. Such configurations maintained, restored, and developed his subjective world.

One pivotal session occurred when Bob wanted to explore his inability to make contact with an admired adviser. He immediately identified feelings of unworthiness. I suggested that he allow an image to emerge that could express these feelings. Spontaneously entering into a trance state, Bob began to re-enact a vivid but forgotten memory:

BOB: I'm in my room on my bed. I'm about two or three years old. I feel crazy somehow, like in my body . . . I'm frustrated, feeling very restless and my bowels are funny. [*Bob's eyes are closed but he moves his body position as if to release tension, and his face becomes visibly anguished.*]

T: What are you noticing?

B: My mother just came in. She's angry with me. I had messed up my room or something. I feel bad about it. She's angry. [*Pause. Bob's breathing becomes restricted.*] I feel like I'm choking. [*Like he feels during an asthma attack.*]

T: Is there something you would like to say to her?

B: I'm angry, I want you to go away, yet I want you here . . . [*pause*] but who I really want is my father. I want my father to hold me. [*Cries silently, pauses, and continues.*] I see myself beginning to hold me. It's me both as a parent and as a child. I'm holding my son. [*Bob sobs deeply for about five minutes, then breathes more easi-*

ly.] I feel like a deep letting go of frustration is happening, like two parts of myself are beginning to come together.

T: Two parts of yourself?

B: [Sobbing] Yea! My *self*—two parts of me here together [cups right hand into left hand]—the adult me embracing the child me. The confusion . . . I was left-handed and my parents wanted me to be right-handed. I didn't even know if I was right- or left-handed. Oh, the confusion and frustration! [*Sobs loudly and deeply for five minutes then quietly continues.*] I feel as if a white light is surrounding me. It's soft and warm. It feels like the light somehow is Christ's presence.

T: The light is Christ's presence surrounding the two sides of you?

B: It's like my former image of Christ was like a wedge between these two parts of myself, keeping them separate. Like the composite image of my parents—my father's distance and my mother's constant intrusiveness—kept these two sides of myself from coming together. It's like these old images have to be thrown out, outside the white light, this presence. [*Moves arms to embrace himself and then cups hands together.*] I want to bring them together and feel them surrounded by the presence.

T: Throughout the coming week, you will understand more fully the meaning of this experience as you are ready to understand it. When you become anxious, you will be able to feel this presence more and more within you.

B: [*Comes out of trance.*] The sermon I'm planning to give this week is on the words of the psalm, "Let me seek your face, do not hide your face from me." Face is presence!

The kinesthetic imagery of a soft, warm light ascribed to Christ's presence surrounding (holding or containing) the various parts of himself (unintegrated good and bad images of self and other) functioned like the glass bubble that protected Bob from intense anxiety during his trance imagery of meeting the man in the forest. In the imagery of this reactivated memory, however, the intrusive demands of Bob's mother, whom he needed and hated, aroused a rage that he could neither tolerate nor express for fear of retaliation. Bob's aggressive urges provoked feelings of guilt that overlaid his fear of retaliatory abandonment by mother. That left Bob in a diffuse somaticized state of confusion, longing to be held by his father. At this point, Bob ingeniously created a kinesthetic image of Christ's presence to function as the wished-for "good mother/father." Bob created his own "object" which acted as an alternative to his former image of Christ as demanding and distant. Thus he provided himself with a "presence" that would allow the split off or separated "good and bad" self-other images to come together.

Before Bob could integrate the good and bad aspects of self and other representations, he first had to recognize and own his aggressive impulses triggered by demanding-mother and disappointing-father representations. To do this work, Bob needed a new presence or a holding matrix to associate with "face": "Face is presence." The features of this face would be recognized, differentiated, and integrated only after Bob removed the mask of his "false self" and developed a positive foundation for his "true self." It is not surprising, therefore, that in the months that followed Bob became preoccupied with faces, especially an idealized maternal face symbolized by the religious imagery of the Madonna and Child. We will see how Bob removed his mask and established a positive foundation for his representational world through transformations of the Madonna and Child imagery.

The Madonna and Child

Bob received a gift from his admired Catholic professor: a large poster reproduction of *The Virgin of Vladimir,* considered the holiest icon of Russia. In this icon, the Virgin holds the Christ child in her right arm and points at Him with her left hand. The child puts His left arm around the Virgin's neck and presses His cheek against hers. This type of composition is known as the

"Virgin of Compassion" or the "Virgin of the Sweet Embrace" (Taylor 1979:22).

Fascinated by this portrayal of the Madonna and Child, Bob often gazed at it while meditating. He brought the picture to a therapy session to explore the intense feelings it aroused. Bob was intrigued by the wide throat of the Madonna. He once imaged "a white-hot iron coming from the madonna's chest and entering my own." Bob identified with the child in the picture, pressing his cheek against the Madonna's, "desperately wanting to make contact." Instead he found her wide throat and the white-hot iron terrifying. Bob spontaneously entered into trance and described the white-hot iron changing into a throbbing heart. He felt the vitality of the heartbeat and wanted to press his heart against it to take in as much as he could of this "vital heart-giving life." Then an image of bread and wine appeared, evoking a desire to "incorporate and devour it so that it becomes a part of my body."

Upon coming out of trance, Bob associated his experience with the words of the prophet Jeremiah: "Your word delighted my heart and I devoured it." Reflecting on the entrance of the white-hot iron/throbbing heart into his chest, Bob said it was like a "word being written in my heart. There's something within me that is growing that feels rather organic and powerful, but I don't know what it is."

In this episode, Bob reconstructed in fantasy his need to merge with the good, powerful mother. He established a base of positive images from which his representational world could be reconstructed, just as he had done earlier with his images of a "containing" bubble and Christ light (Brown and Fromm 1986). Bob transformed the terrifying image of being pierced with a white-hot iron coming from the chest of the Madonna (intrusive mother introject) into a vital substance like mother's milk that he wanted to "incorporate" or "devour" to make his own. Bob spoke of something growing in him that felt organic (of and from himself) yet powerful (the other, nurturing this life). Such regressive incorporative fantasies filled Bob with sustenance from an idealized, powerful other, experienced as part of the self (Meissner 1971, 1979, 1986).

The poster of the Madonna and Child functioned as a transitional self-object (Adler 1985) for Bob. Although an admired professor had given Bob the poster, his decision to bring it to therapy reflected his idealizing transference to me. By looking at the picture and projecting his split representational world onto it, Bob experienced the "intrusive mother" and "bad me" which he readily transformed into images of the "nurturing mother" and "good me." At this point, Bob's treatment focused on the introjection of the good, nurturing mother (therapist) that allowed him to experience himself as a "good me." Before Bob could deal with the intrusive or "bad" self and other representations, he had to incorporate, introject, and internalize the soothing and nurturing qualities of the good mother (therapist) to build a positive foundation for his subjective world.

After Bob gained internal solidity in his reconstructions of a more positive representational world, he transformed the image of the Madonna and Child, indicating his readiness to rework distorted or "bad" self and object representations. Bob imaged "Mary holding the child and her foot stepping on a snake." He did not want to look at the snake that seemed to possess "alive" qualities because he feared that he would "get out of control." Bob's dream of Hercules battling a three-headed snake precipitated this image. "Hercules was frightened, but he was taking an active stance to deal with the snake," reported Bob. Associations to snake images evoked Bob's memory of being sent to bed because he had refused to eat when he was about seven years old. He remembered standing at the top of the stairs yelling down at his parents. He desperately wanted attention. "I wanted my father to come up and spank me. They were ignoring me and I was angry. My father would do nothing." That evening as a child Bob had a dream, which he said recurred many times:

> Huge luminous snakes were crawling up the stairs with open mouths. They were coming up to swallow me up. I was terrified and woke up and still kept seeing them crawling onto the foot of my bed. Their mouths were huge. I began to scream and pound on the bed. My mother came in and turned on the light and asked what was wrong. I

wouldn't tell her. I just said that I wanted a glass of water. She kept pressing me to tell her but I wouldn't. I didn't want to tell her about the snakes because they were very real to me and she would deny it, saying that it wasn't real, deny my feelings, and try to make it all go away. There was something sacred about those snakes—it was between me and them—and I wasn't going to let her interfere.

Bob's rage about being punished and ignored was complicated by his fear of his parents' retaliating anger. His fear of being devoured by the snake image "represents a projection of his own aggression, linked to the rage caused by his frustration by mother" (Kernberg 1986:240). Bob hid his anger from his mother so that she could not deny or take away the sense of power arising from his aggressive urges. Once again, Bob transformed a terrifying image (of being devoured by snakes) into an attachment to the "sacred" quality (of the "luminous" snakes from which he derived power).

Neither of Bob's parents had affirmed or harnessed his aggressive urges. Consequently, whenever Bob felt aggressive impulses of anger or rage, he feared that he might lose control of himself. Rageful feelings could fragment the fragile sense of a positive self that Bob was developing (Adler 1985). After reflecting upon his dream images, Bob stated: "I feel a paralyzing terror around an inner sense of chaos. Something is falling apart, like I'm shedding something." Bob did not say that *he* felt like *he* was falling apart, but rather that he was "shedding something." It appeared that aspects of Bob's defensive structure were crumbling so that his more primitive oral conflicts and structures of experiencing could come to the surface. Bob, like Hercules, had to battle these conflicts despite his fright. Bob's identification with Hercules revealed an idealized self image that both protected him from dangerous, aggressive relationships with others and contained a hopeless yearning and love for an ideal other to rescue him. This idealization was also evident in Bob's fascination with the image of the Madonna stepping on the snake while holding the child. Eventually, "the deep aspiration and love for such an ideal mother and the hatred for the distorted, dangerous mother have to meet at some point, in the transference, and the patient has to become aware that the feared and hated analyst-mother is really one with the admired, longed-for analyst-mother" (Kernberg 1986:240).

In the following weeks, Bob noticed that he greatly identified with his three-year-old daughter. "I feel like a little child who gets assertive and then falls apart and wants to be held. But at the same time, I want to be myself." He reported intense periods of anxiety followed by guilt. Unable to deal with the intensity of these feelings, he felt paralyzed. Bob admitted that his developmental vicissitudes were similar to those of his daughter. Thus he attested to his struggle in resolving his "rapproachment crises" described by Mahler (1972) and Mahler, Pine and Bergman (1975) in the process of separation-individuation. Bob was trying to develop the structural capacity to integrate partial good/bad, giving/denying, satisfying/frustrating images of self and other.

The last transformation of the image of the Madonna and Child emerged after Bob became exhausted with the struggle. All he wanted was for the Madonna (therapist) to "look at me and accept me. Just look at me and see me for who I am." As I reflected and affirmed Bob's yearnings to be seen and accepted for who he was, with both his "good" and "bad" aspects, Bob felt "something vital growing" in him. Constricting parts of himself loosened, and an intense desire to be himself welled up. "The core of me wells up and cries out, 'I want to be me.'" Bob began to dismantle the constraining mask of the "bad" small child and parent and to see the unfolding good potential within himself more realistically (Brown and Fromm 1986; Eisen and Fromm 1983).

Through the mirroring images of the Madonna and Child, Bob removed the mask from the shadowy figure explored in his second visit. The various transmutations and transformations of this religious imagery reflected Bob's inner reorganization of his representational world. At the outset the mask and featureless face were alternately representations of father, God, and self. In removing the mask, Bob turned away (temporarily) from an idealized, undifferentiated father to a found, good mother. The process of reestablishing his representational world on a foundation of positive self-other images, however, necessitated a regression to the earliest point of the development deficit. Having merged with and incorporated the "vital, life-giving substance of the mother" (therapist), Bob established mirroring and idealizing transferences underlying his images of the Christ light and the Madonna stepping on the snake. Only when Bob found himself in the mirror could he move beyond the mirror to the mirroring person, the real mother and the real therapist (Rizutto 1979). Concomitantly, Bob established a more solid, positive self representation, manifested by his last transformation of the image of the Madonna into one who could "look at me and see me for who I am."

One does not tear off a mask without a sense of loss and sadness for what had previously organized one's subjective world (Robbins 1990). Bob described his sadness as also containing hope: "Something is falling away, or apart, everything around me, but *I'm* not falling apart." Although Bob no longer feared falling apart, the structures of his subjective world were still fragile and needed to become more differentiated and integrated to relate to others as "other." Bob now needed to develop specific features of the face of self, father, and God. Bob did this by struggling to own and integrate his love and hate toward his father and those aspects of his self connected to his father. Bob utilized religious imagery drawn from the story of the prodigal son to facilitate his process of structuralization.

The Prodigal Son

Bob had recently taken the TAT (Thematic Apperception Test) as part of a clinical pastoral education program and was haunted by a picture of a little boy sitting at the doorway of an old, empty shed. Bob envisioned the boy watching his father build something in the distance. Bob wanted to help his father but felt that getting close was too dangerous. Memories of his father's repeated rebuffs for "being in the way" activated a profound longing and a sense of emptiness: "I feel empty of my father; I have yearned to know him." Bob said that he often cried out to God to fill that emptiness. Inherent in Bob's yearning for God was a sense of basic trust (Erikson 1950) or confident expectation that his plea would be answered. Bob restored himself by gratifying his deepest wishes during meditation with an image of God (Fraiberg 1969; Rizutto 1979). From the perspective of psychoanalytic phenomenology, Bob needed a God representation to perform the functions that his real and internalized father-imago failed to do. The creation of a God representation, whose felt presence indicated acceptance, love, and self-worth, enabled Bob to better tolerate the disappointments and frustrations of the real world.

As his observing ego developed, Bob reflected upon his pattern of needing and using external structures (self-objects) to provide an internal sense of structure. "When I was in a painting course, I couldn't create anything, only copy what I saw before me. If there was no external structure, I couldn't create a painting." Similarly, he noted how he needed others to give him a sense of self-worth. "In the various jobs I've had, I've been attracted to strong male personalities whose relationship to me gave me a sense of worth and value." As Bob developed his capacity for self-hypnosis, he worked with his own images and their associated affects arising from dreams and meditation. This achievement of distinguishing his symbolic representations from his act of symbolization indicated a critical transformation in his internal subjective world. Rather than entering into trance during therapy sessions, Bob wanted to gain further insight into his discoveries through dialogue and interpretation. I affirmed his request because dialogue could enhance his capacity for a more conscious integration of his subjective world. Such dialogue also would necessitate that he relate more immediately to me.

Bob meditated on the biblical story of the prodigal son. This story stirred within him the longing to go home to his father. He recognized, however, that the "home" he really sought could be found only within himself. Identifying with the prodigal son, Bob became aware that he had spent his "whole life distancing from his father" as a defensive reaction to his profound hurt and rage at feeling "pushed aside." Bob had internalized the "distant father" representation. At the same time he had learned how to distance himself from himself by denying or rejecting his yearning for connection with his father. Bob realized that he had wanted to be an architect but, because his father was an architect, Bob denied his own desire and talent. The seed of this awareness aided Bob to unravel and let go of distorted and painful identifications with his father. This was the beginning of what Osherson (1986) calls "healing the wounded father within, an angry-sad version of ourselves that feels unloved and unlovable" (14). The image of the father-God waiting for the return of the prodigal son empowered and sustained Bob, as it held out promise of healing and reunion.

Bob then had a dream in which he heard himself being called "Robert." He searched through many empty houses for the caller. In one house he met a "scientific sort of man" who was having trouble repairing a pipe. That man called Bob by another name, to which Bob answered, "My name is Robert." After some dialogue, Bob showed the man how to fix the pipe.

Hearing his name called—and affirming that name after being misnamed—pointed toward Bob's growing stability and continuity in self-representation. Thinking that he was searching for the father who called his name, Bob was surprised to identify the "scientific sort of man" as his former self, a self whom he thought he had lost or disowned when he decided to become a minister. By showing the man how to repair the broken pipe, Bob reestablished a connection and continuity with his former self-image. This reconnection intensified his longing to reconnect with the wounded father within and his real father. This longing was manifested, once again, in Bob's religious imagery.

Reading chapter 3 of Philippians, Bob was struck by Paul's words: "All I want is to know Christ and the power of his resurrection so as to share in his sufferings." Bob showed me his journal entry written after meditating on this passage:

> I want to know you, Christ. Who are you? I want to grasp, to obtain, to embody within me that which you have already obtained. I feel my imperfection. I see, I catch only

glimpses of your profound truth. I want *to know* you, Christ, I want to know the promise of your resurrection, I want to know the *fellowship* of your sufferings. I feel afraid but let me find the strength to continue the struggle. I want to know you as you know me.

The direct address to Christ in this prayer/response reveals an intimate dialogue with a symbolic other whom Bob yearns to know even as he is known by the other. To have a relationship (fellowship) with an other, that other must be seen as separate from oneself. Bob wanted to embody (internalize) what he later clarified as "a profound connection with the source of being whom Jesus called Father and a connection with other human beings." Here, Bob's desire for "connection and relationship with others" is qualitatively different from his frustration over being unable to "make contact" with admired others. Rather than merging with the Christ light, Bob sought an identification with a more differentiated and profoundly relational Christ image. Experiencing such desires, however, evoked ambivalent feelings in Bob.

In the weeks following this meditation, Bob had dreams of "foreboding and disaster," which he understood as his fear of getting too close to others (and to me). As Bob realized that he could recognize and better tolerate his anxiety and fear, he felt a new power growing within. He struggled to internalize this new sense of power, as can be seen in these dream fragments. Bob was standing near the ruins of a large public fountain which was dry. The stonework was crumbling. The dream image changed, and Bob saw himself in his doctoral robe getting ready to preach an unprepared sermon. The robe did not fit, and Bob felt uncomfortable. As he spoke to the congregation, Bob felt a different quality in his voice. "I feel a strange power within me, a power that I am not entirely comfortable with. I continue to speak even though I feel very awkward." Another image followed in which Bob witnessed the wedding of two old people near a river. After the ceremony, Bob felt as if he had to get to the other side of the river. He asked a man who was about his own age how to cross the river. The man pointed the way. On the other side of the river, Bob confronted a strange robot made of heavy plastic. The head of the robot looked like a television monitor mounted on a set of tractor crawlers.

> It is able to move about slowly and ponderously with its all-seeing, though blank, eye screen. Although small, it is larger and more powerful than I am. It had the power to engulf and annihilate me. It wanted to know me. I am terrified yet I want to deal with this omniscient robot. I want to be able to confront it, to wrestle with it, to engage it *as an equal.* I examine its undercarriage to see how it moves and what its real capabilities and limitations are."

Bob's dismantling of negative self-images (the crumbling walls of the fountain, the robe not fitting) and speaking spontaneously in his own voice with a new (although awkward) power revealed the possibility of blending or mending the negative and positive parental imagos (wedding of two old people). However, for Bob to claim this power, he had to cross the river and battle the aggrandized all-powerful and all-knowing robot (impersonal father representation) to bring it to more realistic proportions.

In reflecting on these dream images, Bob recognized his desire to be seized and grasped by the all-powerful robot (father representation) but resisted "surrendering" to this desire. Bob wanted to engage the robot figure "as an equal," to confront it on its own terms, to discover its strengths and limits. By trying to identify the specific, differentiated features of the robot, Bob confronted his propensity for indiscriminate idealization of "authority figures." He reclaimed the power provided by his scientific self-image, knowing he had been "trained in fixing and mastery." It is no wonder that Bob represented his "all-powerful" father imago as a mechanical robot. Still, the impersonal quality of the robot with its attribution of magical power suggested that Bob needed to contend with unrealistic fantasies of parental imagos to achieve solid, separate self and object constancy and to gain control of splitting as a defense (Brown and Fromm 1986). Working with the dream fragments and their associated affects allowed Bob to identify and talk about those unrealistic feelings and fantasies that had a destructive (paralyzing) effect on him, thereby making them more ego dystonic.

In the following weeks, Bob reported foreboding dreams of danger. While he felt the danger, he also experienced excitement and hopefulness in facing the danger. This series of dreams culminated in one in which Bob attended a national board meeting of his denomination. He was a young priest, dressed in a white vestment. The bishop and other officials were also present. Two organizations were presenting proposals for a water project in an underdeveloped country, and a question of commissions arose. Bob spoke powerfully, angrily, and passionately: "NO! Commissions paid by the people is a form of slavery."

This was the first time that Bob recalled saying "no" to authority figures, even in a dream. He noticed how he continually gave away his "power" to those in authority and thus "enslaved" himself "like the prodigal son who squandered his own inheritance." Bob recalled that he did not attend his doctoral graduation and had not fully claimed this achievement for himself. Working with this insight, Bob affirmed his talents, qualities, and achievements. As I affirmed his realistic self-appraisals, Bob felt a growing sense of internal self-worth as he began to sort through what *he* wanted to do.

As Bob's self-esteem became internalized, he dreamed that he was looking for office space. His father offered him the space if Bob would agree to paint it. He awoke feeling sadness and grief. Bob's affect was of a different quality as he discussed the dream. His sadness was triggered by the awareness that he had put "a lot of space between" himself and his father, that the failure in relationship with his father had "been my fault as well." This acknowledgment led to deep remorse and contrition.

Bob reported another dream in which his father took an active interest in Bob's activities. Bob's images of the approachable "good father" modified those of the "distant" father. Bob developed his capacity to see the pervasive pattern of his own "distancing" defenses that prevented him from being close to significant others. Bob's feelings of contrition deepened and extended to include deep regret and sorrow for "misusing" his parents, wives, and children. In reflecting on the pattern of his relationships, particularly with his wife and children, Bob stated: "I needed them to be there for me so desperately that I could not be there for them in an adult way." Such a recognition convinced Bob that his "life had been a lie," and evoked in him "a pervasive sense of sin." With this shattering feeling of shame and anguishing aloneness, he turned to God in meditation and cried out for mercy, praying the words of Psalm 51: "Have mercy on me, O God, according to thy steadfast love; blot out my transgression. Cleanse me from my sin." Bob did not hide his shame and guilt behind a mask. Rather he presented himself as he was to God and to me (therapist), exposing his sense of shame and taking full responsibility for his actions, desiring to be forgiven and healed (Morrison 1986).

At this crucial time in his therapy, it was important that I be with him in his pain but that I not reassure him prematurely (Kernberg 1986). I was steadfast in my regard toward him in his shame, guilt, and grief, and Bob eventually understood that he had not "destroyed" me (or others) and that I was still available to him as a good and forgiving person.

That Bob had begun to internalize a good and forgiving object could be seen in dream images in which he moved emotionally toward his father: "Daddy, I love you. I want to be with you. I want to know you." During his meditation, Bob repeated the words of Psalm 27: "Show me your face. Hide not your face from me." Bob then recalled the prodigal son's longing to return to his father's house, but stated again that he couldn't go back to his parents. "I must come to birth within myself." Although these pleas to know the face of the other echoed Bob's earlier yearnings, it is significant that here Bob did not create an image of self-protection. Having acquired a more stable and whole sense of self and other, Bob could admit his yearning for closeness and relationship. As Bob became more immediately present to himself and to others, he was more open to discovering the real features of the other. Bob actively sought to differentiate the features of his actual parents, as well as his internalized parental imagos. Bob wrestled with experiencing himself as both wounded and blessed and subsequently drew upon the biblical image of Jacob wrestling with the angel to further the structuralization of his subjective world.

Jacob Wrestling with the Angel

I suggested to Bob that he might need to forgive *himself* for what he had called "the profound lie of his life." This triggered feelings of intense sorrow and grief. The quality of Bob's longing and sadness was different, however, indicating that Bob had achieved a developmental milestone. True longing and grief can be experienced only in relation to a more or less whole and separate object (not one that serves predominantly as a self-object) (Kohut 1971, 1977; Lachmann and Stolorow 1980). Bob's struggle to internalize this forgiveness became manifest in his meditation on Jacob's wrestling with the angel. "Even though you wound me, I will wrestle with you until you bless me." True forgiveness meant that Bob would experience a blessing in and through his being wounded.

In the following weeks, Bob took an active interest in learning more about his father and mother as people shaped by their own unique histories and psychological makeup. He realized that reestablishing a relationship with them did not mean that he was "going back to his parents' home" (Osherson 1986; Robbins 1990; Williamson 1981). He took a special trip to visit his parents and to talk with them about their experiences. Although feeling awkward and self-conscious, Bob was surprised at his ability to "see them and hear their stories. It was very different being with them. Yet, they only could or would share external details about their lives—some of which was very new for me."

As Bob pieced together the "facts" of his parents' lives as they intersected with his own, he forgave them for wounding him, and he forgave himself "for the profound lie" of his life. In doing so, he was able to accept and appreciate his parents for who they were and are (Osherson 1986; Robbins 1990). Gradually, Bob perceived himself as wounded yet blessed by those he most loved. Likewise, he perceived that he had wounded others who yet chose to remain in relationship with him.

Bob was developing a deeper awareness of his own emotional life and an ability to feel real concern for and interest in others as well as in his own internal life. During the weeks in which we worked on termination issues, one of Bob's former mentors was dying. Bob felt great sadness over this loss, but noted that he still had in himself what his mentor (and therapist) had given him. Bob reflected on his "power to make choices" and stated, "We have the ability to hold images that change our lives." This empowered Bob to reweave the threads of connection of self in relation to significant others in a more complex and richly textured pattern, both in his internal representational world and in his actual relationships (Robbins 1990). The featureless face of the unmasked man now had differentiated features. Bob was able to know and be in relationship with this man—his self, his father (and significant others), and his God.

This paper has shown how religious imagery in dynamic hypnotherapy facilitated the process of psychological structuralization in the case of Bob. His various uses and transformations of religious imagery—particularly those of the masked/unmasked man, the Christ light, the Madonna and Child, the prodigal son, and Jacob wrestling with the angel—illustrate the relationship between the symbolic object, transference relationship, and internalized object (Randour and Bondanza 1987). The dynamic interaction of these components generated movement and structuralization.

At the beginning of treatment, Bob wanted to identify (differentiate) the features of an "unmasked man" who he confusedly thought represented his self, father, and God. He also wanted to make and maintain a sustained connection with those whom he loved, to relate to them as distinct human beings with their own scars and giftedness. To do this, Bob had "to come to birth" within himself; he had to discover and develop his "true self."

Before Bob could discover and develop his true self, he had to face the masked/unmasked man. This was frightening, so Bob had to find a way to protect himself. He created a glasslike bubble to contain and protect various parts of himself while he faced the undifferentiated features of the unmasked man. He then faced the process of structuralizing the self and the other. In this process, Bob continued to create ways to protect himself from intense affects. He drew upon religious imagery for help. Bob imaged a soft, warm light—Christ's light—surrounding various parts of himself (unintegrated, good and bad images of self and other). This light protected Bob from his aggressive urges. Bob's use of the religious image of Christ's light, and later the Madonna and Child, revealed his need for a self-object that would be protective as well as soothing.

Before Bob could integrate the "good and bad" self-other images, he had to recognize and own his aggressive impulses triggered by demanding-mother and disappointing-father representations. Bob needed to internalize soothing functions provided by a new kind of presence or holding matrix. He turned to the imagery of the Madonna and Child. To establish a more positive foundation on which to build his subjective world, Bob regressed to the earliest point in his developmental deficit—the symbiotic phase of the separation-individuation process (Mahler, Pine and Bergman 1975). After regressing to incorporative fantasies of merger with a powerful yet compassionate mother, Bob began to take incremental steps in structuring his representational world through symbolizing the Madonna as the good mother who could see and accept him for who he was in both his "good" and "bad" aspects. I took on the role of the nurturing and mirroring mother, affirming him in his successes in real life and in therapy. Bob began to integrate his split images of the "all good" and "all bad" mother with those good and bad self representations rooted in his relationship to his mother.

Having internalized the good mother imago, Bob turned toward dealing with the loved and hated aspects of his father representation. Recognizing dimly that he had distanced himself as a defense from the hurt and rage provoked by his "distant father," Bob turned to the various images in the biblical story of the prodigal son. Believing that the father in this story (wished-for father and God representation) truly desired reconciliation, Bob realized that he must establish a different relationship with his father within his subjective world. By reclaiming his scientific self representations as well as his real talents and accomplishments, Bob differentiated the features of his own face as distinct from his father's. Bob realized how he had enslaved himself, "squandering away my own inheritance," by alternately idealizing and devaluing authority figures. While I continued to provide empathic mirroring, I pointed out that Bob could love and be loved by those who hurt and disappointed him. Bob recognized and affirmed himself in more realistic ways, thus consolidating object constancy.

Having established a sense of his self as distinct from others, Bob focused on working through his deep sense of shame and guilt for having "misused" others to alleviate his own desperate neediness. Wounded himself, he wounded others. The religious imagery provided by Jacob wrestling with the angel challenged and sustained Bob during this period of deep grief and mourning. Believing himself to be forgiven by God, Bob began to forgive himself and others—especially his parents. As he did so, he experienced himself as one who had been wounded *and* as one who had also been blessed. I was with him in his pain, but I did not reassure him of forgiveness prematurely. If I had done so, I could have aborted the process of his recognizing and working through his shame and guilt. I believe that Bob's inability to tolerate or regulate these feelings early in his life had led him to put on a "mask" and prevented him from knowing and distinguishing the features of his own face from those of significant others.

I utilized the hypnotic techniques of imagery and fantasy production, age regression, free association, and hypnotic and posthypnotic suggestion most extensively at the beginning of treatment. Bob easily entered into trance, partly because of his regressive state at this time. Hypnosis also facilitated this regression at a faster rate, disclosing the core therapeutic issues (developmental deficits) that needed to be treated, and suggesting the next step toward the structuralization of Bob's subjective world. As Bob began to integrate his split images of self and other, he became less interested in working with hypnosis. Rather than use a "trance" during therapy sessions, Bob wanted us to discuss the varied and rich images that arose during his meditation and from his dreams.

Bob's receptive listening to, engagement with, and reflection on the words of scripture actively facilitated his therapeutic process. This was due to four factors: (1) Bob was adept at choosing scriptural passages to meditate on that addressed his inner state, whether actual, desired, or both; (2) Bob believed that God was addressing him in his particular situation/state; (3) Bob believed that God wanted him to know and be in relationship with God as well as with others, and that God wanted him to be genuinely himself; and (4) Bob trusted that the therapeutic process was a crucial part of his "spiritual journey" insofar as it would help him deal with those defensive patterns or developmental deficits that prohibited him from attaining and maintaining the quality of relationship (with self, others, and God) that he so desired. Bob's rich illusionistic world undergirded and fueled each of these four points.

"Reality and illusion are not contradictory terms" (Rizutto 1979:209). Without that transitional space for illusion and play, human beings would be deprived of what makes them most genuinely human: engagement in the creative symbolic processes of art, culture, and religion. "That is the place where man's life finds the full relevance of his objects and meaning for himself" (Rizutto 1979:209). Although Bob's religious imagery evolved from a tutored fantasy rooted in the collective imagination of the Judeo-Christian scriptures and tradition, we can see traces of significant internal and external objects in its form and content. Many other factors gracefully interconnected with such religious imagery to facilitate Bob's psychological structuralization. Aided by the therapeutic context, Bob was ready to create more complex and richly textured representations of his self in relation to himself, significant others, and God.

References

Adler, G. 1985. *Borderline Psychopathology and Its Treatment*. New York: Jason Aronson.

Atwood, G. and R. D. Stolorow. 1984. *Structures of Subjectivity: Explorations in Psychoanalytic Phenomenology*. Hillsdale, N.J.: Analytic Press.

Bowers, P. and K. S. Bowers. 1972. Hypnosis and creativity: A theoretical and empirical rapprochement. In E. Fromm and R. E. Shor, eds., *Hypnosis: Research Developments and Perspectives* pp. 255–91. Chicago: Aldine-Atherton.

Bromberg, P. M. 1986. The mirror and the mask: On narcissism and psychoanalytic growth. In A. Morrison, ed., *Essential Papers on Narcissism* pp. 438–66. New York: New York University Press. [Originally published 1983]

Brown, D. and E. Fromm. 1986. *Hypnotherapy and Hypnoanalysis*. Hillsdale, N.J.: Lawrence Erlbaum Associates.

Eisen, M. R. and E. Fromm. 1983. The clinical use of self-hypnosis in hypnotherapy: Tapping the functions of imagery and adaptive regression. *International Journal of Clinical and Experimental Hypothesis* 31: 243–55.

Erikson, E. 1950. *Childhood and Society*. New York: Norton.

Fraiberg, S. 1969. Libidinal object constancy and mental representation. *The Psychoanalytic Study of the Child* 24: 9–47. New York: International Universities Press.

Fromm, E. 1977. Altered states of consciousness and hypnosis: A discussion. *International Journal of Clinical and Experimental Hypnosis* 25: 325–34.

Hilgard, E. R. 1973. The domain of hypnosis, with some comments on alternative paradigms. *American Psychologist* 28: 972–82.

Horowitz, M. J. 1970. *Image Formation and Cognition*. New York: Appleton-Century-Crofts.

Kegan, R. 1982. *The Evolving Self*. Cambridge: Harvard University Press.

Kernberg, O. F. 1975. *Borderline Conditions and Narcissism*. New York: Aronson.

——. 1976. *Object Relations Theory and Clinical Psychoanalysis*. New York: Aronson.

——. 1986. Factors in the psychoanalytic treatment of narcissistic personalities. In A. Morrison, ed., *Essential Papers on Narcissism*, pp. 213–44. New York: New York University Press. [Originally published 1970]

Klein, G. S. 1967. Peremptory ideation: Structure and force in motivated ideas. In R. R. Hair, ed., *Motives and Thought: Psychoanalytic Essays in Honor of David Rapaport*. New York: International Universities Press, pp. 80–130.

Kohut, H. 1971. *The Analysis of the Self*. New York: International Universities Press.

——. 1972. Thoughts on narcissism and narcissistic rage. *The Psychoanalytic Study of the Child* 27: 360–402. New Haven: Yale University Press.

——. 1977. *The Restoration of the Self*. New York: International Universities Press.

Krystal, H. 1974. The genetic development of affects and affect regression. *Annual of Psychoanalysis* 2: 98–126.

——. 1975. Affect tolerance. *Annual of Psychoanalysis* 3: 179–220.

Lachmann, F., B. Beebe, and R. Stolorow. 1987. Increments of separation in the consolidation of the self. In Jonathan Bloom-Feshbach, Sally Bloom-Feshbach, and associates, eds., *The Psychology of Separation and Loss: Perspectives on Development, Life Transitions, and Clinical Practice*, pp. 396–415. San Francisco: Jossey-Bass.

Lachmann, F. and R. Stolorow. 1980. The developmental significance of affective states: Implications for psychoanalytic treatment. *Annual of Psychoanalysis* 8: 215–29.

Mahler, M. S. 1972. On the first three sub-phases of the separation-individuation process. *International Journal of Psychoanalysis* 53: 333–38.

Mahler, M. S., F. Pine, and A. Bergman. 1975. *The Psychological Birth of the Human Infant*. New York: Basic Books.

Meissner, W. W. 1971. Notes on identification: 2—Clarification of related concepts. *Psychoanalytic Quarterly* 40: 277–302.

———. 1979. Internalization and object-relations. *Journal of American Psychoanalytic Association* 27: 345–60.

———. 1986. Narcissistic personalities and borderline conditions: A differential diagnosis. In A. Morrison, ed., *Essential Papers on Narcissism,* pp. 403–37. New York: New York University Press. [Originally published 1959]

Modell, A. 1986. A narcissistic defense against affects and the illusion of self-sufficiency. In A. Morrison, ed., *Essential Papers on Narcissism,* pp. 293–307. New York: New York University Press. [Originally published 1975]

Morrison, A. 1986. Shame, ideal self, and narcissism. In A. Morrison, ed., *Essential Papers on Narcissism,* pp. 348–69. New York: New York University Press. [Originally published 1983]

Niebuhr, H. R. 1963. *The Responsible Self.* New York: Harper & Row.

Ornstein, A. 1980–81. Transferences as differential diagnostic tools in psychoanalysis. *International Journal of Psychoanalytic Psychotherapy* 8: 115–23.

Osherson, S. 1986. *Finding Our Fathers: The Unfinished Business of Manhood.* New York: The Free Press.

Parks, S. 1986. *The Critical Years: The Young Adult Search for a Faith to Live By.* New York: Harper & Row.

Piaget, J. 1970. *Structuralism.* New York: Basic Books.

Randour, M. L. and J. Bondanza. 1987. The concept of God in the psychological formation of females. *Psychoanalytic Psychology* 4: 301–13.

Reyher, J. 1963. Free imagery: An uncovering procedure. *Journal of Clinical Psychology* 19: 454–59.

Rizutto, A.-M. 1979. *The Birth of the Living God.* Chicago: Chicago University Press.

Robbins, M. 1990. *Midlife Women and Death of Mother: A Study of Psychohistorical and Spiritual Transformation.* New York: Peter Lang.

Shor, R. E. 1959. Hypnosis and the concept of the generalized reality-orientation. *American Journal of Psychotherapy* 13: 582–602.

Silberer, H. 1951. On symbol formation. In D. Rapaport, ed., *Organization and Pathology of Thought: Selected Sources,* pp. 208–23. New York: Columbia University Press.

Stolorow, R. D. and F. M. Lachmann. 1980. *Psychoanalysis of Developmental Arrests: Theory and Treatment.* New York: International Universities Press.

Surrey, J. 1985. The "self-in-relation": A theory of women's development. *Work in Progress, Paper No. 13.* Wellesley College: Stone Center for Developmental Services and Studies.

Taylor, J. 1979. *Icon Painting.* New York: Mayflower Books.

Williamson, D. S. 1981. Personal authority via termination of the intergenerational hierarchical boundary: A "new" stage in the family life cycle. *Journal of Marital and Family Therapy* 7: 441–52.

Winnicott, D. W. 1953. Transitional objects and transitional phenomena. *International Journal of Psycho-Analysis* 34: 2.

———. 1965. *The Maturational Processes and the Facilitating Environment.* New York: International Universities Press.

Myth and Symbol as Expressions of the Religious

ROBERT GOODMAN

> I think what we are looking for [in myths] is a way of experiencing the world that will open to us the transcendent that informs it, and at the same time forms ourselves within it. That is what people want. That is what the soul asks for.
>
> —Joseph Campbell, *The Power of Myth*

> The symbol is not a sign that veils something everybody knows. Such is not its significance: on the contrary, it represents an attempt to elucidate, by means of analogy, something that belongs entirely to the domain of the unknown or something that is yet to be.
>
> —C. G. Jung, *Two Essays on Analytic Psychology*

Human beings inherently seek order, purpose, and truth, consciously and unconsciously. We seek to create meaningful reality in our personal lives, in our families, community, society, culture and now, of necessity, on our planet. Finally, we seek meaning on the level of existence and ultimacy. Religion and faith can be thought of as being the human activity of constructing meaning on the level of ultimacy (Parks 1986:9–19). The idea of religious experience as a human, constructing, meaning-making process is one of the core concepts of this paper. This constructing of meaning is both a conscious and unconscious act; in this paper I shall focus on the latter.

Jung was deeply interested in the personalized rituals of religious experience, so-called mental methods of self-training such as yoga or contemplative prayer. Jung's psychology of religion stems in part from his belief that established forms of religious ritual have lost their efficacy for many people in the West in part because of the emphasis on highly structured rather than personalized experiences of the religious. For Jung this direct experience of the religious means the "spontaneous encounter with the living symbols of the unconscious psyche . . . the quest for a highly personalized experience of wholeness, the quest for a highly personalized experience of the truth" (Aziz 1990:10).

Campbell, a neo-Jungian educator, mythologist, and anthropologist, also locates our present day religious yearning in the individual, away from the tribe, group, and culture. He too emphasizes the role of the unconscious. He claims that historic inherited religious formulae have disintegrated and the center of gravity has shifted to wonder:

> The descent of the Occidental sciences from the heavens to the earth (from seventeenth century astronomy to nineteenth century biology), and their concentration today, at last, on man himself (in twentieth century anthropology and psychology), mark the path of a prodigious transfer for the focal point of human wonder. Not the animal world, not the plant world, not the miracle of the spheres, but man himself is now the crucial mystery. Man, understood however not as "I" but as "Thou": for the ideals and temporal institutions of no tribe, race, continent, social class, or century, can be the measure of the inexhaustible and multifariously wonderful divine existence that is the life in all of us.   (Campbell 1949:391)

In this essay I shall concentrate on the idea that the religious or spiritual (I shall use these terms interchangeably) is experienced through one's inner life, and that the unconscious or inner life, as Jung and Campbell contend, is the primary, though by no means the only, seat of symbolic and mythic meaning. I specifically focus on the client's spontaneous creation of myth and symbol and on the therapist's role to jointly construct with the client the deepest meaning of these symbols and myths on behalf of the client's evolving spiritual and psychological development.

My definition of the religious contains two essential elements: 1) the direct expression of symbol and myth through the unconscious, and 2) the integration of the universal meanings of these symbols and myths into the person's evolving development toward wholeness. Generally, the first element involves sensing and imaging while the second involves thinking, evaluating, and intuiting. This definition emphasizes process, i.e., the spontaneous creative act of symbol and myth formation (not the symbols themselves) and the person's understanding and experiencing of the meanings of these symbols as psychologically and spiritually integral (not the meanings in and of themselves). These processes lead the individual to an experience of wholeness, by which I mean the integration of one's conscious realities and unconscious potentials through imaginal creations. The definitions of these terms will be discussed further in more detail.

Jung wrote, "The religious need longs for wholeness, and therefore lays hold of the images of wholeness offered by the unconscious, which, independently of the conscious mind, rise up from the depths of our psychic nature" (Aziz 1990:11). I contend that psychotherapy should be a context for this depth exploration, in which the therapist assumes the responsibility for welcoming and facilitating the client's spontaneous unconscious productions, viewing them not only as historical but also as prospective signs. The therapist facilitates a full understanding of these symbols and myths, joining with the client's efforts to create personal and ultimate meaning.

Myth and Symbol

Myths have been used by people since ancient times as a way to organize and transmit their deepest sentiments to future generations. Campbell has said the they are the clues to the spiritual potentialities of life, that they are the experience of life itself (Campbell 1988:5). Furthermore, he has claimed that "the prime function of mythology and rite is to supply the symbols that carry the human spirit forward, in counteraction to those other constant human fantasies that tend to tie it back. . . . It may well be that the very high incidence of neuroticism among ourselves follows from the decline among us of such effective spiritual aid" (Campbell 1949:11). To live mythically "is to seek guidance from your dreams, imagination and other reflections of your inner being . . . to cultivate an ever-deepening relationship with the universe and its great mysteries" (Feinstein and Krippner 1988:1).

Symbols, the building blocks of myths, have been studied exhaustively by Jung. As defined by Jung, symbols are

> the expression of transcendent content, i.e., information which can't be completely explained by logic and analysis. The rational mind recognizes a symbol without being able to apprehend its meaning. Symbols hint at a mystery, but always rank below the mystery they seek to describe. Symbols are shorthand for a com-

plex of factors; never do they mean one thing—the depth of meaning, in fact, is only limited by the resources of the interpreter [and inventor of the symbol]. (1989:152)

Because symbols point to the not fully knowable they imply a transpersonal dimension of reality. By emphasizing the symbolic, the Jungian approach thereby accepts such a dimension as a basic concern of psychic life. In the terms I have set forth, the symbolic dimension is a manifestation of the need for meaning in life on the level of ultimacy. Although the dream may lead the dreamer to new understandings of his or her past and current life, it also leads him or her to a spiritual dimension of meaning when interpreted symbolically or mythically.

According to Jung, myth and symbol originate from the collective unconscious and commonly surface in nocturnal dreams, but may also appear in daydreams, visions, and as part of the creative imagination. Jung conceptualized the unconscious as composed of two aspects, the personal unconscious and the collective unconscious. "The personal unconscious contains lost memories, painful ideas that are repressed (i.e., forgotten on purpose), subliminal perceptions, by which are meant sense-perceptions that were not strong enough to reach consciousness, and finally, contents that are not yet ripe for consciousness" (Jung 1966:65). This is similar but not identical to the unconscious and preconscious of Freud. Jung believed that the personal unconscious contains more than repressed material, thus his phrase, "contents that are not yet ripe for consciousness." In other words the personal unconscious could contain material that never was in consciousness and the coming into consciousness of this new material defines the individual's potential. Freud's unconscious was historical and pointed to conflictual material repressed from the past.

In contrast to the personal unconscious, the collective unconscious is a primitive psychic structure which is impersonal or transpersonal because its contents are found everywhere. It is often referred to as a universal unconscious. "The collective unconscious is better conceived as an extension of the personal unconscious to its wider and broader base, encompassing contents which are held in common by the family, by the social group, by tribe and nation, by race, and eventually by all of humanity. [It contains] all the legend and history of the human race" (Singer 1972:94–95). Jung's two types of unconscious are not distinctly realized. The "personal material brought up by individuals in therapy shows the effects of its collective background and often is as a personal voice giving expression to an age old liturgy" (Singer 1972:95). I shall offer several examples which illustrate this interrelationship.

Edward Whitmont, a distinguished Jungian analyst, makes a distinction between allegory and image on the one hand, and myth and symbol on the other.

> Allegorical descriptions widen and correct our view in respect to personal and mentally accessible facts which we have overlooked or preferred not to see. The imaginal form of representation is merely an expression of the fact that the message comes from the "image seer" in the psyche. The message—even though it may use poetic license and dramatic exaggeration—can in principle, be rationally interpreted and understood. Its subject matter is directly observable facts, external or psychological, even though unconscious, outside of the dreamer's awareness. These are constituents of what Jung called the personal unconscious.   (1987:58)

Much of the therapist's work with a client resides on this level, that is, making accessible the meaning of one's personal history, exposing and articulating what I consider to be life themes—core issues that the individual has organized into stories, albeit unconscious or partially conscious. According to the Jungian view, these life themes can be understood by the rational mind. Symbol and myth, in contrast, are not rationally understood, and cannot be apprehended logically. In physics, the idea of electrons moving around a central nucleus is posited as a model only approximating the true essence of an atom. Scientists can only "know" an atom to be thus, yet are aware that this is "as if" language. The same is true for myth and symbol.

Many years ago, in face-to-face therapy, I viewed the analyst's couch every week for two years before I finally asked to lie on it. In a matter of seconds, I had an *image* of my grandmother, and seconds after that I experienced a tingling sensation on my arm. When I put words to this experience, I spoke of how good it felt to sit in her lap as a young child and how soft her skin felt against mine. I recalled times when as a nine-year-old, I would stroke her arm, no doubt evoking the soothing and comfort she provided me when I was an infant.

I was struck by the immediacy of the sensation and how quickly I remembered something theretofore forgotten. The kinesthetic sensation and the visual image of my grandmother represented nurturance and care. The place of this memory in the context of my therapy and the associations with my therapist became the content of the allegory that began as this image. I understood the meaning of this image rationally, and it came solely from my personal history and past. It stands in contrast to a symbol, which embodies universal meaning.

Whitmont, (1987:59) provides another example of an image: "A middle-aged businessman in a state of depression dreamed: I was in bed with a young girl and had just finished intercourse. Then I heard a voice saying in Hungarian—my mother tongue—that I did not deserve the *fa* or *fasz*. (In Hungarian, *fa* means wood, *fasz* means penis.) I was not sure which, perhaps both." The personal allegory of this dream, when checked with the client, was not about how the dreamer undervalues sexuality or represses his sexual potency or masculine aggressiveness. In his life the dreamer was aggressive and reported that in the dream he had enjoyed the sexual encounter and performed it satisfactorily. He was unable to speak at all about the wood, and his only association was to some woodcarving he had done as a child. Viewed symbolically or mythologically, by equating the penis with wood, the dreamer opens up a possible representation of a transpersonal reality. Jung calls such structures archetypes, or

> "a priori motivational energy configurations which express themselves in typical representational images, typical emotions and behavior patterns characteristic of the human species, analogous to the instinctual patterns observed in animal behavior."
>
> Archetypal images appear most often in contemporary form, not in historical costume. One can recognize them by their thematic analogy to myth, fairy tale, religious tradition and artistic imagination." (cited in Whitmont 1987:59)

After exploring the personal meaning of the dream, the therapist always asks the dreamer for his or her mythologically oriented associations and, if none occur, the therapist has to draw upon knowledge of humankind's associations, i.e., the collective historical understanding of such symbols. This requires that the therapist have a knowledge of mythology, religion, and anthropology (all of which have important implications for the therapist's role). Returning to the dream, the "phallus that is also wood is a widespread cult object" used in Indian and Egyptian cultures:

> The wooden phallus represented the generative power of Osiris, restored to life by Isis from death and dismemberment; his natural phallus was lost and Isis substituted a wooden one by means of which he begot the child, Horus, on her. The wooden phallus, then, is not naturally, unconsciously and automatically grown but deliberately created. It signifies creativity that is not of the flesh, of natural being, but of striving of the spirit, of immortality . . . It is to the mystery of spiritual renewal that the symbol of the wooden phallus points, and in respect to this, not to overt sexual prowess, the worthiness of the dreamer is questioned by the dream. (Whitmont 1987:60)

The validity of this assumption seems borne out, since the dreamer described the young girl as opportunistic, unscrupulous, and repulsive. She can be thought of as representing the unconscious aspect of the dreamer's psyche, "representing (allegorically) the opportunistic tendencies with which he is so deeply involved (depicted by sexual union) so as to become almost incapable of a creative renewal in his life" (Whitmont 1987:60).

If this dreamer's therapist had maintained a theoretical stance that interpreted the dream on a purely sexual level, the fullness of its meaning would have been reduced to fit the interpreter's theory. Alternatively, if the therapist had rightly interpreted the dream according to the dreamer's associations and experience of the dream and not gone further, he or she would have missed the deeper significance of the dreamer's myth. This would have been a less serious "error," to my mind, for the personal meaning of the dream would still have been adequately understood and the dreamer could have made use of the interpretation. However, the deeper significance of the myth would have been missed if the seemingly irrational or irrelevant detail of the wooden phallus had gone unanalyzed.

In this example, Jung's view of the unconscious is of a resource and ally that dynamically informs the ego or consciousness, and vice versa. The Jungian unconscious is at the center of the personality where it compensates for the ego, primarily through dreams, by illustrating what has not yet been considered. The unconscious of Jung has a compensatory effect that balances and heals conscious preoccupations, possessing future-directed capacities that point toward solutions for the dreamer. Jung claims that everything we can be is *in potentia* in the unconscious; thus leading us into the realm of hopes, aspirations, and yearnings bridging the psychological and spiritual domains.

The Therapist's Stance

In accepting the importance of a person's unconscious life as the bed-rock of spiritual development, the therapist must assume a particular stance with clients to facilitate understanding of the deeper significance of the client's unconscious processes. The therapist must be schooled in mythology, anthropology, folklore, and the great religious traditions, as well as in the discipline of psychology. This is quite a charge and I view this breadth of knowledge as a lifetime goal. For the therapist to be able to facilitate the client's deepest understanding of the transcendent aspect of these symbols, we must go beyond typical training requirements for therapist education.

Campbell speaks of the analyst as "mystagogue . . . or guide of souls, the initiating medicine man of the primitive forest sanctuaries of trial and initiation . . . His role is precisely that of the Wise Old Man of the myths and fairy tales whose words assist the hero through the trials and terrors of the weird adventure" (Campbell 1949:9). It is hard to know if this is the role Jung envisioned for himself and his followers, though it is true that Jung studied these disciplines thoroughly in his lifetime.

The idea of therapist as mystagogue is an intimidating one; to many, it connotes that the therapist is an agent of the divine. This is more than most therapists are willing or able to assume. It is not necessary to think of oneself in this way in order to interpret the symbolic nature of dreams; in fact it could create problems if it drew the therapist's attention away from a client's personally felt dilemmas. The therapist seeks to delve beneath the apparent meaning of things to the lesser-known and understood aspects of life, reflecting on each symbol and myth carefully, analyzing and researching its meaning. It is essential that the therapist feel comfortable addressing spiritual issues and themes.

However we envision our role, I believe there are certain functions that must be fulfilled by the therapist who is concerned with deciphering symbols. I shall speak of three of them: welcoming, facilitating, and amplifying. As in any model of therapy, the first order of business is to establish safety and trust. This dynamic process takes time. Generally in the beginning of a therapy relationship, the therapist supports the client in her or his concerns through acceptance of the client's construction of her or his issues (I am not discussing here delusional or psychotic people), actively inquiring into the nature of the problem(s) and the feelings associated with them, all the while refraining from interpretation. Regardless of the therapist's knowledge and skill in interpreting symbolic unconscious meaning, it will be of little value to the dreamer unless there is a good therapeutic relationship. Development, the primary goal in therapy, occurs when this interpretive work is performed carefully in the context of genuine empathy honoring the client's meaning making on all levels.

Early in therapy, I inform my clients that I work with dreams and practice collaborative hypnosis (Brown and Fromm 1986) as a method of insight-oriented therapy. (Collaborative hypnosis can also be used for the treatment of behavioral issues.) Since most of my clients do not come to me for hypnotherapy, if they express interest I then spend some time educating them about hypnosis, distinguishing it from the prevalent and historical stereotypes. This requires some exploration into the fantasies and real experiences that people have had with hypnosis. Never is a client pressured into working in this modality if he or she feels uncomfortable. It is both antitherapeutic and unnecessary, since there are other means of working with unconscious material.

Welcoming also includes imparting to the client (in a way that is natural to the therapist) the idea that it is valuable to increase awareness of one's inner life and that through this awareness, the self moves naturally toward integrity (individuation, in Jung's term), regardless of the disintegration that necessarily occurs in the process of therapy. For the severely troubled client, as with psychotic process, I might not recommend this process of uncovering or, if I do, it might not be until quite some time after a stable relationship between therapist and client is developed.

I hold out to my clients the view that their unconscious is a resource and ally that can aid in the discovery of new ways of acting and of understanding and feeling about the self. Often, this is met with some resistance. One does not easily overturn a client's belief that the unconscious is to be approached with extreme caution because it contains conflictual repressed material. There may be good reason for the client to feel this way, as for example with the person who has been abused but has no memory of it, or the Vietnam veteran who has suffered torture. Good judgment is critical on the therapist's part. The idea that one's unconscious self can be accepting, compensatory, and positive spiritual force is an idea that the therapist offers, rather than a fact to be believed.

I recall in my own therapy being particularly upset about a very disturbing image that appeared in a dream. It made me feel "crazy" to have produced such an image. With one statement, which I will never forget, my therapist altered my stance permanently. She said, "What you feel so badly about, a poet could be jealous of." She reframed my disgust as potential creative inspiration, helping me to look more carefully at this disturbing issue. In the same moment she also delivered a message: I can use my unconscious as a creative force.

After welcoming, the therapist must function as a facilitator. In this role, the therapist actively promotes the client's unconscious productions. Techniques may include such things as the appropriate use of silence (these can be longer periods of silence than we are used to; I often suggest to my clients that they close their eyes to promote this process), a dream journal or, at times, a direct suggestion to the client that he or she will have a dream that he or she will remember and that will illuminate a particular issue. I have been impressed by how often my suggestion has resulted in my client bringing in a dream. Active imagination (Singer 1972:331–65), a Jungian technique, can also be used to facilitate unconscious material. This technique may be verbal or nonverbal, e.g., drawing. In my clinical work, I facilitate activation of my client's unconscious through free association, dream analysis, guided imagery, and collaborative hypnosis.

I will illustrate the processes of welcoming and facilitating with a case example. I worked with a computer programmer in his early thirties, whom I shall call Ian, who had great difficulty identifying and experiencing his feelings. I offered to use hypnosis with him toward this end; he was interested. After the induction and deepening phases, I did a hypnoprojective, the "theater" technique, as a way to explore his feelings about hypnosis. In this technique, the client imagines himself sitting comfortably in a seat in a theater where he witnesses a play. He began to view the first act before the curtain was fully opened:

> I am on a cloud overseeing the action below. An actor is playing me, sitting in a barber chair. The barber has slicked-back black hair, scissors and comb in hand. He is an old-fashioned barber with a black bow tie, starched white shirt, with garters on his sleeves. He looks somewhat like you [therapist].
>
> Now there is a World War I biplane hanging from the ceiling on thin wire lines.
>
> Now I am floating in the cloud to a very private place . . . I am lying on pine needles in the woods and still watching the play. My body is stretched out, it feels fifty feet long.

His experience of being able to produce such rich visual and kinesthetic imagery and our dialogue about his feelings during and after trance, were extremely therapeutic. He was pleased "that there was something inside"; previously he had considered himself devoid of feeling or an inner life. Though we largely made our interpretations in the personal and familial domains, his discovery that he had a rich inner life was a profound, enlivening, and what I would term "spiritual" experience. This experience existed *in potentia*. Together we welcomed his unconscious creations facilitated by the hypnosis and set the stage for his future work.

The Jungian idea of amplification is critical to the client's experience of the religious in psychotherapy. Amplification is the process whereby the therapist and the dreamer understand the meaning of the dream through the dreamer's associations on the personal, natural, cultural, and archetypal levels. The last two levels, especially the archetypal level, hold spiritual or religious meaning. Some theorists reserve the concept of amplification to refer only to the universal meanings that can be ascribed to the symbols in the dream; for them, amplification refers only to meaning constructed on the archetypal level.

My clinical experience has led me to believe that it is not only the meanings (on whatever level) that we ascribe to the client's symbols but the very process of generating the symbols themselves that has spiritual significance. This is the client's felt experience of producing images, sensations, and thoughts which heretofore had not existed and which now do. "Wow! Where did this come from?", is an exclamation I often hear. The client has a sense of "bigness" inside, a feeling that there is so much that can be experienced and understood about one's inner life. This feeling of "bigness" makes the client feel rich and enlarged and it also connects the client to the rest of humanity.

According to James Hall, a Jungian analyst and hypnotherapist:

> Archetypal amplifications are found by locating a particular dream motif in mythology, folklore, or religious images. These are considered repositories of archetypal meaning because their motifs have been meaningful for extended periods of time to a large number of individuals . . . I have seen among others, images from Greek, Egyptian, Babylonian, American, Indian, Buddhist and Pythagorean sources. (1989:84)

Whether it be personal or archetypal amplification, the goal is to integrate these meanings into the client's ongoing development. In my practice, I first explore the client's past and present associations to the symbol, any feelings that accompany the symbols or myth when it is generated, and any feelings and associations that the client may have while reporting the dream to me. I then feed back to the client any nonverbal cues I might notice while the client speaks, such as changes in affect or fluctuations in speech. The emphasis during this phase is on the client's meaning-making efforts and constructions. At this point, I refrain from interpretation. I often ask my client questions based on our prior conversations in order to suggest a possible connection to other life themes or issues.

When dealing with symbolic material, and after the dreamer comments on the symbols, the therapist offers universally held meanings from his or her own knowledge. These meanings, though *impersonal,* are always offered in light of the personal development of the client. These universal meanings are not the primary consideration; rather, they should in some way illuminate the client's development. (When these symbols are interpreted in and of themselves, there is a risk of what Hall has termed archetypal reductionism, in which everything is seen as carrying an archetypal meaning, and the tension between the personal and the archetypal is lost.) When a chord is struck, i.e., a felt experience of "Aha!", the meaning is thought useful and the therapist and client then continue the task of integrating it further into the client's present self-understanding.

For example, the appearance of a cross in a client's dream may relate to some aspect of his or her experiences growing up in a Christian home, but depending upon how it appears in the dream and when the dream occurs in the life of the person and in the course of therapy, the therapist may suggest other meanings. Through the ages, the cross has symbolized: the tree of life, emblematic of rain and fertility; union; or a powerful charm for averting evil. Any one or all of these meanings may be useful for the client in coming to a fuller understanding of his or her own spiritual and psychological development, if they resonate with the client *and* if they provide another life perspective not previously considered.

Case Illustrations: Franco and James

In the following two case vignettes taken from my clinical practice, I focus on the process of symbol and myth creation through one's unconscious and how the therapist facilitates, understands, and amplifies such myths. In each of these cases, the hero/journey myth is evoked and essentially understood as a spiritual or universal passage. I define this as a religious experience because the symbols and myths (1) are spontaneously generated by the client through the unconscious, (2) contain both personal and universal meanings, and (3) contribute to the client's development toward integration and wholeness.

Both clients are men. It is interesting to speculate whether this myth is gender related. Campbell speaks about the hero as both male and female. In my clinical experience, the particular form of the myth in which the lone individual departs for an adventure into the unknown where he experiences union, appears more frequently in men's dreams than in women's. Perhaps the female form of this myth is less solitary, the perils having more to do with the risks of inclusiveness at the expense of differentiation.

THE CASE OF FRANCO

The first case concerns a client named Franco (pseudonym), a white male in his early thirties. He entered therapy to "find a

125

way to lead a more vital life." He spoke of feeling isolated, empty, and unable to "really make decisions on my own . . . I float into things, like my work, which I don't feel gives me very much." He also complained of experiencing difficulty conducting an "honest" relationship, fearing that if he were honest, it would create conflict. He knew of my work as a hypnotherapist and was eager to use it in therapy. He had experience with guided relaxation and martial arts, which he associated positively to hypnotherapy.

In our third or fourth session, he asked to use hypnosis for the purpose of exploration. After the induction phase, I deepened the trance by asking Franco to walk down a flight of stairs: he was able to achieve a deeply relaxed state. I used the "theater technique" as a hypnoprojective. Here is a verbatim account of his experience while in trance:

> It is a dark theater, the lights are dim. The stage is big. The opening behind the stage is big and dark . . . I have a sense that it is a kind of an old place, there is a lot of stage—dark wood . . . the walls surrounding the stage are dark wood. There is a balcony level, the boxes are close to the stage, high up, special people sit there . . . it is very quiet.

I then suggested to him that a play would begin shortly and that if he felt comfortable, he would share it with me as it unfolded. Act I follows:

> Part of the stage is very bright . . . a powerful white light. There are two people in the light, a man and a woman. The woman is wearing a bright white long gown, like Cinderella, she's dressed up for a ball. The man is wearing clothes out of the Middle Ages, ballet tights. He is wearing a coat with vertical stripes, he has a beard and hat. He is a big, powerful man.

> They are both standing, holding hands, they know each other. It seems like someone will go away. The man will go away. The woman is upset, not crying, but doesn't want him to go away.

I then asked my client what the man in the play is feeling:

> He is torn, doesn't want to leave her, but feels he must go.
> They are still standing, holding hands . . . it is difficult
> for the man to leave, he wants to spend more time with the
> woman. No one is making the move to leave.

He then paused for a long time, and I suggested to him that if
Act I seemed finished, the curtains would close while he continued to sit comfortably in his seat. In a few moments, the curtain would open again and Act II of the play would begin:

> The man is off, he's someplace walking, through the
> woods, outside . . . the trees are all around, he's off on
> an adventure, he's thinking about what he has left behind,
> but very clear he must go on . . . not clear where he's
> going, but it seems very important to him. It may be im-
> portant to others too. It seems like he's going to meet
> some people . . . the man is going to meet some people
> very much like him, who are also part of this adventure or
> event . . . and sense that they know each other in a cer-
> tain way that binds them together, in com-
> mon . . . seems like [he is] clear about some purpose in
> whatever they will be doing . . .

I ask again what the man feels:

> He's very clear he has something to do and committed to
> doing this, a source of strength to go on, he's not thinking
> about what he left behind . . . he's very sure he wants to
> do it.

Franco reported his initial associations and comments about
the myth immediately after the hypnosis experience. As Act I
opened, he said that he was struck by the brightness of the light
which shone on the man and woman, as if they were "spotlighted." He associated purity to the whiteness of the woman's
dress and reported that the man felt sad. He said, "the image of
my mother pops into my head," and that "issues of loss and separation, letting go, seem to be present." With regard to Act II,

my client was struck by how the man had left the woman and was "on his way to his adventure." He emphasized that the man "is doing something important with people who are like him." This adventuring "is not an easy or fun thing, but is *absolutely* [his emphasis] the thing to do." There is "no looking back or going back."

Franco's myth can be thought of as the archetypal journey of the hero. The journey, in all mythic traditions, exists for personal transformation, though there are countless examples of epic myths in which societies and cultures are also changed. The journeyer undergoes trials and tribulations and is often tested by the gods. He or she must relinquish the familiar and safe through arduous decision and enter into the unsafe. The journeyer constantly weighs what is to be gained against what is to be lost and often battles with the feeling of wanting to turn back.

Franco's dream is more specifically about the initial stage of the journey, i.e., the necessary and painful separation and departure, which Campbell terms the "call to adventure" (Campbell 1949:36). Franco must first detach in order to initiate the crisis through which he will eventually attain spiritual renewal. This detachment releases the energy that will eventually lead to a more creative life. In this first step, there is a transfer of emphasis from the external to the internal (I must do this!) world. Franco's entry into therapy signified this shift. This internal world of journey, expressed in contemporary analysis, is precisely the world of the unconscious with all its early associations, fixations, and magic and, from a Jungian point of view, all the life potentialities that await realization. As Campbell has said, "such golden seeds do not die" (Campbell 1949:17).

Franco's dream appeared so early in the therapy because he had entered therapy ready to take the journey (this is not always the case), with the knowledge that he must go forward; it was very "clear" what he must do. In psychoanalysis a great many of these ritual trials appear in the dreams of the patient at precisely the moment when the dreamer begins to abandon his infantile fixations and progresses into the future (Campbell 1949:10). Franco came into therapy ripe to make this journey, and to some extent had already begun the process of leave taking. It is not unusual in mythology and ancient rite for the boy to cling to his mother just before he leaves her to enter the world of men, for instance, in many circumcision rituals. Holding onto the mother or comforting female protects the boy from serious future harm. He will undergo many trials, but he will ultimately emerge a "victor" in part because of the woman's care and protection.

The therapist must honor and understand the larger function of the holding on as well as the letting go. In this case, this translated into my acknowledging Franco's feelings of loss, sadness, and ambivalence. As in the myth of circumcision, the boy can only leave when and if the mother has wailed, those sounds protecting him from the great snake of adventure; he will differentiate only if he has been allowed the opportunity to experience the feelings attendant to separating, namely, sadness, fear, perhaps even anger. We as therapists must honor this need, even if our "boy" is thirty-five years old, and it seems to us that the leaving is overdue.

Most if not all myths emanating from the unconscious contain significant personal and universal symbolism. We have discussed the universal myth of the hero/journey. From Franco we discover that he is not separating from just any woman, but from his mother. In this "powerfully spotlighted" scenario, he portrays the idealized relationship of the oedipal myth. He is the medieval gentleman and she, his Cinderella. They are holding hands, a sweet and innocent moment. His portrayal reveals his child-like perspective. "He is a big, powerful man"—he spoke these words during trance as if he were a young child. In Act I he is unable to leave her, while in Act II he begins his adventure, still thinking about her as he leaves.

Unknown to Franco consciously, he was in a powerful relationship with his mother who, as long as he could remember, has had an unhappy relationship with his father. He describes his father as a passive, unavailable man who is lost to his work. Franco's rescuer does not appear in the myth, instead it is Franco who feels that he must rescue himself. Though he is alone, he feels he will join a group of like-minded people in the future.

This myth is more than a reenactment of the oedipal myth; it is a vivid imaginary statement of an unconscious reality in the process of dissolution. The drama is located in the "call to adventure" which the dissolution heralds. At this point in therapy, he began to think about the meaning of his relationship with his mother, though this was by no means an "Aha!" experience. Even with these images before him and with our conversation, he was slow to integrate this experience. It was the need to leave that was most compelling.

It is imperative that we see Franco not as the fixated child but as the hero who, through his own efforts, courageously embarks on a journey of profound significance. As he said when beginning therapy, he wanted to lead a more creative and vital life. He has taken the first steps to make this happen. The relationship between therapist and client will allow him to go further in his journey. Franco felt hopeful because we were able to construct the meaning of his "play" as a sign that he had begun his journey of creative renewal, and not merely an indication that he was "stuck" in his relationship with his mother. Here, we wove universal and personal meanings together into a single strand, using his unconscious images of wholeness to further him psychologically and spiritually.

THE CASE OF JAMES

The second case vignette is taken from my work with a man in his late twenties whom I shall call James. James is a white research physicist, married with no children, who works in an academic setting. We began working in hypnosis because he had become increasingly frustrated with his inability to experience his feelings. He described distancing himself from a feeling and judging his actions or feelings. He often did not know *that* he was feeling and *what* he was feeling.

Several months into the therapy and only the third time we utilized hypnosis, this session was done for the purpose of exploration, with no particular goal in mind. James experienced kinesthetic sensations while producing vivid visual images, as is evident in this passage:

I see a path, the opening is in the brush on the edge of the sand and leads up to the cliff. I am walking through the brush on the sandy path. I am climbing toward the cliff and it is a bright, sunny day, not much wind. The path crests toward the bluff up ahead and I can't see it now. The top of the bluff will be a precarious spot to stay in. I'm walking towards it. Now I'm on the top, the view is for miles, it is a clear day and the ocean is far below.

The geography is changed on the other side of the bluff where the path continues to wind through the trees. I can't see the terrain.

(Therapist asks him if he wants to continue on the path; he says yes).

It's slow going now and I'm scrambling down the path, now it levels. The path goes under gnarled branches and I have to duck as I enter the region. I've lost contact with the sky, it's gotten darker and I can't see where I am.

Now I'm viewing myself from a helicopter above and I can't see myself on the path anymore. I'm back on the path now, sitting on a chair which is sinking down slowly through the earth. My head is alone on the path without my body or hands. My head is wriggling along without the help of my body or hands. The path goes on for quite a while as I inch along. My head tips over and is bleeding through the neck where by body is usually attached.

My head rights itself and slowly it rises up attached to my body as it comes up through the ground, but I am stuck at the knees. I can't move but I feel much more whole right now than a while ago but there is no movement forward. Now I am rising gradually out of the soil and in a little while I'm all the way out. My feet are underground and the rest is above. Now I'm completely out.

In this vignette we again witness a journey, though James has progressed further than Franco both in the journey and in terms of therapy. Again, there are elements of the personal and collective unconscious contained within the symbols. In subsequent sessions we examined these symbols separately and the myth taken as a whole. I regard this material as illustrative of one of James' central life themes; it is simultaneously personal and universal in its meaning. This myth embodies his struggle and indicates a possible solution. I have divided this "dream" into four sections, indicated by the breaks in the passage, to facilitate analysis and discussion. My client reported the dream in one continuous stream.

The first part of James's ascent is symbolic of his consciousness. He commented that this part of the journey represented the work he has already done in therapy and the part of himself he already knows. He is content with what he can see; it is familiar and safe. He says, "it is sunny . . . clear . . . for miles," bright and relatively peaceful, "not much wind." He can easily see where he is going. I commented to him that in his life James is often blind to potential "storms"; he tends to move along in his intrapsychic and interpersonal life unaware of any problems, or alternatively he may know that there is a problem but denies it for fear that it might overwhelm him. Conflict, in short, is equated with disastrous consequences. In this dream, he is forewarned: the spot at the top of the bluff is precarious. He senses before he gets there that from this vantage point he will be able to view his descent into unknown terrain; this causes him apprehension.

Part 2 describes the descent. It is mysterious, unfamiliar, and evokes panic: "I am scrambling." He loses contact with the light and enters the darkness. I interpreted the "gnarled branches" as symbolic of the knotty, twisted, complex nature of his underworld with its many dangers awaiting him as he makes his journey. Unlike the terrain on the ascent, it is not straightforward and needs to be deciphered. In myth, when the hero undertakes the perilous journey into darkness by descending intentionally or unintentionally into his own spiritual labyrinth, it is for the purification and cleansing of the self. When this is accomplished, energy can be utilized for spiritual or transcendent goals.

In part 3 of the myth, he finds himself in a helicopter, symbolic of the dissociation from his feelings which he described as the initial reason for doing hypnosis. This adaptation or defense has helped him get through his life, providing a kind of safe harbor from the perceived threat of contacting another person or, as the myth suggests, from contacting his innermost feelings. I suggested that for him relationship is fraught with loss and rejection. Being intimate with another is like entering "unknown territory" and it is safer to remove himself. Further along in his narrative, James describes in vivid detail the consequences of this kind of separation of body or heart from mind. He describes how it is to live with only his head: painful, unbalanced, and alone. He is literally and figuratively disconnected, and he is saying to the therapist that it is impossible for his intellect to do all the work. In other words, there can be no satisfying relationships or spiritual life where there is no integrity, no contact with the heart and soul.

In part 4, James is presented with a possible solution; in fact, it charted the course of our work together. His head must be reunited with his body, his intellect with his heart—a literal and metaphorical symbol of his need for wholeness. It is not "forward movement," as he says, but vertical or downward movement into the depths of his feelings. Descent is required before reunion is possible. The myth suggests a role for the therapist: to be like mother earth as she steadily holds parts of the self in their reconstitution of the whole.

In the course of therapy, we elaborated the personal and spiritual meaning of this session for his development. James recounted numerous times the pain he experienced as a child as he "inched along" alone, unaware of and confused about his feelings, trying to experience life solely through his mind. He experienced considerable difficulty imagining what his life would be like were he to give up his adaptive, if somewhat limiting, response of intellectualization; fear dominated him and often in therapy he retreated. But in the end he was able, after many struggles and setbacks, to overcome his fears and risk the joining of the opposites. He eventually came to know his "signs" of dissociation and was able to find a way to resist the split. He discovered that commenting on what was happening inside him often helped him to change. The spiritual dimension of this dream lies in his universally based solution: wholeness and unity of the self must be achieved, or at least set forth as an ideal to be achieved, before one can lead a full life. A full life is a spiritually renewed life.

This central life theme of James's is at the same time a metaphor for human growth in the Jungian sense. The movement toward wholeness, integration, and unity is the end point in development, an ideal archetype that all people attempt to realize consciously and unconsciously. This is the archetype of the Self, as represented by Christ or the Buddha. The yearning for wholeness defines the spiritual element in the individual, perhaps in all of nature. Like any noble aim, the journey is fraught with crisis, dark nights of the soul, and ecstasy. While James fears the downward movement, he nonetheless takes the risk. And perhaps it is when we "take the risk" that we are most able to make use of the images of wholeness offered by our unconscious.

Joseph Campbell believes that it is the burden of the modern hero to move the society forward, through this exploration in depth. The culture, he contends, no longer guides or saves the creative hero; rather, the hero redeems the tribe. I have witnessed and experienced meaningful community and therefore believe Campbell's proposition to be only partially true, yet I am intrigued enough by this idea to reconsider its application to the therapeutic endeavor.

Psychotherapy can be an experience that enlivens the client and therapist by what Jung termed the "warm red blood" of "immediate experience" (Aziz 1990:10). Here the therapist-guide connects the dreamer's spontaneous, personal, and unique images with the rest of humanity's symbols and myths, enlarging the context of therapy to include community, society, and culture. Through this connection, the client's experience of wholeness, Jung's telos, extends beyond the personal into humanity's collective consciousness.

I daresay that most of us would not see "moving society forward" as our expressed therapeutic goal. Therapy is an undertaking usually begun for more personal reasons. Yet those whom I have accompanied in their explorations in depth have returned to families, friends, and colleagues with renewed vitality and hope—essential ingredients for moving others forward. Viewed in this way, it is inevitable that some of the tribe will move forward with them.

References

Azia, R. 1990. *C. G. Jung's Psychology of Religion and Synchronicity.* Albany: State University of New York Press.

Brown, D. and E. Fromm. 1986. *Hypnotherapy and Hypnoanalysis.* New York: Lawrence Erlbaum.

Campbell, J. 1949. *The Hero With a Thousand Faces.* Princeton: Princeton University Press.

——. 1988. *The Power of Myth.* New York: Doubleday.

Feinstein, D. and S. Krippner. 1988. *Personal Mythology: The Psychology of Your Evolving Self.* Los Angeles: Jeremy P. Tarcher.

Hall, J. 1989. *Hypnosis: A Jungian Perspective.* New York: Guilford Press.

Jung, C. G. 1966. *Two Essays on Analytic Psychology.* Princeton: Princeton University Press.

——. 1989. *Psyche and Symbol.* New York: Doubleday.

Parks, S. 1986. *The Critical Years.* San Francisco: Harper and Row.

Singer, J. 1972. *Boundaries of the Soul: The Practice of Jung's Psychology.* New York: Doubleday.

Whitmont, E. C. 1987. Jungian approach. In J. L. Fosshage and C. A. Loew, eds., *Dream Interpretation: A Comparative Study,* pp. 53–77. New York: PMA Publishing.

Religious Imagery in the Clinical Context:

Access to Compassion Toward the Self—Illusion or Truth

Sharon Daloz Parks

A t the beginning of the now-classic story of the journey from madness to health, *I Never Promised You a Rose Garden,* Dr. Fried reviews the testing, interview, and family history of sixteen-year-old Deborah Blau and wonders whether to take on another patient. It is the girl's age that makes the decisive difference: "If we succeed . . . [she will have many] good years yet to live." She then reconsiders the facts and numbers, remembering that a report like this had once caused her remark to a colleague, "We must someday make a test to show us where the *health* is as well as the illness." Her colleague had responded that with ametyls, pentothal, and hypnotism such information could be obtained more easily. "I do not think so," Dr. Fried had answered. "The *hidden* strength is too deep a secret. But in the end . . . in the end it is our only ally" (Greenberg 1964:19).

This essay, intended to be read less as an argument than an act of contemplation, could proceed simply as a reflection upon the question of whether Dr. Fried is wise or deluded. But our agenda as therapists requires more. Broadly construed, this essay is an exploration of and critical reflection on "the hidden strength" upon which every therapist is absolutely dependent. Specifically, this essay examines the relationship of religious phenomena to that hidden strength and explores how religious imagery, particularly God imagery, may open or inhibit access to "our only ally." Finally, I beg the question, "Is our only ally compassionate?"

In accord with the theoretical and social norms of clinical psychology, many practitioners have tended to uphold a perception of religious phenomena as maladaptive and pathological. This view can be attributed in general to the Enlightenment philosophical culture that gave birth to modern psychology, and, more particularly, to the influence of Freud. Freud made vivid the pathological manifestations of religion, especially the desire to seek solace in the illusion of a projected God.

At the same time, however, Freud himself was preoccupied with religion. R. Melvin Keiser argues that Freud's preoccupation persists "because the religion he attacks is different from the religion he continues to explore." He then suggests that beneath Freud's critique of "manifest" religion there are "latent" resources for a fruitful conception of religion. Freud's "'manifest religion' is objectified and 'critical'—in Polanyi's sense of a dualistic split between subject and object, mind and body—seeking consolation in the illusion" (1988). Thus the projected illusory God of Freud's manifest religion "functions morally as a prohibitive and protective father resolving guilt and helplessness, whom we believe in on external authority rather than experience—basically a manifestation of the super-ego" (1990). Keiser recognizes that Freud's solution is to withdraw expectations from another world and to be educated to reality so as to liberate our energies into "life on earth." In contrast, "'latent' religion . . . is 'postcritical'—a dimension of ultimate mystery in the depths of existing selves."

Keiser observes that Freud is captivated by nonobjective religious elements in his own experience, although he does not identify them as religious. For example, in *The Interpretation of Dreams* Freud speaks of a fundamental mystery underlying every dream: "There is at least one spot in every dream at which it is unplumbable . . . its point of contact with the unknown" (1971:143). This recognition of unfathomable mystery (which is fundamentally religious) is significant, Keiser contends, because Freud sees it not as separate from, but as a dimension emerging within, the psyche, the very matrix in which psychic life originates.

Two elements are critical for my reflection. First, the notion of an ultimate mystery constituting the matrix in which psychic life originates is deeply resonant with some of the conversation emerging within the discipline of constructive-developmental psychology. The cognitive evolution of constructive, creative, meaning-making activity in human beings, initially mapped by Jean Piaget, has been recognized by Fowler (1981) as finally participating in the construction of an "ultimate environment" and by Kegan and others as partaking in the "restless creative motion of life itself," a relationship of the "meaning-we-compose to the ground of being which is doing the composing" (Kegan 1980:407–11).

Second, Freud's critique of manifest religion rests in part upon his resistance to an illusory protection, believed "on external authority rather than experience," inhibiting our living "life on earth." It may therefore be the case that the central issue is most fittingly understood in terms of the development of the locus of authority—a context for understanding the issues of an "illusory protection." The dichotomy Freud assumes between external authority and experience suggests to the constructive-developmental psychologist that Freud is addressing a failure of development in adulthood, a failure to compose a locus of authority within the self. If this is what Freud refutes, he is making an appropriate refutation of stunted human development. Kegan has described an evolution of self-other differentiations essential to the development of mature patterns of meaning-making, and Fowler has described an evolution in the locus of authority in the life of faith—each suggests a normative maturing process in the formation of meaning and faith that would likewise resist any simplistic infantile projection used to obscure "reality" (Kegan 1982; Fowler 1981). These two points of resonance between Freud's discourse and constructive-developmental perspectives disclose a path by which clinicians may be able to rejoin psychological and religious-theological insights in ways both truthful and useful in relation to clinical phenomena without lapsing into the naive projection that Freud refutes.

Human beings are meaning-makers; moreover, we have a need to make meaning in ways that create a correspondence with the reality of both our inner and social worlds, achieving an equilibrium between them. Piaget observed an ongoing dynamic process of assimilation and accommodation by which the self in interaction with his or her world composes reality. But human beings do not seek reality in rational, empirical terms narrowly defined. Human beings seek a meaningful reality that embraces the sensibilities and affections of the whole of their being and the whole of Being. Not only do we seek to make meaning of our immediate, mundane, personal experience, we also require a sense of the whole. We seek order, pattern, significance, purpose, truth, and trust-worthiness in the largest frame we can conceive. Human beings must continually compose and recompose a sense of self, world, and cosmos.

When we compose meaning in these most comprehensive dimensions, embracing all that is ultimate and intimate, we are engaged in an act of "faith"—the act of composing our sense of what is finally trust-worthy, dependable, true, and real. To speak of faith in this fashion is to provisionally distinguish faith from dogma, belief, and religion. As the historian of world religions Wilfred Cantwell Smith has shown, faith is an activity prior to belief—although in modern English usage faith has become inappropriately conflated with religious belief (Smith 1979). Faith is the prior and composing activity by means of which we apprehend and participate in the ultimate, unfathomable mystery that is the matrix of life itself. In this most deeply human sense, faith is, then, not merely a matter of belief understood as dogma or the superego (though both dogma and the superego may contribute to the composition of faith); nor is faith simply the activity of those who identify themselves as religious (though faith seeks religion). Rather, faith is meaning-making at the level of ultimacy, something that all human beings do, whether they express it in secular or religious terms.

Piagetian psychology offers a theoretical perspective from which to recognize the intricate, intimate process by which we come to compose and to see "reality." Piaget practiced an extraordinary respect for the dynamic processes we use to develop enhanced capacities to receive, engage, and know the complex wonders of self and world. He meta-phorically described the underlying "structures" or "operations" of thought formed and transformed over time as necessitated by the ongoing interaction of self with world. He identified each new, more complex, and adequate structure as a particular "stage." But as important as these stage descriptions are, their significance derives from their capacity to hold and act upon "representations" or images—the contents, the stuff, of life itself.

Thus the formation of meaning and faith cannot be understood through theories of stage development alone, essential though they may be. Theories of stage development must be joined with an understanding of the role of images and the process of imagination, because human beings compose meaning and faith by means of the imagination, which is conditioned by both structures and images (Parks 1986).

In this context, what we mean when we speak of imagination is drawn from the insight of Samuel Taylor Coleridge. Fundamental to Coleridge's understanding of imagination is the sharp distinction he drew between imagination and fantasy. Fantasy he recognized as a mere (though powerful) associative activity; in contrast, imagination serves as the highest power of the knowing mind, the highest power of reason. Imagination is the composing activity of the mind, seeking correspondences and unity. For example, imagination seeks a proper fit between inner and outer reality.

Central to this discussion is the recognition of four dynamics integral to the process of imagination: (1) Imagination is provoked into motion by dissonance. (Indeed, most of those who seek therapy do so because some dissonance or contradiction has become intolerable.) (2) The task of the faithful imagination is to imagine as adequately as possible the one reality there is in all its most comprehensive dimensions, including its manifold complexity. (3) The imagination is vulnerable to the images to which it does or does not have access. (An image is any object or act of the sensible world that is employed as metaphor and symbol to give form to more than the object itself; by extension concepts and theories function as complex forms.) (4) The faithful imagination is dependent upon a community of confirmation (or contradiction) to affirm (or refute) the images it employs in its formation of the real.

To summarize my reflections thus far: Freud refutes the image of a projected God believed in on the basis of external authority; Freud remains preoccupied with the unplumbable mystery of the matrix of life itself; constructive-developmental psychology is likewise preoccupied with human meaning-making, which can be described as the activity of faith and is composed by means of the imagination—the utility by which we apprehend the real.

Note that my exploration here is epistemological. At least since Kant, we practically, psychologically, and philosophically recognize the fact of the composing and finite mind. We know that human beings do not *comprehend* reality; we can *apprehend* reality. The central questions for my purposes here are: How do we as clinicians recognize, name, and know what is real, true, and worthy? How do we recognize a fitting correspondence between the meaning our client is making and the world of "reality," of "life on this earth"? By what authority do we function as a part of a client's community of confirmation or contradiction as he or she is engaged in the perilous and fateful task of making meaning of self and world, thereby composing a faith to live by?

As therapists we join our client's meaning-making as an activity of faith composed of experience and the imagination (Lynch 1973). It has been said that "reality" is a "collective hunch." All of us, clinicians and clients alike, at whatever stage of development, are creating reality. We do so by aligning self with other through images—images that serve as metaphors to name reality in ways we can share with others. The "talking cure" is, in part, a shared search for fitting, right images by which to name our sorrows, delights, anxiety, terror, despair, and hope as we compose meaning together—as we compose a faith to live by. Thus it is by means of images (held and shaped by the underlying structures [stages] of thought and affect) that we gain access to both inner and outer reality in its most mundane and most profound dimensions. To use an example common to many in clinical practice, dream images can become a gift to the faithful imagination (to reason), for they hold something of the truth of our inner, subconscious reality that can then seek correspondence with our outer, social, and more conscious reality—each modifying the other to form a more adequate truth.

But to do this in any dimension of our lives and particularly in the composing of meaning in the most comprehensive dimensions of our experience, we necessarily are dependent, not only upon the process of imagination but also upon a community of imagination. Most clients seek a therapist not only for his or her skills per se but also and even primarily in order to find or augment the client's community of imagination—the client's community of faith. Only with each other can human beings sustain an adequate enough sense of meaning, sufficient to orient both self and other. The members of the whole global community are to one another, sources of images as well as refuters or ratifiers of their adequacy. It is by this means that human beings in their necessary quest for meaning, together with the natural order, create religion. Thus at its best, religion is the distillation of *shared* images powerful enough to create a correspondence between the whole of inner and outer reality—powerful enough to grasp truth. This is to say that images employed in human meaning-making will inevitably become "gods," i.e., anchoring centers of power, value, and affection. Religion at its worst is a collection of images (gods) that sabotages the search for a fitting correspondence between inner and outer reality. Religion at its best is adaptive and fosters life-bearing constructions of reality. Religion at its worst is maladaptive and finally fosters pathological constructions of reality.

In Western culture, "God" is the primary image by which the character of ultimate reality is conventionally named. For many the image of God is anthropomorphic and is personified differently as wrathful, loving, originally creative but now disinterested, judging, caring, abusive, committed, male, female, powerful, all-knowing, all-seeing, limited, preoccupied, chaotic, ordered, and so forth, depending upon people's notions of the ultimate nature of things. Every psychologist, whether of the object-relations school or not, appropriately recognizes that one's notions of God are shaped, in part, by one's sociality, especially by one's experience of primary others. Ana-Maria Rizzuto (1979) has elegantly shown that a *non*anthropomorphic image of God may likewise be shaped by social relations, particularly painful ones. God, ultimate reality, is, at least in part, socially mediated. (Christians have grasped this dynamic in the notion of incarnation, but in the main have yet to fully understand what this means owing to their tendency to collapse the paradox of transcendent-immanent reality into a dichotomy and a hierarchy.) Rizzuto also contends that one's God image is composed not only out of what we experience in our social world but also out of what we need. Extending this insight, I suggest that our "need" is composed not only of finite longing and wish but also of our inner conviction of the character of the wider reality and truth we partake in, the ineffable matrix of life experienced both within and outside the self and for which the self seeks confirmation—a correspondence. The search for an interpretation of the one matrix of life manifest in inner and outer reality is the central passion that fires the human imagination.

Something of this sensibility is echoed in Robertson Davies's *The Fifth Business:*

> Day after day I sat in the basilica for a few hours and wondered. The sacristans and nuns who gave out little prints of the miraculous picture grew accustomed to me; they thought I must be a member of that tiny and eccentric group, the devout rich, or perhaps I was writing an article for a tourist magazine. I put something in every out-thrust box and was left alone. But I am neither rich nor conventionally devout, and what I was writing, slowly, painstakingly, and

with so many revisions that the final version was not even in sight, was a sort of prologue to a discussion of the nature of faith. Why do people all over the world, and at all times, want marvels that defy all veritable facts? And are the marvels brought into being by their desire, or is their desire an assurance rising from deep knowledge, not to be directly experienced and questioned, that the marvelous is indeed an aspect of the real?

Philosophers have tackled this question, of course, and answered it in ways highly satisfactory to themselves; but I never knew a philosopher's answer to make much difference to anyone not in the trade. I was trying to get at the subject without wearing either the pink spectacles of faith or the green spectacles of science. All I had managed by the time I found myself sitting in the basilica of Guadalupe was a certainty that faith was a psychological reality, and that where it was not invited to fasten itself on things unseen, it invaded and raised bloody hell with things seen. Or in other words, the irrational will have its say, perhaps because "irrational" is the wrong word for it (1977:203–4).

If human beings seek and compose meaning in both empirical and "irrational" dimensions, if this is done by means of the imagination, and if the therapist is a part of the client's community of imagination, then the questions for the therapist are further deepened. For example: What hospitality do I, as a therapist, offer to the images of power, value, and affection that center and shape the life of my client, i.e., Father, Mother, Boss, My Child, My Profession, My Drugs, The Holocaust, Nuclear War, and so forth. In other words, What is the range of images that function religiously for the client, whether they are religious images per se, and what measure of hospitality and caring critique do they receive as images of faith? In reference to specifically religious images and the God image in particular, the questions to be posed are: If the client has a God image (and Rizzuto [1979] argues that all clients do), is the image of God that has been constructed by the client in interaction with his or her experience of life given place in the community of imagination constituted by the client-therapist relationship? If so, does it hold adaptive and/or maladaptive potential for the client? If there is adaptive potential, does the clinician facilitate access to that potential? Does the clinician thereby enable the client to have access to truth? Is that "adaptive potential" merely a projected illusion, or is it a faithful manifestation of the ineffable mystery at the core of life? How does the therapist make meaning? What is the therapist's faith? What is the content of the therapist's imagination and its adequacy? *How does the therapist know?*

Consider these questions in relation to a specific issue—the matter of compassion extended toward the self. Most clinicians over time have occasion to ponder why so many clients demand so much of themselves and are so quick to withhold from the self the understanding, care, and compassion that is often proffered much more freely to others. Compassion means the capacity to "suffer with." To suffer means to undergo; in its richest sense it may be applied both to pain and to joy. We suffer gladness as well as despair. Within the therapeutic process clients learn to know, be with, accept, embrace, and make choices about some dimension of the self that has been alien. As they heal, clients learn to recognize and to extend compassion toward (to suffer with) heretofore estranged others, both within and without. Embedded in the dynamics of compassion, then, is a connective dynamic, a unifying function. Compassion restores the fitting connectedness between self and world, the correspondences between self and selves. As this connective, unifying dynamic is necessarily dependent upon the power of imagination, how does the imagination evoke or extend compassion in relationship to the self? Does religious imagery block or illumine the pathway?

As therapists observe and seek to describe the fundamental alienations within the self, some would assert that "God" is often a major component of the problem, that images of a demanding, controlling, judging, harsh, or perfect God (ultimate reality) has informed the parental and communal practices that have shaped and misshaped many of the psyches/souls in this culture—and our clinics are made more profitable "thanks to God." These therapists, I believe, speak a good deal of truth. Yet it may also be that they are contending with Freud's "manifest religion" and projective, maladaptive forms of religious formation. Are we likewise alert to the potentially compassionate features of "the hidden strength" and the full range of images by which compassionate strength may be made accessible to the faithful imagination? Is it possible that for some clients and for some therapists the image of "God" holds truthful, positive content and serves as a primary source of adaptive, corrective reality? Might such an imagination coincide with Freud's "latent religion" and provide ground for a fruitful conception of religion?

I offer two cases as occasions for reflection upon these questions. Both cases focus specifically upon the issue of compassion and care toward the self as it may be manifest in the course of therapy, as it may be conditioned by development in the locus of authority, and as it may be given form by the image of God.

The first case: A few years ago, a young man in his mid-twenties walked into my office. I knew him as a student in the graduate school where I was teaching, though he had never been enrolled in one of my classes. A very bright, attractive, active, and committed student, he lived and worked as a student pastor–social worker in a low-income, crime-ridden neighborhood, yet managed to make high grades in his academic work. He had traveled the globe, he was "streetwise," and he was religious in a liberal fashion.

He came to see me because he was having headaches he could no longer control or ignore. He had tried to cope by working hard, jogging regularly, eating properly, and getting more or less reasonable amounts of rest, but the headaches persisted. He suspected that there was an inner tension building up that could not be explained even by his rather stressful living situation. Over our next several meetings, he seemed to have a good deal of energy for talking about features of his early life—particularly his school years and the events leading up to them.

Gradually the story unfolded as follows: He was the eldest child, and his father, a minister, was actively involved in a number of social issues in the city. The boy's first grade teacher was critical of the father and, unknown to the parents, made school life difficult for the son. The small boy, proud of his father, bewildered and stressed by the situation at school, soon was described as "acting out"—a behavior problem in the school. The family was advised that it would be best to send him away to school. So it was that at the age of seven he was sent to boarding school. At the heart of it all, he remembered, he did not tell his parents that he desperately did not want to go away; it was better to go away believing that his parents would have let him remain at home if they had known that he did not want to go, instead of actually telling his parents what he felt and risking the discovery that they would make him go anyway.

At boarding school he was poignantly, painfully lonely, especially when the new friend he had made in the first year did not return to the school the following year. The pain was eased when he was finally old enough to participate in team sports and earn the favor of a coach; however, as he reported with wry and subtle awareness, his parents did not attend the athletic events in which he participated. Throughout the narrative there was a consistent care for his parents, an insistence that they had done what they could, the best they could.

After the basic outlines of the story were laid out, he returned in a later session to the actual time of being sent away to school, and he shared an image. He had a distinct mental image of himself as a seven-year-old boy wearing a little yellow raincoat, walking down the stairs. At the top of the stairs were his parents. At the bottom of the stairs was the camp counselor who would take him to camp and subsequently to school. The image was very vivid for him, but there was no accompanying affect or further observation. I patiently tried to provide the space for him to explore the feelings that might dwell with the image. It seemed, however, that he could not remember how it had felt to walk down those stairs, nor could he comment on its meaning for him now. And again he took care to affirm that his parents were doing the best they could. Finally, I found myself quietly asking him what he thought God saw when the little boy was walking down the stairs. With no hesitation, this divinity student responded thoughtfully and directly that he thought God saw "sin"—signifying a sense of broken relationships and alienation even in the midst of people's best intentions. I responded by saying gently, "Yes, God saw sin." Then after a pause I said, "But you haven't told me that God wept."

What followed was one of those silences in which the therapist almost forgets to breathe. There was a clear sense, as this young man sat across from me, motionless, saying nothing, that there was a great deal of motion going on inside him, almost as if his insides were being rearranged. In a profound, reordering way, something shifted, as for the first time he was able to extend compassion to the little boy in the yellow raincoat, walking down the stairs. He was recomposing meaning, self, and world; he was recomposing faith.

In the weeks that followed, he was not only able to know more adequately the truth of his own feelings, and especially his own pain, but also able to know the truth of his experience of his parents in a more complex way—a way that acknowledged who they were *not,* as well as who they were. He began to recognize his own disappointment, anger, frustration, and loss. There was, it seemed to me, a more adequate correspondence between the truth of inner reality and the truth of the outer reality. The means of this transformation, it seems, was the juxtaposition of the image of the little boy in the yellow raincoat and the image of a God who wept—both of which were experienced as "true."

I am a theologian as well as a therapist. I critically reflect on the subject of God in a disciplined fashion. I cannot be content with the fact that this young man is now "better" than he was, that the headaches are gone. I must ask myself, How do I know that God wept? What I said was useful. Was it also true? Is this young man better able to live life on this earth? Is compassion a part of the ultimate character of things? Yes, my compassion served to make me something of a "transitional object" whereby this young man could relinquish some of his attachment to his parents so as to recompose them in a more accurate fashion. Yes, the God he brought into my office was not only potentially compassionate but also probably as demanding and self-sacrificing as his minister-father. But the question is: Did I say something true or untrue? Did I facilitate access to something more than the mere illusion of a protective father? Are the care, empathy, and compassion that any good therapist mediates ultimately real or an illusion unfitting to "life on this earth"? Is the motion of a young man's internal reordering a motion that partakes in the movement of the ultimate mystery of life, the object of Freud's "latent religion"? I believe so, but it is a matter of faith—my composing of ultimate reality, my sense of God. If the reader disagrees with me, it is by means of another composing of ultimate reality, another imagination, another faith, another perception of God.

The second case: One morning many years ago, one of my then room-mates, a spiritual director, shared with me over our morning coffee and as a matter of professional confidence her concern about conversation she anticipated in the day ahead. She was guiding the annual retreat of a religious sister who in mid-life was doing some deep, demanding psychological-spiritual work. Over the previous days, this sister had recounted how she had witnessed a terrible and life-altering event when she was five. Apparently unbeknown to her parents, she had been crouched behind a piece of furniture when her father chased her mother around the main room of their home and finally stabbed her with a knife. In the course of the chase, her father also smashed the head of the five-year-old's doll with his foot.

The incident was obviously a powerful one, not only for the client but now for my friend. She was unsure and concerned about "where this was going"—in what direction would she as a therapist and spiritual director be moving. One step removed from the power of the affect, I stayed with the story and, moving with the experience itself, wondered what had happened after the stabbing. My friend had frozen her attention upon the event itself and realized that she had no idea what had followed in the experience of the child—an understanding of which might be a clue to "where this was going."

Indeed, she came to learn that the mother had not been mortally wounded, and both parents had immediately left the room together to seek medical help. Then the five year old, still sitting behind the furniture, remembered forty years later how clearly she had heard God say to her "I will take care of you."

As in the previous case, the image of God served as a means of access to compassion toward the self, but at a very different age. At the age of five, the image of God offered immediate, essential comfort and protection to the little girl, protection necessary and appropriate for the well-being of a five year old. When she was older, she "gave her life to God," becoming a religious sister in the service of the church.

This story prompts two sets of questions. In line with my epistemological inquiry, the first is: Does this story reveal something "true" in the matrix of life itself? Did this woman grasp (or was she held by) something "true" when she was five? I would guess that many clinicians would agree that whatever served to preserve her psychic life—her hidden strength—at the time she was five was "true enough."[1] The second question follows from the constructive developmental perspective: Does the meaning she has composed of that crucial experience of compassion adequately serve and appropriately shape her life at the age of forty-five? Is the functioning of the God image for the five year old fitting for the adult woman?

Most clinicians, I suppose, would intuit that the image of the five year old is inadequate for an adult ordering of meaning and truth. If the five-year-old imagination is inadequate, was the linkage of God and compassion when she was five "wrong"? Or was it "right" but must now be held in a more complex form to adequately take her ongoing experience into account? Does her relationship to ultimate reality, composed and anchored in that five-year-old experience, need to be recomposed if she is to live a life in which a transformed inner and outer reality correspond for the living of an adult life "on this earth"? Did the image "I will take care of you," which was fitting as a grounding center of power, value, and affection at the age of five, now place an organizational constraint upon the imagination of the forty-five-year-old woman? If so, other questions then follow: Are compassion and protection irrelevant to adult life as it must be lived "on this earth"? If the image of God as caring for and protecting her has "held her" until mid-life, has she been held hostage to a false consciousness? Is it "false" that ultimate reality includes a principle of compassion? Or has this truth inappropriately obscured other truths such as the potential development of this woman's capacity for more self-aware thought and choice?[2] Might the "voice" she heard at the age of five healthfully speak and beckon again? Would it still be the voice of God, and would it still be compassionate? How does life take form in us except by means of the imagination? Who controls the religious imagination—an imagination that can be shared?

For example, it may be important to recognize that this woman was undoubtedly particularly vulnerable to and may have initially benefited from ecclesial structures offering an alternative "family," providing place, recognition, shelter, protection, and meaning. It would be especially important, however, that such an alternative sociality should foster an ongoing maturing process. Yet given the patriarchal structures of the Roman Catholic (and other) churches, which sometimes infantilize women and others, any person who like this woman was dependent in a primary way upon the image of God as caretaker and protector might be vulnerable to a variety of forms of exploitation—overt and subtle.[3] A thoughtful therapist would therefore want to provide space in which the client could explore whether, in order to hold her world together, she had to remain a "child" in the care of an exclusively protective God. The client would also need to consider whether this God who protected her when she was a child would likewise care for her and compassionately beckon forth her potential as a mature adult woman. Such work would have as a goal what Rizzuto has described as "keeping faith compatible with development" (1979:213).

For the young man in the first case, there was no "voice of God" articulating compassion and protection at the age of seven when he was sent off to boarding school. He smuggled a stuffed toy monkey into the dormitory and hid this representative of his vulnerable self—and of comfort/compassion—in his bottom bureau drawer. (Is the monkey an image of something both transcendent and immanent—and true?) It is not until the little yellow raincoat has long been discarded and the monkey consigned to his parents' attic that, in his twenties, the image of God serves as a conscious vehicle of compassion extended toward the self. Is the therapist's appeal to a God who weeps and its appropriation by the client as truth a collusion whereby shared, artificial, neurotic dependencies on an illusory father figure are maintained? Or do client and therapist together find themselves dwelling in the midst of the great matrix of life in which psychic life originates, one dimension of which, in that moment, they adequately apprehend through a finite but meaningful image?

According to Freud's critique of manifest religion, a key to answering this question is whether this compassionate God is believed "on external authority" or on "experience" (authority located within the self).

As a constructive-developmental psychologist, I have argued elsewhere that we must now recognize a postadolescent period in human development that is neither a "moratorium" nor fully equilibrated adulthood. In this period, described as "young adulthood," we achieve a self-aware adult self and critical thought, while retaining an appropriate dependence upon authority outside the self. This authority, however, is not merely assumed, conventional authority. Rather, it is authority that makes sense in terms congruent with the critically perceived reality of the young adult as he or she begins to include the self in the arena of authority (and will later locate authority more firmly within, though always remaining dependent upon confirmation outside the self as a necessary corrective to the inevitable distortions of any subjectivity) (Parks 1986). I suggest that this young man in his twenties was appropriately dependent upon the authority of the therapist and of "God," but that at this young adult place in human development, any authority would have to prove credible on the basis of his own perceived experience. External authority alone would be insufficient—even the authority of "God." For example, while his own minister-father (an external authority) may have been a primary image both demanding and compassionate in his experience, the compassion the young man himself actively extended to others in the "name of God" had been tested in notably harsh settings and found to so correspond with the truth of life in his own experience that this compassion was potentially available as truth also for the self. It needed only to be made accessible to the self by means of a legitimating credible-enough-therapist/authority-outside-the-self.

After decades of suspicion between psychology and religion, clinicians are being invited to reckon in new ways with the dynamics of meaning, faith, and imagination, especially the religious imagination. This requires us to deepen our respect for the truth that every image (and by extension every theory) by which we grasp "how things are really" is an image both powerful and finite. Every image and theory has the power both to disclose and to obscure, to illumine and to distort. A central religious image, God, can serve (in both transcendent and immanent forms) as a powerful vehicle of the truth of compassion—suffering with, suffering recognized, suffering confirmed and therefore bearable—reconciling the self with alienated elements within psychic life. The character and function of that image, however, will be shaped both by political-social structures and by the developing personality structures of the individual. The image that serves as a vehicle of compassion toward the self can, as in the second case, be domesticated and exploited by political-social structures and can serve to constrain ongoing growth when the truth of the image is not recomposed in a fashion fitting to the ongoing development of the individual.

We may thus contend that "idols" are those images that serve as centers of power, value, and affection yet, in their failure either to adequately grasp the one reality and/or to keep faith compatible with development, lead to intolerable distortion and death. "God," as revealed in Jewish and Christian traditions, is the "Spirit of Life," the "One Beyond the Many," the hidden strength, our only ally, who suffers with us and yet continually transcends the finitude of inevitably distorting forms and images while at the same time seeking images by which life on this earth may be known. "Idols" are those merely illusory projections of an infantile need for a protective father employed by "adults" on the basis of external authority alone so as to inhibit the development of trust of self—the gods of Freud's manifest religion. "God," in contrast, can be a centering image of power, value, and affection that serves to orient our imaginations to truth, reality and the ineffable matrix of life itself—the God (by inference) of Freud's latent religion. If so, then therapists share with theologians a common vocation, for therapists too participate in the work of assisting the human community in its essential task of distinguishing "God" from the "idols."

Notes

1. Parents care for and protect a child's reality, but even the best parents cannot control their child's experience. Should the child be given access to the image, "God"? Therapists care for and when necessary protect a client's reality, but even the best therapists cannot control or always be present to their client's experience. Should the client, of any age, have access to "God"?

2. This question must be considered along with the recognition that the word *compassion,* in contrast to both *pity* and *mercy,* does not require a disparate power relationship. Compassion means a feeling with, a suffering with, which is not exercised from any superior stance but rather places all participants in a relationship of solidarity.

3. Keiser notes that Freud's fierce contention with illusions that inhibit "life on this earth" likewise partakes in patriarchal, sexist assumptions. He sees Freud's alternative to the illusion as a clearly masculine solution: "a stiff upper lip, hard work, focused on the task at hand, relying on no other strength than one's own, facing the harsh realities of a motherless world where the father's protection, even divinized, is inadequate, because there is no consolation." Van Herik elaborates a yet more complex gender analysis, offering the compelling thesis that Freud discerned similar mental structures in femininity and Christian "illusion"; masculinity and Jewish renunciation of wish; and the human ideal (which is the masculine ideal) and the postreligious, psychoanalytic "scientific attitude." Judith Van Herik, *Freud on Femininity and Faith* (Berkeley: University of California Press, 1982).

References

Davies, R. 1977. *The Deptford Trilogy.* New York: Viking Penguin.

Freud, S. 1971. *The Interpretation of Dreams.* New York: Avon.

Fowler, J. W. 1981. *Stages in Faith: The Psychology of Human Development and the Quest for Meaning.* New York: Harper and Row.

Greenberg, J. 1964. *I Never Promised You a Rose Garden.* New York: Holt, Rinehart and Winston.

Kegan, R. 1980. There the dance is: Religious dimensions of a developmental framework. In J. Fowler and A. Vergote, eds., *Toward Moral and Religious Maturity*, 407–11. Morristown, N.J.: Silver Burdett.

——. 1982. *The Evolving Self: Meaning and Process in Human Development*. Cambridge: Harvard University Press.

Keiser, R. M. 1988. Postcritical religion and the latent Freud. *Zygon* 25, no. 4 (December): 433–47.

Lynch, W. F. 1973. *Images of Faith: An Exploration of the Ironic Imagination*. Bloomington, Ind.: Notre Dame University Press.

Parks, S. 1986. *The Critical Years: Young Adults and the Search for Meaning, Faith, and Commitment*. San Francisco: Harper and Row.

Rizzuto, A.-M. 1979. *The Birth of the Living God*. Chicago: University of Chicago Press.

Smith, W. C. 1979. *Faith and Belief*. Princeton: Princeton University Press.

The Transcendent Moment and The Analytic Hour

R. G. K. KAINER

W e do not usually encounter ideas about transcendent phenomena such as the human spirit and the soul in connection with a psychoanalytic undertaking, relegating them instead to the arenas of philosophy, mysticism, or religion. The exceptions are the well-known works of Carl Jung and the lesser-known works of Otto Rank on the soul and the human creative will (Rank 1930, 1932). The seminal works of these analytic pioneers contain some of the richest ideas on the themes of transcendence, yet they are now systematically addressed only outside the mainstream of psychoanalysis. In this paper, transcendence refers to transformational phenomena in the therapeutic undertaking and the transcendent moment refers to that moment in the therapy hour when such transformations become possible. My use of "transcendence" differs from the more usual reference to a dualistic theory in which matter and spirit are two separate forms of reality. Rather, I am speaking of a moment in which the self is transformed to a higher, more creative, or optimal level of being.

In *Freud and Man's Soul,* Bruno Bettelheim makes an eloquent plea to have us consider Freud not as a medical scientist, but as a "minister" (1984:35) or "midwife to the soul" (1984:36). Nonetheless, history has more consistently assigned to Freud the role of "biologist of the mind" (Sulloway 1979). Bettelheim thought Freud's translators did particular disservice to Freud's intent by rendering his Greek word *psyche* as "mind" instead of "soul." He further believed that mistranslating Freud's direct use of the German *seele* (soul) as "mental apparatus" or "mental organization," overemphasized the body and the intellect over the spirit.

In his work and in his writings, Freud often spoke of the soul—of its nature and structure, its development, its attributes, how it reveals itself in all we do and dream. Unfortunately, nobody who reads him in English could guess this, because nearly all his many references to the soul, and to matters pertaining to the soul, have been excised in translation.   (1984:35)

Psyche, Bettelheim reminds us, was depicted in mythology as young and beautiful, "as having the sings of a bird or a butterfly. Birds and butterflies are symbols of the soul in many cultures, and serve to emphasize its *transcendental* nature" (emphasis added) (1984:14). Psyche as soul, in her fragile beauty, must be approached with respect and care, else she might be violated or even destroyed, and Bettelheim likens this to the care of and respect for the other that must be present in a psychoanalysis (1984:15). The evolution of the concept of the self and the special attention being paid to it in contemporary practice may further reflect this concern. Bettelheim believed that Freud meant psychoanalysis to be the "science of the life of the soul" (1984:72). He regretted the paradox that, although the scientific language of psychoanalysis has made it acceptable to the world of medicine and successful in our country, medicine now holds it in too tight an embrace, making psychoanalysis a mere handmaiden of psychiatry. By interpreting Freud's work only as a science of instinct and mind, and by overemphasizing the sexual, Bettelheim feared that it has been reduced to a narrow and shallow pursuit.

Bettelheim's reading of Freud is a complex mixture of fact and longing. It is hard to reconcile the criticism of Freud's translators with the fact that Anna Freud authorized the official English language translation of the *Standard Edition of the Complete Psychological Works,* as Freud had authorized the earlier translations of his papers. The compilation by Joan Riviere of the *Collected Papers* is also an authorized translation, and while sometimes more graceful than Strachey, yields essentially the same data. It would be hard to reason as Bettelheim did (1984) that Freud's low opinion of America made him indifferent to the translations of his work for that country. It is more likely that his endorsement was based on a very accurate assessment of the appeal of mind over soul for the scientific community, as well as his own need to have psychoanalysis be a reflection of a scientific enlightenment distinct from its philosophic roots. Psychoanalysis may indeed belong more the German tradition of human science rather than natural science, but it is well known that Freud had no wish to place it either in a philosophical or mystical tradition.

Bettelheim's work is among the better known of a problematic revisionist trend which attempts to reconcile the compelling power of Freud's genius and exquisite style with his inevitable mistakes. Among these efforts are other attempts to recolor Freud's scientific determinism, his antireligiousness, and even to place him within the ranks of feminists. I believe that these "bionic attempts" to replace the ailing parts of Freud with new and better parts does a disservice to Freud's actual monumental achievements in the history of ideas and to the advancement of thought in our field. As Stephen Mitchell has said, "We have to move the theory, not the man" (1989).

Bettelheim is right in saying that we have missed the implications of Freud's belief in the dark side of the soul by rejecting the death instinct and not grappling with it more fully. I believe that we should move the theory of human destructiveness from the instinctual realm of drive and defense and rethink its implications in terms of self and object. We will then be able to come closer to an understanding of the meaning of the transcendent in psychoanalysis—the triumph over the destructive internal imagos within the self.

The Object and the Other

We are well aware of the polemics surrounding the developing schools of psychoanalytic thought as each of the "four waves" of drive, ego, object relations, and self psychology unfolded in a continuing dialectic (Pine 1990). Ego psychology corrects for the thesis of the primacy of id in Freud's drive psychology, giving ego its own important place. Self psychology is the antithesis of the negative role accorded narcissism in drive psychology. In particular, object relations and self psychology, in addition to their conscious conceptual purpose, have moved us further from a mechanistic view of the psyche to a more humanistic one. For example, the *object* in object relations theory corrects for the fundamentally mechanistic, autoerotic, and nonrelational meaning of the *object* in drive theory. As Freud conceived it:

The *object* of an instinct is that in or through which it can achieve its aim. It is the most variable thing about an instinct and is not originally connected with it, but becomes attached to it only in consequence of being peculiarly fitted to provide satisfaction. The object is not necessarily an extraneous one: it may be part of the subject's own body. It may be changed any number of times in the course of the vicissitudes the instinct undergoes during life: a highly important part is played by this capacity for displacement in the instinct. (Freud 1915)

In object relations theory, the object shifts from being a mere (and interchangeable) target of instinctual discharge to being the relational "other." In Fairbairn's particularly sophisticated reversal of drive theory, libido is "object seeking rather than pleasure seeking" (1952). For Fairbairn, one's internal world is not fueled by sexual and aggressive instinctual tension states (Freud), but rather it is figuratively "peopled" with objects. Furthermore, object relations theory advances our understanding of the *interactional* nature of self and object in all its introjective and projective aspects. We not only contain mental representations of our introjected objects, we maintain mental representations of our *relationship* to these objects.

It was Hans Loewald (1960), a highly respected classical ego-psychological psychoanalyst, who first suggested that the analyst might become a "new object" for the patient, and that the analysis may create a new "object relationship." His seminal paper "On the Therapeutic Action of Psychoanalysis" transcends the classic concept of the analyst as only a passive and neutral recipient of archaic transferences. The analysis itself has the potential for providing a new beginning for a different interactional matrix. Bollas (1987) recently took a similar idea even further and expressively captured the transcendent quality of the potential for transformation in the analytic undertaking. Referring to Winicott's "environmental mother" he says:

Not yet fully identified as an other, the mother is experienced as a process of transformation, and this feature of early existence lives on in certain forms of object-seeking in adult life, when the object is sought for its function as a signifier of transformation. Thus, in adult life, the quest is not to possess the object; rather the object is pursued in order to surrender to it as a medium that alters the self . . . The memory of this early object relation manifests itself in the person's search for an object (a person, place, event, ideology) that promises to transform the self.   (1987:13–14)

Internal representations of early object relationships permeate thinking and behavior, fueling and shaping both personality and pathology. In the clinical examples presented here, the patients' internal worlds housed various deadened, deadening, unempathic, and murderous objects with which each patient maintained a symbolic and powerful unconscious relationship. These to me are the "dark images of the soul" that function destructively in the self structure. The basic thesis of this paper is that the therapist serves a fundamentally inspirational role as Muse (Kainer 1990) or tranformational object (Bollas 1987) effecting changes in these internal relationships and mitigating their demonic effect. These changes occur through the essentially transcendent medium of the empathic connectedness of vicarious introspection (Kohut 1984) or through the acceptance of the patient's projective identifications (Bion 1977). This allows the split-off or disavowed part of the self to be reclaimed. Similarly, it allows the inchoate bits and pieces of the self to be named (Bion), thereby giving expression to the "unthought known" (Bollas 1987).

EMPATHY, THE TRANSFORMATIONAL OBJECT, AND THE TRANSCENDENT MOMENT

The Case of D

D was a somewhat subdued but nonetheless delightful eleven-year-old who was a misfit in her rather disturbed upper-middle-class family. Her parents had separated. Angry and depressed, the mother was sullen and depriving toward her. D would sometimes ask me for money for the monthly scholastic magazine and carfare. D's sister had been sent to one of the more exclusive private schools in the city, but D was enrolled in a rather rough public school where she was not doing well scholastically or socially. As sometimes happens, the healthiest member of the family was sent for therapy. She came to see me twice weekly and communicated with me by writing "Stupid" on the blackboard (or, when she was feeling affectionate, "My stupid psychologist") in response to any comment I should be so foolish as to make.

My tender maternal feelings for her helped me to avoid experiencing her remarks as her editorial comments on my ability; however, they did puzzle me. I found no need to take notes during the session, for I could easily recall the six or so phrases that passed during the hour. I will confess that at no point during the year's work (which took place at a university clinic) did I ever have a conscious notion of what I was doing nor a rationale to support it. We were together in a simple state of being, which consisted mainly of quiet parallel existence or an occasional word game, at which she would often beat me, sometimes with a little help on my part.

After absorbing this for almost a year, I blurted out one day after she had written "STUPID" in large letters on the blackboard, "Oh, *now* I know—that's how you *feel* when *you* feel something no one else sees!" My hastily constructed words were awkward, but that didn't matter. She then wrote, in little letters, "I love you."

This was the moment when I finally cracked the code of D's silence and her feelings. At some level I had finally "heard" what it was like to be a sensitive child in a markedly obtuse family environment in which she was "different." I felt the impact of that moment, as did D. When I later learned to my surprise that she actually improved her schoolwork and made friends, I was impressed with the power of what I now know to be empathic understanding as a therapeutic agent (Kainer 1984).

The Case of A

Many years ago A came to treatment with a history of severe gynecological pain that was poorly understood and often dismissed by her physicians. She also had a history of inappropriate object choices in men and many failed attempts at passing a professional licensing examination. Both her feminine and professional development were arrested. I found myself using my odd subjective experience of her to further understand her damaged self, for she evoked a giddy mirthfulness in me and an urge to laugh at her, despite a strong bond and therapeutic alliance that was created between us. I mused on my experience of her: I had associations to Charlie Chaplin's little tramp—a sad, tragicomic figure. The way she dressed seemed somehow wrong to me. In reality, except for a somewhat flustered demeanor, there was nothing odd about her gait or her conservative clothes. I experienced her as if she were one of those drawings in a comic book where the color doesn't quite stay within the lines of the figure. Her very being seemed off-the-mark. What I had unconsciously sensed was the projection of her experience of a self that was off center and felt not-quite-right. The result was a hysteric character phenomenon of unbelievability that permeated her emotional and physical bearing.

The source of the disavowed part of herself was unacknowledged grief and forbidden mourning. She had lost a beloved father at the age of thirteen. He had had a quiet but profound regard for her and took considerable pleasure in her intellect. He often expressed the belief that she could surpass him professionally, and this gave her pride and pleasure. She experienced an enormous loss at his death, especially in light of the more narcissistic makeup of her mother. Her mother's response to overhearing her sobbing shortly after his death was the admonition, "No one will want to know your troubles—besides, you may have lost a father but I lost a husband!"

Intellectually and interpretively we were able to link the anxiety which had crippled her attempts to pass her exam to the pact she had made with herself at the time of her unacknowledged anguish: she would become an outstanding professional as compensation for being fatherless. Success would be her consolation in the light of her mother's inability to become a consoling and compensatory object. Her failure to pass the exam the first time (in a jurisdiction with a fifty percent failure rate) was shattering to this ego ideal and triggered latent anxieties around the task. This interpretation was useful to her, but something far more compelling took place.

As I listened to her while she told of her mother's response to overhearing her sob while alone at her bath, I found myself feeling very sad as I had a sudden image of the little girl sitting alone and bereft. At the next hour, she questioned me about the misty look in my eye which her alert glance had caught as she was leaving the previous hour. She expressed surprise at my reaction and I exploded, saying: "If losing the father you love at thirteen isn't the saddest thing in the world, I don't know what is!" It proved to be a moment of profound connectedness.

I later understood that I was experiencing the grief which had been disavowed because her mother could not tolerate it. Her grief was now affirmed by an object who could, and who would sustain the necessary mirroring. Furthermore, via projection, she made me feel the unspoken sadness and loneliness of her adolescence. It was a brief but potent moment in the therapy, where an unconscious exchange was successfully completed and the long-repressed feeling state was allowed expression. Pursuing the metaphor of this paper, we might say that the part of the self that lay buried was given renewed life.

In the ensuing years of painstaking work she was able to pass her examination, find a suitable mate after many false starts, and finally validate that her previously diagnosed "hysterical" gynecological pain was due to large ovarian cysts that she had had since puberty. She later mastered the intricacies of adoption after surgery left her sterile. She balanced marriage, motherhood, and profession in a day when that was not so common. She literally blossomed into a mature and confident young woman. The power of affirmation, which is a well-known clinical precept of self psychology, was particularly striking in this case (Kainer 1990).

PROJECTIVE PHENOMENA AND A
SADOMASOCHISTIC WORLDVIEW

The Case of C

It may seem odd to attempt to illustrate trancendent and transformational phenomena with a case of sadomasochism. I am not referring here to the patient's sexual practices in the classic sense, but to a commonly found "Weltanschauung" or world-view in which one constantly experiences oneself as a rageful victim. I view this patient's capacity to shift from that sado-masochistic worldview as a transcendent act in the sense of rising above or going beyond. With the help of the patient's own notes, reconstructed independently after the therapy ended, we can capture some important moments in achieving this transformation. I will intersperse my recollections with hers (Kainer 1983).

RK: My first recollection was of a telephone call from her late one July, enquiring about the possibility of starting therapy. It came shortly before my summer vacation in August. She reported difficulties relating to pressures at school and I asked her if she could hold on until September since I wouldn't be available if she needed immediate and sustained help. She said yes, and I told her I would try to see her for an initial consultation before I went on vacation. I was able to arrange a consultation, and found her to be a plucky and determined young woman who had previous therapy. She was experiencing difficulties in graduate school but she reported no urgency at that time. It seemed an unexceptional meeting, and we agreed to begin work in September. Her own notes however, are far more revealing:

C: I felt that I had been "holding on" for a long time. I knew much of my resources had been used up. I had encouragement [from a mutual colleague] who hinted about self-esteem issues. I still found it difficult to make the first call to Rochelle to ask for help and begin therapy again. I called once. The call was not returned. I called again. No appointment was available. When making that first [later] appointment, R. asked me if I could hold on until September as she would be on vacation until then. I said "yes" and *felt* nothing pressing. R. asked me if I wanted to see another therapist as she would be unavailable for a month. I said "no"; it had taken me a long time to decide on R. and I did not want to see a "stranger." I wondered if I was acceptable and felt that beginning of a will battle, sure I would be turned away.

RK: The well-known self psychological phenomenon of an *idealizing transference* has begun for, without ever having met me, she uses the little actual knowledge she has of me to imagine that I am not a stranger and am the "chosen one" to help her. She has also positioned herself, through her internal needs and my limited availability, into a vulnerable and somewhat helpless position. She makes me powerful in that I can turn her away, and she feels her own will rise against me. She is determined, but has partially denied the extent of her neediness to both herself and to me. I am completely unaware of the true state of her mind at this time, as is she.

C: R. called with an opening for an appointment at the end of July. The day before the appointment I had an anxiety attack, the second in my life. Saw R. the next day. It was fairly uneventful. I felt that R. did not understand my worries. I thought I expected too much from R. Felt reassured and that perhaps I was exaggerating my difficulties to myself.

RK: It is crucial to her dynamic that I cannot "hear"—nor can she make me understand—her intense inner stress. This will later become meaningful in the light of her history. In retrospect, it is likely that the anxiety attack was related to the impending consultation although she linked it to difficulties at school. For she dutifully repressed the extent of her neediness in response to my unspoken message which she hears (as an archaic parental message) only too well: "I'm tired, I have no time, I'm writing a paper, I'm on vacation, I'm going out of town, you go away too!"

C: I wondered why I was beginning therapy as the meeting was so mild, although I remember many tears. I also remember worrying about what R. would think of me as a professional. She told me that people in the profession are the worst and I wasn't sure what she meant.

RK: This careless comment was addressed to the exaggerated self-diagnoses I have heard over the years, including autism and borderline personality organization! While it was meant to lighten her anxiety about any "judgment" of her and her adequacy, it was a technical error that further served to stimulate her intense self-demeaning tendencies of which I was unaware. Although clearly a frivolous remark, her notes indicate that she:

C: Felt embarrassed, inadequate, self-degrading, looking for warmth. These were not addressed.

RK: In retrospect, it seems astonishing that we both experienced the hour as unremarkable. I was unaware of her unexpressed bad feelings, and I self-protectively turned her off. She was so used to her bad feelings that they had become ego syntonic. She left the hour "feeling happier, having been 'held', 'accepted.'" The stage is set: I am already experienced as idealized, powerful, good— but also hurtful, although that is subordinated to her longing to keep me as the good object. I have already wounded her several times in just one telephone call and one meeting but this gets disavowed. She recalls August as a particularly painful month:

C: Many demands made on me. I felt overwhelmed, underprepared, and anxious. I called R. at the end of August and got an appointment for September. Resources were becoming depleted and panic completely overtook me. I walked around the house in an anxious stupor.

RK: She then called me during August while I was still on vacation and about to go out of town.

C: I finally called R. I felt I couldn't make it alone. I felt a cold reception. R. was annoyed but concerned. She said she wasn't available this month and asked if there was someone else I could see. I said yes. She called back and gave me a name anyway.

RK: She organized a support system for herself, including some interim therapy. The therapist she saw likened her state to her swimming in a river of alligators with "her loved ones watching but not helping her." This too will become significant in the light of her history. By now, I had most certainly become one of those watching from the shore. All this occurred before the session in September when, to my mind only, our therapeutic journey was to officially begin. Because of my own needs, I took her at her word that she could wait until September to begin work. The annoyance that she detected in me was already that of a caretaker whose child is needy at an inconvenient time and who is pulled to respond but does not want to—a typical maternal ambivalence. At some level I sensed her need and was concerned, but resented her untimely intrusion expecially since I had extracted a tacit promise from her that she wouldn't need me until I was ready.

Consciously, I was aware of none of this. Until the September appointment my contact had been limited to the initial telephone call, the "unexceptional" interview, and the telephone call in late August. I'm sure I felt that the work had not begun. One can assume from my awesome density that I was not really yet "on the case." Her notes on the dramatic session after the summer coincide directly with my own recollections.

C: I walked in and fell apart. I cried immediately. I apologized for disturbing R. I apologized for crying. I apologized for feeling so miserable. I cried, cried, cried. Tears are everywhere. I wouldn't ask for a tissue. Tears, tears, tears.

RK: As the hour went on I felt like a cross between a child-beater and somebody dropped into the wrong scenario. I had no idea what was going on, but her reproaches seemed unmistakable. Her incessant crying combined with her apologies were particularly distressing. I tried to get her to tell me what was wrong. We tried to process her disappointment at the emergency call to me. She was surprised that I wouldn't see her and was *sure* that I was seeing other clients. I responded with a series of unhelpful comments and reflections that only made matters worse and which she experienced as:

c: An attack by a barrage of spears. I wanted mercy and felt attacked instead. I cried but I did not leave. R. wonders if we could work together. I felt the door open, almost pushed out. I thought it was all hopeless yet stayed anyway. Was it willfulness? I felt like an ocean wave was washing over me, could get no air, only punishment from a great force. I wanted caring and got a knocking about. I didn't understand why. *I couldn't believe this was happening with a therapist.* (emphasis added)

rk: Her excellent notes perfectly capture the essential awfulness of the encounter. I too felt caught up in a useless undertow of confused and troubling emotion. I did not understand it at all. I felt a rare uncertainty that perhaps I could not work with her. I knew that I was inflicting pain and felt that this should not go on between two human beings. It was at the moment when the whole thing seemed senseless to me that a realization broke through. Although she doesn't report in her notes that I acted oddly at that critical moment, I was seized with manic relief as I blurted out: "Oh, we're just engaged in a sadomasochistic interaction!" Her more appropriately sober notes read:

c: Suddenly, R. realizes sadomasochistic dynamic and the sun came out again. I had been through a hurricane, got drenched in tears, and exhausted. Relieved, although in the aftermath of terror. I left the appointment feeling as above.

rk: The fever had broken. I accepted the projected images of her murderous internal world and reenacted them with her, finally giving them a name. The under-

standing that together we had recreated a sadomasochistic interaction somehow freed me from having to
continue it, and I was able to lift both of us out of it.
The therapy that followed yielded some important
background information that helped me to understand
how this dynamic originated and how she was unconsciously searching for the transformational relationship
that would free her from it.

C's childhood had been made a hell by an older, much larger,
and possibly psychotic sister who chased and terrorized her daily while both parents worked. Of very modest circumstances,
the parents were well meaning but preoccupied with earning a
living. They only sought help for the disturbed sister after she
had threatened my patient with a knife. C had escaped serious
physical harm by using her wits and was to do so again when an
intruder broke into the household. Again, *no one came to her rescue* as she was abused in the kitchen of her own home, too terrified to scream.

This archaic image was deeply embedded in her, resulting in a
sadomasochistic sense of self projectively reenacted in our initial
contact. Her scream was silent and I did not hear it, nor did I
rescue her from the danger she was in. The potential for transformation quite literally began when I was able to receive the bits
and pieces of her inchoate and dissociated state and put them
together in a thought that could then be spoken between us.

Later aspects of the work with her further illustrate my unconscious identification with Loewald's (1960) concept that
the regressive crisis encountered in the transference neurosis of
the work is constructively resolved because the analyst is available not only as a *new* object but also for the development of a
new object-relationship. In a later paper, Loewald states:

> Insofar as the development, flowering, and resolution of
> the transference neurosis requires the active presence of,
> and responsive . . . interaction with the analyst, and is
> the result of the collaboration of patient and analyst, this
> fantasy creation is more than an intrapsychic process, it

has a form of reality different from pure thought or dreaming or remembering . . . such fantasy action is called forth and shaped by present actuality (including the mental life of the analyst), and shapes present and future actuality. (1960:369–70)

We entered a phase of the work that addressed itself to her rather entrenched role of victim. This was complicated by the realities of her life as a "privileged" contemporary woman who ran a household on a modest income, raised small children, maintained a marriage to which she was seriously committed, and pursued an advanced degree in a department where the requirements were in the process of changing! However, every time she came in presenting herself as a persecuted victim, I challenged her assumptions without attacking her being. There was a slightly zany quality to some of the work. The following material arose spontaneously and seemed to work by enabling C to establish a new object-relationship that superseded those of earlier malevolent imagos. For example, her hectic schedule could make getting to my office an ordeal, especially in traffic or snow. One day, after her anxiety about school was somewhat under control, she came in saying that she was overburdened and that there was not *one more thing* she could cut out of the week. I countered by telling her that if she stopped coming to therapy during the winter, she would add three hours to her week and could resume when the snow and her school schedule had let up. It was a suggestion she later accepted with success.

Once, it snowed, and she was fearful that she couldn't get her car moving. I left with her after the hour and helped her shovel out. Although it was a natural gesture under the circumstances, she experienced it as not "what she expected" from a therapist. Perhaps this "unexpectedness" was what had crushed her at the beginning of the therapy when I attacked her in an attempt to extricate myself from her engulfing masochistic posture. Being capable of using and sustaining the unexpected with her became my ultimate resource and the basis of her capacity to eventually shift from her sadomasochistic worldview.

My own capacity to yield to the unexpected also served its therapeutic purpose. Leaving the session one day relieved at our ability to establish a working alliance, she surprised me by saying, "I know you're not a hugger, but I'd like to hug you!" She was quite right about my strong hands-off preference, but I thought "It won't kill me!" I believe that I unconsciously reasoned that if I'm going to ask her to shift out of a lifelong masochistic posture, I'd better be capable of a little flexibility myself. After all, her task was harder than mine.

All these encounters were spontaneous attempts to shake her worldview; the worldview of a terrified young child who felt abused by life's ordinary traffic and snow, or who would unconsciously and naively construct situations that invited abuse. Some time after our work ended and I called her to invite her participation in preparing a paper on our work together, she remarked, "You know, I don't do that anymore." The "that" was vague, but we both knew what she meant.

In all three clinical examples, what I am describing as the transcendent moment occurs in the context of profound empathic connectedness, either in the form of "vicarious introspection," as in the fist two cases, or in the more inchoate primitive communication of projective identification as in the case of C. I believe that these empathic phenomena describe essentially transcendent acts in "scientific" language. They enable us to find our way to the deepest core of the other, where we find the unnamed pathological introjects. But this core also contains what is most essential, vital, and original about the individual—it contains both the pathological and the creative. My imagery of empathic phenomena is of reaching down through the mind of the person, straight through to the heart. Bettelheim's is of reaching down into the soul.

Although I prefer the metaphor of "muse" with its more direct association to creativity to either that of "midwife" or "minister," I did have an association closer to Bettelheim's vision while writing this. I suddenly thought of the final scene of Gounod's opera *Faust:* Marguerite, in a fit of madness and despair, has killed her child. She is about to die for this and sings ecstatically, asking to be carried to heaven. Mephistopheles has won Faust's soul, and as he drags him away from her triumphantly cries out, *Jugée!* ("She is condemned!"). The heavens part, and on the heels of the Devil's basso profundo, the seraphic soprano voices of the choir of angels swell as they sing out *Sauvée!* ("She is saved!") as they reach down and lift Marguerite up to them. I had not remembered, until I recently checked the libretto, that this is immediately followed by the phrase "*Christ est ressuscité!*" Musically it is a sublime moment that I have always found thrilling without being particularly conscious of the words. I do not think it coincidental that the two themes of this powerful moment are those of resurrection and the redemption of the soul. Perhaps we find the spiritual in the creative.

The shift from instinct theory to object relations reflects the growing awareness that we crave the relational other. The hell that we may create for ourselves is not so much the hell of our instinctual conflicts but, as Sartre says in *No Exit,* "Hell is other people." If this is so, we may look for redemption from the same source. Analysis has always been focused on the patient's internal world; its drives, its objects, and its affective states. We are becoming increasingly aware of the relational role of self to object and analyst to patient (Mitchell 1988). We may not only look to analysis for a new object and a new object relationship but secretly hope to find, in the person of the analyst, the actual object who can aid in the transformation of our self or, put self-psychologically, can aid in consolidating self-object cohesion.

In addition to recognizing the crucial importance of the relational other, the emergence and growth of a psychology of the self is further demonstration that within psychoanalytic science, with its sometimes clumsy, cold, and stilted language, fundamental aspects of the human spirit are being recognized. As Kohut suggests, it formally recognizes the human longing for figures whom we can idealize and thereby feel strong; for those who can provide empathic mirroring and the affirmation of our being and thereby feel whole; and for those with whom we can find our alter ego in a twinship of identification and thereby feel connected (Kohut 1984). Transformation, aspiration, idealization, affirmation, and twinship are phenomena of the self in the psychological sense, but they also symbolize transcendent yearnings. If we are not yet a science of the soul, the spirit to become one is strong.

References

Bettelheim, B. 1984. *Freud and Man's Soul*. New York: Vintage Books.

Bion, W. 1977. Transformations. In *Seven Servants*, pp. 1–183. New York: Jason Aronson.

Bollas, C. 1987. *The Shadow of the Object*. New York: Columbia University Press.

Fairbairn, R. 1946. Object-relationship and dynamic structure. Reprinted in *Psychoanalytic Studies of the Personality*. London: Rutledge & Kegan Paul. 1952.

Freud, S. [1915] 1959. Instincts and their vicissitudes. *Collected Papers*. 5 vols. 4:60–83. New York: Basic Books.

Kainer, R. 1983. Shifting the sado-masochistic world view of the patient. *Proceedings of the Eighth Annual Meeting of the D.C. Institute of Mental Hygiene*. Washington, D.C.

———. 1984. From "evenly-hovering attention" to 'vicarious introspection': Issues of listening in Freud and Kohut. *American Journal of Psychoanalysis* 44:1.

———. 1990. The precursor as mentor, the therapist as muse: Creativity and self-object phenomena. In *Progress in Self Psychology*. 6:175–88. Hillsdale, N.J.: The Analytic Press. In press.

Kohut, H. 1984. *How Does Analysis Cure?* Chicago: Chicago University Press.

Loewald, H. 1960. On the therapeutic action of psycho-analysis. In P. Buckley, ed., *Essential Papers on Object Relations*, pp. 385–418. New York: New York University Press.

———. 1980. Psychoanalysis as an art and the fantasy character of the psychoanalytic situation. In *Papers on Psychoanalysis*, pp. 352–71. New Haven: Yale University Press.

Mitchell, S. 1988. *Relational Concepts in Psychoanalysis*. Cambridge: Harvard University Press.

———. 1989. Personal communication.

Pine, F. 1990. *Drive, Ego, Object, and Self*. New York: Basic Books.

Rank, O. 1930. *Psychology and (the Belief in) the Soul*. New York: Barnes, 1961.

———. 1932. *Art & Artist*. New York: Knopf, 1958.

Sulloway, F. 1979. *Freud: Biologist of the Mind*. New York: Basic Books.

Concluding Clinical Postscript:

On Developing a Psychotheological Perspective

John McDargh

T he clinical papers in this collection should, if successful, have the cumulative effect of overcoming one of the major factors that until relatively recently has blocked many clinicians from effectively addressing the religious dimension of their clients' lives in the therapeutic relationship. I refer to the lack of a sufficiently nuanced clinical "listening perspective" from which to hear the dynamic meanings and hence the therapeutic potential of religious material as it may present itself in the clinical situation (Hedges 1983). The various structural developmental, object relational and self psychological perspectives on religion presented in this book propose ways to recognize religious material as yet another "royal road to the unconscious" that may be creatively explored and integrated into the therapeutic process. Clients who may have withheld personal religious preoccupations from analysis because of subtle but clear clues from the therapist that these concerns are not germane to the real work of therapy may begin to share such material with a clinician who appreciates its potential significance for the work of therapy.[1] Such sharing can make a significant difference in therapeutic outcome. The failure to address the area of religion in the psychotherapeutic process may leave some clients with a vague, dissatisfied sense that something rather crucial remains unintegrated (Saur and Saur: in press). More critically, the therapist who does not find a way to listen to the salient religious aspects of a client's life may miss a vital clue to the psychic conflict that is at the heart of the therapy. Finally, a therapist's silence on the subject of religion—experienced by the client as indifference or hostility—may eventually compromise the empathic bond between therapist and client and result in a therapeutic "mis-alliance" (Wolberg 1977).

Is it enough, however, for the therapist to be actively interested in and attentive to religious material simply in order to effectively solicit it in the therapeutic situation? Each of the papers in this collection tacitly or explicitly acknowledges that something more is needed. A therapist's interest in a client's religious experience is perceived as carrying with it a certain valuation. Clients even minimally aware of depth psychology's history with respect to religion may be honestly concerned that what they share of their religious views or experiences may be dealt with unempathically or reductionistically. As Kochems points out in this volume, this fear may also serve certain defensive purposes. It may collude, for instance, in the client's desire to keep his or her religion "pure" and isolated from the sexual and aggressive aspects of human experience. Nevertheless the concern that the therapist's theoretical mapping of religion onto the developmental process may carry with it certain a priori negative judgments is neither illegitimate nor historically unwarranted. Freud's original hypothesis that religion has its roots in the dynamics of childhood projection and must be outgrown in maturity has cast a long shadow. Our authors have sought to identify how the psychological theories or "listening perspectives" they set out represent a more balanced and more irenic analysis of the role that an individual's religious ideation and beliefs may play in the process of psychological maturation.

In this "concluding clinical postscript" I want to add a further question to their not inconsiderable accomplishment. It arises naturally from my own professional identity as a theologian involved both in clinical practice and in the interdisciplinary conversation between psychology and theology. The problem may be framed in this fashion: Is it *therapeutically* sufficient for a clinician to appreciate the *psychological* value of an individual's religion, or may it also be necessary for a clinician to take a position on the *ontological* status of the client's religious inner world? Since it is by no means immediately self-evident why this is a question that should engage clinicians and not just theologians, some explanation is needed.

In much of this book the hermeneutical key to religious material and, in particular, references to "God" is to see in the individual's conscious and unconscious God representation the whole complex history of the vicissitudes of that person's early object relationships. Unlike Freud, our authors do not see that God representation as frozen in the form of the oedipal father. On the contrary its dynamic development can be charted across the life cycle and, like other important cultural creations, it can be shown to exercise a decisive influence in shaping the individual's psychic structure. Optimally, the representation(s) of God may have a crucial psychological function to play in the maintainance of an individual's sense of being a loving and beloved self in relationship to a meaningful world (Rizzuto 1979; Lovinger 1984; McDargh 1983). For the religiously influenced client with a theistic belief structure his or her uniquely personal images of God has ontological significance as well as psychological meaning. In a word, God is experienced as *real*. "More prominent than the sense of the holiness or power of transcendent reality," writes Louis Dupre, "is the sense of its ontological richness—God is eminently *real*" (Dupre 1972:327). For the believing or struggling-to-believe client the word-symbol G-o-d is not exhausted by its psychological functions but includes the conviction that such a symbol has as its referent a superindividual Reality with which the client has some experience of relationship. This may also be true for some who have consciously rejected belief in God but who are able to speak with considerable conviction about the God they do not believe in. Does it make a difference if and how the clinician admits, if only to himself or herself, the possibility that a client's religious convictions do in some way resonate with a reality that is not simply of the client's creation?

The late Paul Pruyser and, more recently, William Meissner propose that the therapist can achieve a sufficiently nonreductionistic position by recognizing that *all* human beliefs are inescapably "illusions"—imaginative constructions informed by fundamental wishes and yearnings. These theorists hold that this act of primal human creativity is essential for psychic well-being and not to be outgrown or rejected (Meissner 1987; Pruyser 1983).[2] More than this psychology cannot say, yet more than this is not necessary. But the question may be asked: what quality of empathy is a clinician who privately judges his or her client's most deeply meaningful felt relationship to be an "illusion" capable of conveying—even in this newer and decidedly more positive use of the term? (The problem of empathy is compounded when the clinician holds the further judgment that the client's beliefs are also "delusions" in Freud's usage.)

The writer who has recently put the matter most starkly is Moshe Halevi Spero, senior clinical psychologist at Ezrath Nashim Hospital in Jerusalem: "I believe that therapists who view the patient's religious feelings simply as 'the patient's reality' ultimately deny the patient's essential experience that his relationship with and feelings toward God are not simply modeled after interpersonal dynamics" (Spero 1985:76). For Spero the practical dilemma is that "a therapeutic relationship cannot be sustained if the therapist views religion and God as merely isolated artifacts of overall psychological development" (Spero 1985:77). The problem of achieving adequate empathy is inseparable in Spero's judgment from some resolution of the philosophical status of the client's religious worldview, if only in the most general terms. He summarizes his case:

> It must matter whether the objects we deal with therapeutically, whose constructive and destructive influences we interpret, are intrapsychically real, phenomenologically real, metaphorically real, or *actually* real. And this is so even if the only directly observable difference such distinctions allow is a more profound empathic bond between patient and therapist.   (Spero 1990:69)

For Spero the issue is not one of explicitly endorsing or condemning a client's religious worldview, or even of the therapist ever sharing his or her own religious views with the client. Such actions risk coercing the conscience of the client and would violate appropriate therapeutic boundaries. What matters is whether the therapist is able to find a listening perspective on religious material that does not exclusively and unilaterally translate its meanings into the interpersonal or intrapsychic language that is the common currency of psychotherapeutic exchange. This may be illustrated by reference to a detail from a clinical case discussed by the British object relations theorist, Harry Guntrip. Guntrip's client brings into the session the following dream:

> I'm looking for Christ on the seashore. He rose up as if out of the sea and I admired his tall, magnificent figure. Then I went with Him to a cave and became conscious of ghosts there and fled in stark terror. But He stayed and I mustered up enough courage and went back in with Him. Then the cave was a house, as He and I went upstairs, He said, "You proved to have greater courage than I

had," and I felt I detected some weakness in Him. (Guntrip
1969:351)

The client's associations to this dream connect the figure of Christ to
both the client's admired but ultimately disappointing father and
Guntrip as therapist. Guntrip views the dream exclusively in terms of its
transferential significance, but in one direction only. That is, for Guntrip
the dream suggests that for the client the therapist is beginning to assume divine qualities and the client is "oscillating between the old fear
that father lets him down if he tries to stand up to his violent-tempered
mother, and the new wavering hope that the therapist will not let him
down in facing the 'ghost' of the angry mother within" (Guntrip
1969:351).[3] But if the therapist is beginning to assume salvific significance for the client, it may also be accurate to observe that the client's
God is becoming more therapeutic, that is, more reliably available to the
client in his struggle for freedom from his negative introjects.

Guntrip's interpretation misses the significance for the client of the
fact that the figure in the dream is not the therapist, but rather Christ. An
interpretation that assimilates the client's relationship to Christ entirely
and without remainder to the transferential client-therapist relationship
or to other internalized object relations ignores the possibility that
something new and *sui generis* may be occuring in the client's relationship with the divine, something that may well have implications for the
therapeutic relationship and for the structure of all other significant object relations.

The troubling questions that Spero raises for our clinical practice are
ones that require us to venture onto the new and uncharted boundary
between psychological theory and theological or philosophical reflection. There the task is to engage in interdisciplinary metamodel building
or the construction of what I term a "psychotheological" listening
perspective.[4] The term sounds both foreign and formidable, but the
project is one that most clinicians already have undertaken with varying
degrees of self-awareness and sophistication. Essentially a psychotheological perspective requires that the clinician identify as clearly as
possible where he or she stands with respect to two sets of questions.
The first is: What is the normative trajectory or path of human development? How does the clinician define "the human good" (health, optimal
human functioning, or maturation)? What does a clinician hope for his

or her clients?[5] The second question asks how this normative understanding of human nature is related to what might be termed the clinician's "metaphysical commitments." If the first question can be sum-
marized by asking, "What does one hope for?," this second question
attempts to name the grounds of one's hope. What does the clinician
believe to be the ultimate character of reality, the seen and the unseen,
the known and the unknowable? Individual therapists will differ widely
in terms of what they feel they are able to affirm with confidence about
the relationship of the human person to ultimacy. Some will have fairly
well-developed metaphysical schemas grounded perhaps in specific religious or philosophical traditions. Others may opt for a respectful
a-gnosis before these questions, taking to heart Hamlet's warning,
"There are more things in heaven and earth, Horatio, than are dreamt of
in your philosophy." Whatever position one assumes, the clinician's burden in developing a psychotheological position is to become self-
conscious of the way in which the answers to these questions influence
the conduct of therapy.

I shall describe three representative contemporary psychotheological
listening perspectives in psychotherapy. These are a "spiritual reality"
perspective, a "God relational" perspective, and a "faith relational" perspective. They are examples of the range of possibilities open to the clinician. It is hoped that in setting them out, with some of their strengths
and limitations, clinicians will be challenged to become more aware of
their own operative psychotheologies and to develop these with greater
intentionality and self-awareness.

The Spiritual Reality Perspective

Arguably the broadest and most inclusive psychotheological perspective
is one that basically challenges the "naturalistic" or "materialistic" bias of
psychology by asserting that "there is a spiritual reality and that spiritual
experiences make a difference in behavior" (Bergin 1988:23). The principle features of such a spiritual reality perspective can best be illustrated
first by reference to the extensive work of Allen Bergin, professor of psychology at Brigham Young University (Bergin 1980, 1983, 1988,
Bergin et al. 1988).

The hypothesis of a "spiritual reality" grounds the research by Bergin
and his colleagues that investigates the relationship between reported

religious experiences and measures of psychological well-being and other positive outcomes (there is a tendency to ignore negative consequences of religious experience in Bergin's research design). The intention behind such research is not simply to argue the *functional* value of such religious experiences, but rather to find in their measurable impact upon behavior evidence for their *ontological* reality. Bergin compares this research to the study of subatomic particles in nuclear physics, which necessarily relies upon tracing the visible effects of elements that are themselves invisible (Bergin 1988). Bergin names this invisible influence the "x factor" and presumes it to be at work in faith healing and in the transformations of personality brought about by profound religious experience. The "x factor" for Bergin is "the spiritual" and he approaches its investigation in ways analogous to the operation of the physical and biological sciences. Thus he writes, "Assuming that there is such a thing as a spiritual substance, it may be possible eventually to harmonize the principle governing it with empirical, behavioral and materialist positions" (Bergin 1988:24). Bergin's hope is that eventually we might be able to chart and identify the "laws" that govern such a spiritual system and that function with the same regularity as the laws of other systems, for example the hydraulic laws of the circulatory system or the electrochemical laws of the nervous system. Underlying so ambitious a project there is in Bergin's work an ethical and apologetic agenda, namely to find a basis for moral rules that grounds them in some form of universally valid "spiritual laws" safe from the perceived corrosion of historical relativity.

In its broadest terms a spiritual reality perspective has certain virtues. It speaks in such inclusive terms about "the spiritual" that it does not limit its scope to specific theistic traditions. It has the further value of opening up clinicians' "accounts with reality" (to quote William James) so that new data may be deposited and new insights withdrawn. As formulated by Bergin however this perspective also has some serious limitations. The basic problem is that Bergin's approach may not be radical enough. It hypothesizes a "spiritual reality" while still maintaining the research methodologies and underlying worldview that were responsible for banishing such a hypothesis in the first place. Underlying Bergin's approach is a naive positivism that presumes to locate spiritual reality "out there" with the same assurance as persons of reason and goodwill agree upon the existence of a new element or a new planet.[6] At the least, one might ask what becomes of the act of faith if Bergin's project is successful.

Fortunately, there are more philosophically sophisticated approaches to "spiritual reality" available to clinicians attracted to this psycho-theological perspective. We might broadly refer to these as "post-modern" approaches.[7] They attempt to overcome the radical subject-object dichotomy that has characterized empirical science since the En-lightenment (Barfield 1965). These approaches argue that, in ruling out subjectivity, experience, value, and feeling as valid dimensions of human knowing, modern science has produced a mechanistic model of the world and of the human psyche rather than an organic, ecological, and interactive one (Griffin 1988, 1989; Berman 1981; Zee 1986). Such postmodern perspectives tend to locate the dimension of the spiritual not "beyond" but rather "within."[8] They regard the unconscious as the source of genuine knowledge or revelation about personal resources for healing and life direction. From this perspective "the good life" or opti-mal human functioning is the knowing integration of all capacities in-herent in being human and this significantly includes the "deep wis-dom" of the unconscious. In actual clinical technique this perspective gives warrant to the use of various forms of hypnoprojective techniques that might evoke "the capacity of the unconscious, through vivid imag-ery, to crystallize a core theme in a person's life and to map out future directions for his life and therapy" (Goodman 1989).[9]

Spiritual Reality and Nontheistic Metaphysics

The spiritual reality perspective sketched out above is deliberately non-specific as to whether that reality is ultimately best spoken of as "person-al" or "impersonal." I would group under that general heading the psychotheological listening perspectives of clinicians whose worldview is largely informed by the nontheistic metaphysics of such traditions as Theravada Buddhism (see note 5). Though the further development produced by meditative practice is quite beyond their own therapeutic agenda, these clinicians nevertheless hold that the fullness of psychologi-cal and spiritual development (the purview of the spiritual master and not the clinician) eventually requires the individual to leave behind the illusion of a personal God along with the constructions of the self that are allied with that God. Enlightenment involves a process of "seeing through" the constructed character of all human identities and the withdrawal of all projections, including those by which we construe "God." Again, clinicians such as Engler and Brown would not view the achievement of enlightenment as the appropriate goal of psychotherapy. Thus in actual practice they may differ little from other psychoanalytic object relations theorists, though their appropriation of that theory takes place within a wider horizon of what is envisioned as humanly possible.

Arguably there are traditions of apophatic or negative mysticism in the West that may be interpreted as privileging a similar developmental sequence, i.e., the movement beyond particular images of God and of the self towards an imageless knowing (or better, an "unknowing") of that divine reality that is beyond all thought or representation but which is also the true ground of the self.[10] Nevertheless, for many clinicians who more or less self-consciously work out of Jewish, Christian, or Muslim contexts, the formulations of apophatic mysticism overleap both their own experience and that of most clients raised in the same religious culture. These clinicians find themselves in agreement with William James when he argues that for the religious individual "the universe is not an *it* but rather a *Thou*." It is the irreducibly *interpersonal* character of the individual's relationship to the ultimate that most deeply impresses these clinicians and they are at pains to defend the potential integrity and *sui generis* reality of the individual's relationship with the God of his or her understanding.

The God Relational Perspective

Clinicians who chose to adopt what I term a "God relational" perspective, which is in many respects deeply congruent with the spiritual intuitions of the major monotheistic faiths, will find that they are challenged by new problems of both a psychological and theological nature. One such problem is how the clinician discerns when an individual's religious experience is genuinely "of God" and when it reflects analyzable projective dynamics. Here clinicians vary greatly in terms of how much they believe they are able to specify about what they believe God to be like, and also how actively they introduce their own theological judgments into the therapeutic situation. At one extreme one finds clinicians who exhibit a kind of "revelational positivism" philosophically not unlike the position of Bergin though more explicitly indebted to biblical sources. As an example one might consider the work of the evangelical Christian psychiatrist, Daniel Heinrichs (Heinrichs 1982).

Heinrichs presumes that God exists as "an object in external reality" whose features have been revealed to humankind in God's definitive self-revelation first in the Hebrew scriptures and subsequently in the New Testament. The New Testament is further regarded as "the historical record of God revealing God Himself in His person and character, in Jesus Christ, and the validity of these writings is that of an eye-witness account" (Heinrichs 1982:122). Because God is a "real object" in this psychotheological perspective, our object representation of God is subject to "parataxic distortion . . . by our state of mental health, by the developmental status of our capacity for object relatedness, by our relational experiences with significant others, and by the quality of interpersonal experiences we have with those who propositionally teach us about God" (Heinrichs 1982:122). The task of the psychotherapist, from this point of view, is to help clean up these parataxic distortions by tracing them back to their developmental origins but also and importantly to provide in the therapeutic relationship a corrective experience of unconditional acceptance that most nearly reflects the revealed nature of God in Christ.[11] Clearly this particular understanding of the task of therapy is unapologetically confessional.

Henrichs' version of a God relational listening perspective obviously can only serve clinicians who share his particular theology of revelation. Even some Christian psychotherapists may register serious reservations about an approach that emphasizes correlating an individual's God representation with a God "out there" who it is presumed can be known with the same precision with which we believe we can know another person in the world. Practically, it is not clear how this approach can work with clients who do not share the religious universe of the believing clinician. Morally, it also must be asked whether these religiotherapeutic interventions do not violate the integrity of conscience of the client and the client's own unique relationship with the God of his or her understanding. Theologically, this approach ignores another equally venerable principle within the Christian theological tradition, *Deus semper major* (God is always greater)—greater than we can imagine or conceive, more creative, more inexpressible, and more unpredictable in the means by which God wills to be present to creation.[12]

From my own point of view, the God relational perspective is illustrated less problematically in the work of Moshe Halevi Spero. Spero offers a critique of those psychotheological positions that allow for the "psychological reality" of God but interpret that reality almost entirely in terms of its transference features in relation to actual human interactions past and present. His own position in contrast acknowledges the "uniqueness of interpersonal conflicts and feelings that are based on the real impact of God on human experience" (Spero 1985:80). For Spero, as for Martin Buber, God is in search of the human person. God is an actual dialogue partner, an actor who is capable of initiating and responding to human beings. In sum, something psychically new can happen from what William James would have called the "Godward" and not just the "humanward" side. At the same time Spero has a fundamental respect for the privacy and essential mystery of that human/divine interaction. In the actual conduct of the therapy his psychotheological listening perspective does not prescribe interventions that directly address this relationship and, unlike Heinrichs, Spero would certainly not presume to name what "the very God" should or should not be to the client. Spero limits himself to helping the client, where appropriate, to identify the transferential elements in his or her representation of God while remaining himself reverently and tactfully silent about what may or may not manifest itself when those transference aspects have been worked through. The case that Kochems presents in this volume illustrates the tacit adoption of this perspective. In that case while there is no direct intervention made that challenges or questions the individual's God representation, neither does the clinician collude in the client's desire to keep his religious life split off from and unintegrated with the rest of his experience. The clinician monitors the ways in which the client experiences him as similar to his God (and similar to his father) but also identifies the client's own efforts to work through the transferential aspects of the God representation. Thus Kochems is prepared to recognize that shifts in the client's independent life of prayer reflect new initiatives and movements in the client's relationship with his God that are also significant indices of growth and development. The apparent success of this case may in part be accounted for by the clinician's careful attention to these dynamics, guided by this perspective.

The characteristic strength of the God relational perspective is its recognition that for a great many persons the most salient figures organizing their felt relationship to the ultimate conditions of their existence are their object representations of "God." The God relational perspective concerns itself with the complex correspondence between such object representations of "God" and the individual's genuine, evolving relationship to what the client, and also the therapist, may be able to ontologically affirm as—and here language limps badly—the very God, the "God beyond God" (Tillich), God in God's Self. Therapists have spoken about the nature of this correspondence with differing degrees of assuredness, from the revelational positivism of the Christian evangelicals (correspondence as the literal comparison of two mental pictures, one biblical, the other of human construction) to the more modest and indirect formulations of Spero and certain contributors to this collection who look for evidence of the activity of that very God in subtle movements beyond the transference features of God to something more genuinely new.

The Faith Relational Perspective

Ana-Maria Rizzuto has cogently argued that no one comes to awareness in Western culture without some conscious and unconscious psychic representations of God, although the uses to which those representations are put vary tremendously (Rizzuto 1979). Some persons experience object representations of God as irrelevant or even inimical to their construction of a sense of being a "loving and beloved" self (Schafer 1960). With such persons inquiries after a "God" representation produce either incomprehension or incredulity. The "faith relational" perspective attempts a more inclusive formulation of what constitutes "religious material" in order to accomodate the widest range of human spiritual experience. In the God relational perspective primary attention is directed to particular religious contents, especially the object representation of "God" or other divine figures. The "background of safety" (Sandler 1960) of such figures may be described as the individual's fundamental sense of the quality of his or her relationship to self, others, and ultimacy as symbolized, secured, and mediated by those object representations. In the faith relational perspective it is this "background sense" that is of paramount interest. The focus is not upon the *what*, i.e., specific religious contents, but rather upon *how* the representational world functions, regardless of content, as a factor in an individual's construction of his or her relationship to whatever is experienced as an ultimate ground of personal meaning and value.

The faith relational perspective is the product of the critical correlation of a theological viewpoint and one or more psychological models of development. Theologically it is indebted to an approach to faith that resists identifying faith with a set of particular doctrinal beliefs, namely the notion of faith that people commonly have in mind when they inquire, "What is your faith?" By contrast, as we are using the term "faith" it is intended to be descriptive of a person's most foundational and encompassing experience of relationship to what is most deeply trustworthy and valuable in life. Wilfred Cantwell Smith, scholar of comparative religions, defined faith as "an orientation of the personality, to oneself, to one's neighbor, to the universe; a total response; a way of seeing whatever one sees and of handling whatever one handles; a capacity to live at a more than mundane level; to see, to feel, to act, in terms of a transcendent dimension" (Smith 1979:12). This definition of faith, Smith argued, is in fact more congruent with the oldest traditions of most major world religions insofar as these traditions are primarily concerned with the cultivation of a particular quality of *relationship* towards the divine, and not with cognitive assent to this or that set of doctrines or beliefs.

Theologian James Fowler, in a project that to date has had its greatest impact in the area of religious education rather than clinical or pastoral counseling, has integrated this theological perspective on faith with the structural developmental perspective of Piaget and Kohlberg to develop a research paradigm for the study of "faith development" (Fowler 1981). Out of his extensive Piagetian semi-clinical interviews Fowler has posited discrete and observable stages of "faith development." These describe in highly formal terms the ways in which individuals construe their relationship to an imaginatively conceived center or source of ultimate meaning and value. The various "developmental lines" in an individual's total faith perspective describe the individual's relationship to authority, his or her manner of using symbols and of constructing a life narrative, and the evolving and expanding capacity to take the perspective of the other.[13] This faith developmental model has been explored and further nuanced by Sharon Parks as a "tool to think with" about the crises of meaning typical of the young adult years (Parks 1986). Her work is one illustration of some of the uses that may be made of a faith development perspective to direct counseling interventions at a particular era of the life cycle.

The more specifically clinical applications of a structural developmental model are those that make the formation of the "sense of self" (rather than "faith") the central issue. Here the work of Robert Kegan represents the most significant theoretical breakthrough. In his book *The Evolving Self*, Kegan has observed that human beings optimally undergo over the course of life an orderly series of self-other differentiations that dynamically balance what counts as "self" and what is known or experienced as "other" (Kegan 1982).[14] In an elegantly written but little known essay, "Where the Dance Is: Religious Dimensions of a Developmental Framework," Kegan expressed the conviction that there is also a profound spiritual significance in what the structural developmentalists have discerned to be the "deep structure" of human consciousness—this ever-evolving tension between being included (a part of) and being distinct (apart from), of losing and reconstituting a progressively more inclusive sense of self (Kegan 1980). Such a motion or "cosmic dance," he argued, is the "meaning-constitutive evolutionary activity" of the human species and points toward a fundamental human relatedness to a Source or Ground of Being (Tillich 1951:280).[15]

Other researchers have similarly found in the neo-Piagetian work of Kegan, in the neopsychoanalytic writing of Heinz Kohut, and in the research of Jean Baker Miller and colleagues a vision of the human person that is at base deeply congruent with a religiously derived understanding of life (Miller 1976, 1984).[16] Mary Lou Randour's *Women's Psyche, Women's Spirit*, for example, is written from what I would term this faith relational perspective (Randour 1987). She maintains that the experience of "being a self-in-relationship" is psychologically foundational to human persons, though her focus is on the nature of this experience for women. Arguably this view of human motivation is convergent with a Judeo-Christian view of human beings as constituted for and by relationship. From Augustine's "You have made us for Yourself O Lord and our hearts are restless until they rest in You" to Martin Buber's "all real living is meeting," a stream of thought developing out of the biblical tradition has consistently understood the drive for relationship as the primal motive force for all human action. A developed faith relational perspective attempts to work out the correlations between such a theological position and a psychological analysis, either psychoanalytic or structural developmental, that focuses on the primacy of relationality in human development. A brief clinical vignette may suggest its potential value.

"Michael," a middle-aged man, the adult child of two severely narcissistic parents, made the pointed and unsolicited assertion at the beginning of his therapy that he was an atheist. Sometime further into the therapy after a working alliance seemed to be established, his therapist, in response to a remark Michael made about his atheism, invited him to describe "the God you don't believe in." Quite to the therapist's surprise, and apparently even to Michael's, the question provoked a welling-up of strong and complex affect. Michael was able to describe in considerable detail the features of this God he claimed "didn't exist," with particular attention to the severely punative and intrusive aspects of this omniscient God. It became apparent to the therapist and eventually to Michael himself that he was in fact deeply and tenaciously engaged with this God—an engagement that often took the form of angry monologues directed against this God, rather like negative prayers. A God relational listening perspective would have focused attention upon the transferential aspects of that God representation. Some therapists operating within a circle of explicit and shared religious conviction might have intervened to challenge the adequacy of that God representation by contrasting it with more benign and gracious images of God found in the Hebrew or Christian scripture. In this case however, the therapist assumed the psychotheological posture we have termed a faith relational perspective. This shifted the focus away from the nature of Michael's God and moved into the foreground the client's self-experience as linked to this and other symbolic representations. The guiding question then became, "How is this God part of a total schema of faith or comprehensive meaning-making that Michael somehow needs in order to be a self?"

As the therapy proceeded it appeared that Michael's fiercely defended grasp on this God whose "existence" he had to deny kept intact an inner world, and a correlative perception of the outer world, that legitimated his sense of himself as somehow cosmically wronged and victimized. This mode of "faith" maintained a sense of relationship to an overarching meaning and value, albeit one characterized more by mistrust and enmity than confidence and assurance. We explored the developmental antecedents of this worldview in the vicissitudes of his early childhood experience. The faith relational perspective respected the integrity of Michael's way of making meaning and did not directly challenge his formulation of God or the self. Nevertheless, as the work entered into its final phases Michael began to possess important and valid aspects of his own self-experience that had been hitherto split off and unintegrated. These included the anger he felt for an entire history of psychological abuse and disappointment from his family and the deeper underlying sense of sadness and attendent mourning. Michael began to more directly appropriate the authority of his own inner experience and the painful but full sweep of his own feeling life. Other aspects of self-experience emerged, including certain feelings of hopefulness, of inner expansiveness and generosity, and of being cared for "in spite of everything." Michael began to link these to long-forgotten moments walking by the seashore with a beloved grandfather as a small boy, and in the present, to other contemplative moments in nature. Less clearly he identified them with changes that were part and parcel of his therapeutic relationship. By the end of the therapy Michael had come to connect these experiences with what he named, borrowing the language of twelve-step programs, a "higher power"—a power that he still maintained (but not strenuously) was "not God." In this abbreviated description of a complex case, the normative dimension of the listening perspective was not organized by the perceived validity or truth of the client's representation of God, but rather by a judgment upon the adequacy of the client's experience of self.

George Bernard Shaw once quipped that "the world is divided into two kinds of persons—those who divide the world into two kinds of persons and those who don't." His remark points up the inadequacy and presumption of all efforts to sort a complex world into limited categories, whether of two or three. Nevertheless, it is hoped that the typologies represented here will invite the reader who is a working clinician to reflect more intentionally and more critically upon his or her own working psychotheological perspective. The range of possibilities is scarcely exhausted by the options sketched here; the necessary function of a psychotheological perspective to provide normative bearings for the conduct of psychotherapy is, I hope, a bit clearer.

Notes

1. For a discussion of the impact of therapists' religious beliefs on the conduct of therapy see Kochems (1983) and Ragan and Beit-Hallahmi (1980).

2. Pruyser was also interested in trying to formulate a psychotheological perspective for the conduct of psychotherapy that did justice both to the insights of psychoanalysis and to the enduring significance of religion in human culture. For an appreciative assessment of Pruyser's accomplishment see David Barnard (1990).

3. Spero discussing this particular case in Guntrip writes: "Doubtless, the patient's image and experience of God was colored by the same sense of disappointment or anger for previous let downs and perhaps the hope of future strength. What is most important is that the human object relationship influences the divine object relationship and *vice versa*. These mutual and complimentary influences can be expected to show up in the individual's attitude towards prayer, God's role in the evil in the world, repentence and reward and punishment, and so forth" (Spero 1985:23).

4. The term *psychotheology* is first used by E. Mark Stern in a book by that title where it refers to what is held to be an accomplished fact, namely the convergence of insights from depth psychology and theology in such a way as to create a single world view (Stern and Merino 1970). While adopting Stern's term, this essay holds that the development of a psychotheological perspective remains an uncompleted project still requiring methodological care and mutual criticism. See also Stern (1985).

5. That psychotherapy is inextricably though often uncritically involved in the provision of normative models for human development is a point made by both London (1964) and Browning (1987).

6. Psychoanalyst Stanley Leavy has perceptively observed that a positivism such as Bergin's is at base the same as Freud's. This is also the critique that Leavy raises with respect to the appropriation of the notion of transitional object phenomena by William Meissner and others. Leavy writes: "In the background of this application of the transitional object shimmers the baleful commentary of 'The Future of an Illusion,' Freud's revenge on bad religious teaching. It seems that we must be content to keep the diagnosis of illusion, but to change its sign to a positive one. I find that approach affected by an epistemological naiveté that neither Meissner not his protagonist Winnicott surpasses. 'Illusion' is a deception, in which someone's perceptions are literally 'played upon' (from *ludere*, to play), either by misinterpretation induced by an accident of nature (a mirage), or by a thaumaturgic design (rabbits out of the hat). Once we remove the term

from its latter connection with purposeful deception by someone else, we imply in its use that we might perceive reality in itself, independently of any prestructured symbolic schema. Such a radically positivist empiricism runs through much of Freud's philosophical view. For him the basis of perception is not in the symbolic system, but in the primitive and direct encounter of receptors with stimulating agency. Freud's anti-theology owes much to the reflex psychology of Chapter VII of *The Interpretation of Dreams*." (Leavy 1986:154–55)

7. For a discussion of "postmodern" psychoanalysis see Holland (1983).

8. Other variations on a spiritual reality perspective propose a "spectrum model" of human development in which depth psychology is held to accurately and helpfully describe a certain range of psychic functioning, but this account is regarded as incomplete. The most sophisticated and inclusive of such models are those proposed by Ken Wilbur and Jack Engler (Wilbur, Engler, and Brown 1986). For these writers contemporary developmental psychology is able to explain the processes by which human beings construct a sense of being autonomous and internally coherent "selves." What Western psychology does not know how to describe is the development further along the spectrum whereby the "self" is deconstructed and the individual comes to experience him or herself in terms of participation in a greater spiritual reality. To chart that portion of the developmental spectrum, it is argued, one must turn to such sources as the Abhidhamma texts of Buddhism which offer different, but arguably equally empirical, accounts of human development.

9. Goodman offers the clinical case in which a client is invited to use the "theatre technique" to access the meaning of chronic back pain. In a light trance she is given an open ended suggestion to imagine herself viewing the events of her own past life as if from the safe vantage of a theatre seat. In that condition she comes upon an image from her past that in subsequent therapy becomes a master metaphor for the sadness and grief which she had been burdened with in her adult life. What is relevant for our purposes is that from this psychotheological perspective this interpretive image is not regarded solely as a repressed memory but also as a "revelation" that has implications for the future of the client (Goodman 1989).

10. For a discussion of the congruence and points of difference between Western and Eastern mystical systems see William Johnston (1970).

11. Perhaps the most extensive efforts at working out theologically the relationship between secular psychology and traditional Protestant Christian doctrine have been from an evangelical Christian perspective. *The Journal of Psychology and Theology,* published by the Rosemead Graduate School of Professional Psychology, La Mirada, California is a good current record of the status of that dialogue in the evangelical tradition. See also Fleck and Carter (1981).

12. Respecting that principle, the clinician whose starting point is either Jewish or Christian revelation may yet hold that while nothing to be discovered about God will contradict what we know of God in and through Torah, or the life and teaching of Jesus, God's loving self-communication to the human family

is not limited to or limited by the symbols and stories of that particular revelational tradition.

13. In more recent work, James Fowler has gone back to look at the developmental antecedents to faith in the vicissitudes of early childhood experience. See Fowler (1989). For a critical discussion of the status of faith development theory see McDargh (1984).

14. For other examples of the *clinical* uses of a structural developmental model see Kegan et al. (1982) and Lee and Noam (1984).

15. Theologically, Kegan's method is inductive: he begins with attention to certain putatively universal human experiences and finds in them "clues to transcendence" that suggest statements about God. In contrast a deductive method would begin with certain statements about the nature of God and proceed to interpret human experience in terms of these statements.

16. For an example of a direct appropriation of Kegan's model of self development as a normative basis for the assessment of maturity in spiritual life see Joann Wolski Conn (1989).

References

Barnard, David. 1990. Paul Pruyser's psychoanalytic psychology of religion. *Religious Studies Review* 16: 125–31.

Bergin, A. E. 1980. Psychotherapy and religious values. *Journal of Counseling and Consulting Psychology* 48: 95–105.

——. 1983. Religiosity and mental health: A critical re-evaluation and meta-analysis. *Professional Psychology* 14: 170–84.

——. 1988. Three contributions of a spiritual perspective to counseling, psychotherapy, and behavior change. *Counseling and Values* 33: 21–31.

Bergin, A. E., R. Stinchfield, R. Gaskin, K. S. Masters, and C. Sullivan. 1988. Religious lifestyles and mental health: An exploratory study. *Journal of Counseling Psychology* 35: 91–98.

Barfield, Owen. 1965. *Saving the Appearances: A Study in Idolatry*. New York: Harcourt Brace & World.

Berman, M. 1981. *The Reenchantment of the World*. Ithaca: Cornell University Press.

Browning, Don. 1987. *Religious Thought and the Modern Psychologies*. Philadelphia: Fortress Press.

Conn, Joann Wolski. 1989. *Spirituality and Personal Maturity*. New York: Paulist Press.

Dupre, Louis. 1972. *The Other Dimension: A Search for the Meaning of Religious Attitudes*. New York: Doubleday.

Fleck, J. Roland and John Carter, eds. 1981. *Psychology and Christianity: Integrative Readings*. Nashville: Abingdon Press.

Fowler, James. 1981. *Stages of Faith: The Psychology of Human Development and the Quest for Meaning*. San Francisco: Harper & Row.

———. 1989. Strength for the journey: Early childhood development in selfhood and faith. In Doris Blazer, ed., *Faith Development in Early Childhood*, pp. 1–36. Kansas City: Sheed and Ward.

Goodman, Robert. 1989. Revelatory knowledge and the capacities of the unconscious: A post-modern view of psychological health. Unpublished manuscript.

Griffin, David, ed. 1988. *The Reenchantment of Science: Post-modern Proposals*. Albany: State University of New York Press.

———. 1989. *God and Religion in the Post-Modern World*. Albany: State University of New York Press.

Guntrip, Harry. 1969. *Schizoid Phenomenon, Object-Relations, and the Self*. New York: International Universities Press.

Heinrichs, David. 1982. Our Father Which Art in Heaven: Parataxic distortions of the image of God. *Journal of Psychology and Theology* 10: 120–29.

Hedges, Lawrence. 1983. *Listening Perspectives in Psychotherapy*. New York: Jason Aronson.

Holland, Norman. 1983. Postmodern psychoanalysis. In Ihab Hassan and Sally Hassan, eds., *Innovation and Reflection: New Perspectives on the Humanities*. Madison: University of Wisconsin Press.

Johnston, William. 1970. *The Still Point: Reflections on Zen and Christian Mysticism*. New York: Fordham University Press.

Kegan, Robert. 1980. Where the dance is: Religious dimensions of a developmental framework. In James Fowler and Antoine Vergote, eds., *Toward Moral and Religious Maturity*. Morristown, N.J.: Silver Burdett.

———. 1982. *The Evolving Self: Problem and Process in Human Development*. Cambridge: Harvard University Press.

Kegan, Robert, Gil Noam, and Laura Rogers. 1982. The psychologic of emotions: A neo-Piagetian View. In D. Cicchitti and P. Hesse, eds., *New Directions in Child Development: Emotional Development*, no. 16. San Francisco: Jossey Bass.

Kochems, Timothy. 1983. The relationship of background variables to the experiences and values of psychotherapists in managing religious material. Ph.D. dissertation, George Washington University (*Dissertation Abstracts International*, order no. 8311196).

Leavy, Stanley. 1986. A Pascalian meditation on psychoanalysis and religious experience. *Cross Currents* 36: 147–55.

Lee, B. and G. Noam, eds. 1984. *Developmental Approaches to the Self*. New York: Plenum Press.

London, Perry. 1964. *The Modes and Morals of Psychotherapy*. New York: Holt, Reinhart & Winston.

Lovinger, Robert. 1984. *Working with Religious Issues in Psychotherapy*. New York: Jason Aronson.

McDargh, John. 1983. *Psychoanalytic Object Relations Theory and the Study of Religion: On Faith and the Imaging of God*. Lanham, Md.: University Press of America.

———. 1984. Faith development theory at ten years. *Religious Studies Review* 10: 339–42.

Meissner, William. 1987. *Psychoanalysis and Religious Experience*. New Haven: Yale University Press.

Miller, Jean Baker. 1976. *Toward a New Psychology of Women*. Boston: Beacon Press.

———. 1984. The development of women's sense of self. *Work in Progress*, no. 84–01. Wellesley College: Stone Center for Developmental Services and Studies.

Parks, Sharon. 1986. *The Critical Years: The Young Adult Search for a Faith to Live by*. New York: Harper & Row.

Pruyser, Paul. 1983. *The Play of the Imagination: Toward a Psychoanalysis of Culture*. New York: International Universities Press.

Ragan, Malony and Benjamin Beit-Hallahmi. 1980. Psychologists and religion: Professional factors and belief. *Review of Religious Research* 21: 208–17.

Randour, Mary Lou. 1987. *Women's Psyche, Women's Spirit: The Reality of Relationships*. New York: Columbia University Press.

Rizzuto, Ana-Maria. 1979. *The Birth of the Living God*. Chicago: University of Chicago Press.

Sandler, Joseph. 1960. The background of safety. *International Journal of Psychoanalysis* 41: 352–56.

Saur, William and Marilyn Saur. In press. Religious illusions: A psychoanalytic object-relations perspective. In Mark Finn and John Gartner, eds., *Object Relations Theory and Religion: Clinical Applications*. New York: Praeger.

Schafer, Roy. 1960. the loving and beloved super-ego in Freud's structural theory. *Psychoanalytic Study of the Child* 15: 163–88.

Smith, Wilfred Cantwell. 1979. *Faith and Belief*. Princeton: Princeton University Press.

Spero, Moshe Halevi, ed. 1985. *Psychotherapy of the Religious Patient*. Springfield, Ill.: Charles C. Thomas.

———. 1985. The reality and the image of God in psychotherapy. *American Journal of Psychotherapy* 39: 75–85.

———. 1987. Identity and individuality in the noveau-religious patient: Theoretical and clinical aspects. *Psychiatry* 50: 55–71.

———. 1990. Parallel dimensions of experience in psychoanalytic psychotherapy of the religious patient. *Psychotherapy* 27: 53–71.

Stern, E. M. 1985. *Psychotherapy of the Religiously Committed Patient*. New York: Haworth Press.

Stern, E. M. and B. Marino. 1970. *Psychotheology*. Paramus: Paulist Press.

Tillich, Paul. 1951. *Systematic Theology*. Vol. 1. London: Nisbet.

Wilbur, Ken, Jack Engler, and Daniel Brown. 1986. *Transformations of Consciousness:*

Conventional and Contemplative Perspectives on Development. Boston: Shambhala Press.

Wolberg, L. 1977. *The Technique of Psychotherapy.* Vol. 1. New York: Grune & Stratton.

Zee, A. 1986. *Fearful Symmetry: The Search for Beauty in the Modern Physics.* New York: Macmillan.

Psychology and Spirituality:

Forging A New Relationship

GIL G. NOAM
MARYANNE WOLF

F ew topics are as central to the lives of those seeking therapeutic counsel as spirituality, especially if we define spirituality as the search for meaning in the face of mortality. Yet most psychotherapists remain hesitant to enter into these essential and often unconscious quests when framed in religious terms. A reevaluation of the stance of "secular propriety" is long overdue.

In a domain where language often fails to clarify, the sharing of ideas and experiences by a group of committed clinicians is most welcome. Mary Lou Randour, an established authority in shaping the interface between psychotherapy and spirituality, has assembled an impressive group of clinicians, theoreticians, and theologians to explore this new territory. Of the many ideas put forward in this book we will discuss a number of central themes from our own developmental and clinical perspectives.

We begin with a brief reexamination of Freud's and Jung's positions on the relationship between psychotherapy and spirituality and the influence of these positions on modern therapy. Next we consider recent changes in openness towards the inclusion of spiritual content in the therapeutic relationship. A clinical case study from the senior author's practice illuminates the potential differences in process and outcome that can result from this openness. In the third section we delineate some of the difficult central questions that must be addressed in any contemporary consideration of the role of spirituality in therapy and vice versa and we propose several "first principles" to guide future discussions.

Origins: Freud and Jung

Most of the contributors to this volume seem to agree that Freud's rational model unnecessarily dismisses religious concerns by equating them with childhood illusions. For Freud, interpreting the unconscious is not an act of magic, but part of the great project of enlightenment, in which human beings battle evil inner and outer forces with only their reflective powers and the ability to generate truth. Freud took the scientific method to its radical conclusion—the dedication of all psychoanalytic principles to the discovery of truth and "the love for insight" for the purpose of overcoming symptoms. Like Marx before him, Freud rejected the wealth and power of spirituality and its power for insight (see, for example, work on insight in spiritual development in Buber 1970; Dunne 1967). Freud (1927) erred in relegating religion to immaturity of the self and lack of conceptual sophistication. Spirituality was walled off from psychoanalysis by this fundamental mistake.

Jung, Freud's former student and vigorous partner in a dialogue about religion and psychoanalysis, sought to unite spirituality and daily life to provide new meaning for modern men and women (e.g., Jung 1938/1940). This unity is at the core of his developmental telos in which maturity is defined as the integration of spiritual life into the personality. Jung viewed unconscious forces as the mysterious source of myth and archetype. With his concept of the collective unconscious, Jung attempted to discover the universal aspects of the unconscious and to validate the intuitive and symbolic aspects of different religious forms. This broad perspective places psychology and spirituality in a continuously evolving relationship, and understandably accounts for Jung's renewed popularity among therapists and theologians.

However, Jung underestimated the usefulness of the boundaries drawn in Freud's work. For example, Jung liberally uses cosmology, alchemy, and divine reincarnation. These concepts are not suspect because they are unscientific (has "drive" as a core organizer of psychological development ever been demonstrated scientifically?); they are problematic because they place psychology and psychotherapy outside the realm of enlightenment and logic. The feudal relationship between church and state, between science and religion, was forever altered in the West through the period of Enlightenment, but the nostalgia for a unified spiritual-secular life was and continues to be an understandable desire.

195

The existing split, however, is not a matter of neurosis alone, but a core condition of a world committed to the principles of rationality and logical coherence. The many postmodern attempts at dignifying the irrational are only a new version of a long strand in philosophy that had its peak, arguably, in Nietzsche. Totalitarian attempts to create a fundamentalist unity between spirituality and political life have been the major tragedies of our century. Indeed attempts continue to exist in varied forms throughout the world today. "Being at two with nature," as Woody Allen has so poignantly put it, is part of our daily existence. The split between our lives as citizens of the world and as men and women of faith must, however, be reckoned with. No romantic desire to return to a state of unity, understandable as it is, will create the necessary bridge. It is an essential truth of psychotherapy that integration results from a recognition of contradictions, not from a romantic yearning for a lost time.

We do not wish to suggest that those who pursue an integration of spirituality and daily life follow an unenlightened position; far from it. It is nevertheless imperative to dispassionately scrutinize all such endeavors, lest we fall into the many traps of unreflective religious zeal cautioned against by religious contemplatives from the third century desert fathers to Thomas Merton (1968). We therefore must keep in mind the dangers implicit both in Freud's position and in Jung's religious romanticism as well. The Freud-Jung duality is not only a historic chapter in the emergence of the practice of psychotherapy, but also a living part of our dialogue about the relationship between spirituality and psychotherapy.

There is little doubt that Jung spoke to some deep truths and human yearnings and should not have been marginalized by mainstream psychoanalysis. Contemporary psychotherapy has incorporated many ideas and techniques for which he has not been given appropriate credit (e.g., the centrality of adult development, the use of art in therapy, the introduction of face-to-face psychotherapy).

During its vigorous struggle in this country to gain acceptance as a medical-scientific subspeciality, mainstream psychoanalysis rejected both Jung and spiritual concerns. Few analysts or therapists over the last decades have been willing to enter the "soft" and speculative pursuits of faith and religion. In a discipline in which the humanistic concerns of love are translated into "cathexis" and the creative mind into "mental apparatus," one could hardly expect an attitude of openness toward the transcendent notions of spirituality.

A number of trends in psychotherapy have, however, generated a greater degree of openness toward spirituality today: current psychoanalysis is forced to free itself from a complete association with medicine due to the increasing predominance of biological directions in psychiatry. Even a medically focused psychoanalysis would not be considered scientific enough to become part of the new neuropsychiatric trends. At the same time, the psychotherapeutic field as a whole has significantly diversified, allowing for a great deal of experimentation and alternative approaches. While psychiatry is becoming increasingly less open to psychoanalysis, psychology has become more so. What is considered scientific today in the psychological sciences is not confined to positivistic hypothesis testing but includes approaches to text, meaning, and construction. This opens some areas in psychology that traditionally had viewed psychoanalysis as unscientific to the psychoanalytic hermeneutic approaches.

In this atmosphere of evolving alliances and the decline of one unitary world view or general paradigm, a reassessment of the individual's spiritual issues and their place in psychotherapy is emerging. The first step in this emergence is confronting the taboo itself.

The End of a Taboo

For most therapists it is far easier to discuss the joys and aberrations of sexual life, the honest and deceptive uses of money, or the creative and petty elaborations of intimate love than it is to explore the role of prayer, meditation, and the discovery of meaning in the face of mortality. This difficulty in most clinical encounters can without exaggeration be called a taboo, first introduced during the training of the therapist and then transmitted in the clinical encounter with the patient.

This taboo cannot be solely attributed to Freud's basic stance toward religion. It is similarly enforced in other psychotherapies, including those that advance the traditions of "value-free" positivist psychology and share little with psychoanalysis. Trainees, like patients, take subtle and not-so-subtle cues about what is proper or improper to address in therapy. No one ever told us not to pursue spiritual issues, but not one of our many gifted teachers ever suggested we do so. Does any typical psychiatric and psychoanalytic anamnestic interview ever include an exploration of the transforming images of God or the content and meaning of prayers across the lifespan? To this day, Harry Stack Sullivan's "The Psychiatric Interview" (1954) includes the most detailed account of how to "take a life history" with clinical goals in mind. It includes questions relevant to self and interpersonal development, to family life, and to schooling; however, religion and spirituality are totally absent as topics for exploration. This omission is particularly poignant because one cannot imagine that someone as developmentally aware as Sullivan would be oblivious to the significance of religion in the lives of children and adults.

Today we are more likely to explore new "foreign territories of the mind" and to trust less in established truths handed down within any clinical subspecialty. The field of psychotherapy has entered a post-dogma period that is more sensitive to the developmental needs of the patients and *their* (in contrast to the theorists' and therapists') reality. For example, the feminist critique of male biases in developmental and clinical theory exposed a unidimensionality in perspectives that ultimately concerned not only male/female issues but also such issues as ethnicity, class, and religion.

An example illuminates how subtle shifts in listening produce very important clinical results. (The "I" voice refers to the first author, who was involved in the psychotherapy.) Joan, as I shall call her, a Jewish professional, was forty-two when she first requested psychotherapy four years ago. She was depressed about the conflicts experienced with her lover, whom she represented as both weak and demanding. She discussed her inability to overcome a sense of betrayal experienced in her relationship to her parents. Her mother had been unable to nurture her as a girl and her father had treated her in simultaneously seductive and abandoning ways. Over time Joan became highly intellectual and received considerable acclaim. Essential aspects of herself, however, were left behind: artistic expression, music, parental affection, and simple play between friends were relegated to distant, unclear memories of a time before age five. These early childhood memories were superseded by memories of intellectually demanding, remote parents who were at war with each other, but united in their demands of their daughter.

Psychotherapeutic treatment revolved around images of "true self" and "false self"—terms that she introduced into the treatment and that animated her descriptions of past memories, present relationships, and most prominently, the emerging transference. She placed impossible demands on her therapist, vigorously interrogating me upon every topic, and equating patience and a nonjudgmental attitude with weakness. With every incremental gain of emotional expressiveness she would cancel the next session "to gain control." Despite the pace, the process continued to move forward, insights emerged, and the therapeutic relationship strengthened and deepened.

Throughout treatment religious and spiritual issues were only background variables. She described her Jewish background, which became an important aspect of my understanding of her. However, it was a "dry" understanding, concerned with ethnic group rather than spirituality. After three years she had to move from the area and the treatment was terminated prematurely. We were aware that a great deal had been accomplished and that more was needed; in our review of the work spiritual issues were never mentioned.

Two years later she returned to the area. She had not continued therapy elsewhere and was eager to resume. I immediately became aware of important changes that had taken place in her. After a serious love affair, she was less defended and felt more open in relationships and less anxious about losing control. She was both less angry at her parents and also able to acknowledge more significant injuries. (I had also changed in those years, becoming, I believe, more reflective and open concerning spiritual exploration. I had thought myself "open" to issues of spirituality earlier when in reality, like most of my colleagues, I largely translated those experiences into the dynamics of family life.)

One day Joan shared a great deal of sorrow and pain concerning her lover's serious illness. In the context of our discussion a question about prayer was not out of place, even though her hint could have easily been missed. My question led to a very surprising set of associations about her reemerging spiritual questions and her readings of Merton and Buber. Even more important than her readings were the memories of her childhood in temple. She began to describe her prayers when she went to synagogue. She began to reveal that her relationship with Judaism was not limited to living in a Jewish neighborhood but involved a rich dialogue with God throughout her childhood.

It could be argued that Joan had not been ready to reveal her relationship with God, a relationship which had become even more important after her relationship with her father and mother derailed. This interpretation deserves consideration, especially because since I had last seen her she had begun both a new love-relationship and a process of active self-reflection. New experiences "produce" new memories, as the psychoanalyst Loewald (1958) so beautifully describes. This would also let me "off the hook"—that is, I as therapist was ready to receive her emerging self when she was ready to share and develop it. However, another interpretation is that I had missed an entire dimension of Joan's development in the first treatment.

Indeed the truth probably incorporates both interpretations. I was now more open to hear and understand a set of experiences that Joan was also more ready to communicate. With her history of disappointments in communication, I am sure that she had tested my willingness to listen to her spiritual experiences long before. Reading my notes about the treatment, I found that she had mentioned Thomas Merton's work and waited for a response from me. My response was limited to mentioning that I had read his work on contemplation and was interested in her experience concerning his books.

It must be emphasized again that the cues between therapist and patient are very subtle and to a great degree unconscious. Either party can leave out essential parts of experience. But we also know that theory and therapeutic stance can block the way to important explorations. Rediscovering real, rather than fantasized, sexual abuse is one example of therapeutic approaches that have changed dramatically in recent years. Discovering spirituality in our patients may well be another.

Joan had, in fact, already introduced a spiritual dimension into the earlier therapy. I had been largely unaware of it and can only now understand it. One dream stands out. Somewhere by the Mediterranean, she and I climb a mountain, first by foot, then by car. On the top of the mountain is a great view, a perspective of sky, water, olive trees, and all nature. The way up is full of obstacles, mules getting in the way. I drive the car and she wants to take over the wheel but is at this point afraid to drive the car. When she sees the mules, she is afraid of crashing.

She had interpreted the content of the dream in the earlier treatment as the wish to be more in control, asking whose therapy it really was, and discussing the sexual dimensions of the mules and the road up the mountain in terms of her own development of self. She interpreted the Mediterranean as a setting of freedom, of sun, and remembered trips to Greece and Israel. Neither of us mentioned the potential spiritual dimensions of the dream: trying to find harmony in nature, moving beyond the daily bustle of earthly reality to gain not only insight but also a deeper perspective into the meaning of life. Neither of us discussed the potential biblical associations to the Mediterranean as the birthplace of Judaism and Christianity or the associations between heights and heaven or afterlife.

I am not suggesting that the dream in fact had those meanings, but the view that associations are born only within the head of the patient and have nothing to do with the active mind of the therapist or the openness of the therapeutic field ignores an important component of the interactive nature of the therapeutic relationship. The fact that these meanings now entered my hypothesis-generation process influenced the degree to which Joan would allow herself to ask particular questions. Her questions, in turn, led to a greater radius of exploration within the therapy.

My own changes in these areas are part of a broader change within the field. We consider these developments in openness to spiritual content as being potentially as important to progress in the field as, for example, understanding gender differences or typical vulnerabilities of the self, two areas in which we have significantly altered our attitudes and our clinical work during the past decade. We believe a new approach to spiritual content will have meaningful consequences. Mapping the scope and limits of this approach, however, poses many formidable questions.

Psychology and Spirituality: Different Domains

At a recent meeting of psychoanalysts in Boston, a seasoned teacher reviewed the clinical work of a candidate whose patient was a deeply religious Catholic woman. The patient's psychological language incorporated many spiritual metaphors about the relationship between God and guilt. Picking up on the insecurity of the analyst who mentioned that she had difficulties dealing with the religious experience of her patient, the consultant said with authority and conviction: "Why should you treat her religious concerns differently than you deal with any associations that emerge in psychoanalysis?" He meant his remarks to encourage the young analyst to enter all experiences of her patient and to try not to remain aloof from the religious ones. Although he sounded convincing and had a positive impact on the treatment, the remark is troubling. Are spiritual associations really the same as any other associations? Should they be treated in the same way as other associations? The desire for unity, earlier described as the romantic yearning to return to pre-Enlightenment times, is exchanged for a new romantic vision: the notion that a scientific perspective can unify biography, an understanding of self, object relationships, and spirituality within one basic conceptual scheme, the unifying assumption being that all mental processes are "created equal."

We believe that this romantic version of science as unification of all human experiences clouds the possible links between spirituality and psychotherapy, by *a priori* viewing separate domains as belonging together (see also Wulff 1991 and Timpe 1983). The context, meaning, and function of religion, faith, and God are not the same as the development of sexuality, ego, and psychopathology. As Anna Freud (1936) has shown, postulating different domains with separate developmental lines does not deny possible relationships among them, but fundamental distinctions must first be drawn.

Unfortunately, both psychoanalysis and developmental psychology have in the past tended to view multiple psychological functions in terms of overarching processes. Consider, for example, Kohut's work on the self in psychoanalysis and Erikson's tradition of a board identity concept that encompasses multiple developmental processes. We have critiqued this trend in developmental psychology in the work of Loevinger, Kegan, and Fowler (e.g., Noam 1990). Present research in human development has become far more respectful of multiple developmental domains, each with its own functions and trajectories (see, for example, Gardner 1988; Noam in press). From this perspective, one domain may be evolved or immature without predetermining the developmental complexity and adaptational styles in other domains. The reason for these discrepancies lies in the fact that development occurs both through experiences and our constructions of them. If we have not had the opportunities to explore new relationships and challenge the limits of our knowledge, we are not likely to expand our capacities and gain new insights. The specific experiential context determines the developmental trajectory in each psychological and spiritual domain (e.g., Meadow and Kahoe 1984).

When we focus on the developmental context, we refer not only to external conditions, but also to intricate systems of language, meaning, and interaction (e.g., Mead 1950). A person who has grown up in a religious tradition will be dealing not only with universal issues of identity and self, but with religious beliefs that produce a specific grammar of experience. For many religious people, God is not just another object relation but a relationship that follows its own rules, logic, and direction. To frame images of God and our parents solely in terms of their commonality—that is, as self and object representation—does not address the fundamental differences in images of God across different cultures and in the rituals with which the child learns to communicate.

In considering the implications of this domain perspective, it cannot be assumed that every psychotherapist is suited for reworking spiritual experiences and for entering a basic dialogue on the topic of God (see for example Hunter 1990). There is an important difference between learning how to listen, as exemplified by the case of Joan, and acknowledging either disbelief or a fundamental lack of knowledge, either of which could disqualify one from being the appropriate therapist to a client. The taboo mentioned earlier serves an important function: it shields clients from the lack of capability most therapists have in this area. Although the taboo is waning, a spiritual knowledge base for most therapists has not increased.

This lack of conversance, coupled with the notion that modern psychological and spiritual domains are distinct not only in the social world but also in the intrapsychic world, raises the question whether some issues of spiritual concern should be pursued solely within spiritual counseling. The choice is difficult. Many therapists lack a language of spirituality and many—but not all—spiritual counselors lack a fundamental knowledge and training in how to uncover unconscious processes and deal with difficult transference relationships. The willingness of the therapist to listen is no guarantee of understanding the basic language of religion. We can not automatically assume that we are the proper persons to do the work. Neither should we assume that a religious person should seek counsel only from someone similarly religious and within the same tradition. From this logical perspective, women should see only woman psychotherapists, and men should be seen only by males, given the fundamentally different experiences of the two genders. Just as there is no consensus concerning gender choice for therapists, there is a similar lack of consensus around issues of spirituality. Clear guidelines cannot be expected at this stage of our understanding. Let us, however, consider certain principles that may advance our thinking.

Development in the Relationship Between Psychology and Spirituality

A developmental perspective might prove pivotal in working toward a new relationship between psychology and spirituality. Spiritual and psychological domains develop throughout life, transforming the nature of the relationship between spiritual life and psychological life, between religious and worldly concerns, and between God images and object representations.

The past decade has benefited from an emerging group of scholars (many represented in this book) who systematically study faith as a developmental process in normal life. Cross-sectional, cross-cultural, and longitudinal research has shown (e.g., Oser & Scarlett 1991; Fowler 1991; Reich in press) that the evolution of the images of God parallels the development of other relationships and psychological representations. There are fascinating phylogenetic precedents to this parallelism. This concept was first discussed at the turn of the century by Herman Üsener, who traced the developmental history of the move from polytheistic to monotheistic religions through the names and images given to deities by different civilizations (see a discussion of Üsener's *Götternamen* in Ernst Cassirer's philosophical work on symbols, 1946). A more ontogenetic parallelism is found in current object-relations psychoanalysis, which has shown that parent images do not extend only to persons but also to transcendent beings (e.g., Rizzuto 1979; Vergote and Tamayo 1980). There is little understanding, however, of how the psychological and spiritual worlds become differentiated, or of the lifelong tensions and integrations between these worlds in different individuals. Understanding these developmental dynamics will aid our clinical work and help guide decisions concerning the relationship between psychotherapy and spiritual counseling.

In their excellent Piagetian research on the development of faith Oser and Gmünder found that, at a developmental stage associated with early formal operations, adolescents and adults tend to differentiate strictly between their spiritual and worldly lives (see also Scarlett and Perriello

1991). Oser (1991) describes this stage as follows: "The human being is solipsistically autonomous, responsible for his or her own life and for secular matters. The Ultimate Being, if its existance is accepted, has its own domain of hidden responsibility (p. 10). In our own observations, this stage differs from earlier developmental levels in which the spiritual domain is far less differentiated from other psychological ones. It also differs from later developmental positions in which psychological life is often couched in spiritual terms. At this intermediate developmental position—which indeed characterizes most of our clients—the person psychologically takes a perspective on early identifications and develops multiple voices as he or she moves to a more cohesive self identity (Noam 1988). It is crucial to support the process of differentiation and the need to separate spiritual and worldly lives. During such a transition, we think that it can be valuable to separate therapy and spiritual counseling and to offer both to the client. An analogy is the decision to suggest individual therapy and couples therapy (with separate therapists) at the same time.

We have also found it especially important at this developmental level to support a dialogue within a person's religious tradition to help transcend a somewhat concrete and conformist approach to spirituality and encourage a more individualized, more complex, and ultimately more flexible relationship to God and religious institutions. Such a trajectory poses many difficulties. Helping a person become more flexible with conventions requires a firm understanding of those conventions. Without this knowledge the counsel remains untrustworthy to the client. The therapist must also strike a complex, delicate balance in helping a client to think more clearly about his or her own personal relationship without dictating any aspect of that relation or image to the client.

At later developmental positions, particularly at a stage of development associated with "postformal operations," spirituality and worldly matters often become more integrated. The psychological experience is often framed in spiritual terms similar to what Erikson described as the "stage of wisdom." The self transcends its own boundaries of identity and becomes more firmly committed to the world, the next generation, and hopes for the future. Daily life and everyday decision making gain a spiritual dimension. Therapist and client are typically viewed as being part of this larger world so that, in addition to the complexities and vicissitudes of the transference, therapist and client also join in the process of change.

In early life the spiritual and worldly domains and images of parent and images of God are relatively undifferentiated; these become more and more differentiated and separate into different domains in development, and then become reintegrated later. The relationship between spirituality and psychotherapy must also be flexible and developmentally focused on this evolving relationship (beginning with a certain unity, then differentiating, and finally reuniting). At one time we may have to support the unity, whereas at other times our client may need help in differentiation and synthesis as the recognition of different spiritual and worldly domains changes developmentally. These movements are relevant within each treatment.

In this essay we have examined a number of different themes that emerged in the present book as well as reactions to this volume: an impatience with unidimensional theoretical dogma, a related phase of experimentation in psychotherapy, the systematic research in faith development, and spiritual questions within psychotherapy and/or spiritual counseling. We believe that these developments are in the process of coalescing into a new climate for both the telling of life histories and spiritual searches and the listening we offer our clients and ourselves.

References

Buber, M. 1970. *I and Thou*. New York: Scribner's.

Cassirer, E. 1946. *Language and Myth*. New York: Dover.

Dunne, J. S. 1967. *A Search for God in Time and Memory*. New York: Macmillan.

Fowler, J. W. 1981. *Stages of Faith*. New York: Harper and Row.

Freud, A. 1936. *The Ego and the Mechanisms of Defense*. New York: International Universities Press.

Freud, S. [1927] 1964. The Future of an Illusion. Garden City: Anchor Books.

Gardner, H. 1983. *Frames of Mind*. New York: Basic Books.

Hunter, W. F. 1990. *The Case for Theological Literacy in the Psychology of Religion.* Special Issue of Journal of Psychology and Theology, 17(4).

Jung, C. G., 1938/1940. *Psychology and Religion* (The Terry Lectures). New Haven: Yale University Press.

Loewald, H. 1974. Current status of the concept of infantile neurosis: The psychoanalytic study of the child 29: 183–88. New Haven: Yale University Press.

Mead, G. H. 1934. *Mind, Self, and Society.* Chicago: University of Chicago Press.

Meadow, M. J. and R. D. Kahoe. 1984. Psychological versus spiritual maturity. In M. J. Meadow and R. D. Kahoe, *Psychology of Religion: Religion in Individual Lives.* New York: Harper and Row.

Merton, T. 1968. *Faith and Violence.* Notre Dame: University of Notre Dame Press.

Noam, G. G. 1988. The theory of biography and transformation: Foundation for clinical developmental theory. In S. R. Shirk, ed., *Cognitive Development and Child Psychotherapy.* New York: Plenum.

———. 1990. Beyond Freud and Piaget: Biographical worlds—interpersonal self. In Thomas Wren, ed., *The Moral Domain.* Cambridge: The MIT Press.

———. In press. Ego development: True or false? *Psychological Inquiry.*

Oser, F. K. 1991. *Gmünder: Stages of Religious Development.* Birmingham: Religious Education Press.

Oser, F. K. and G. Scarlett. 1991. Religious development in childhood and adolescence. Special Issue of *New Directions for Child Development,* vol. 52.

Reich, K. H. In press. Religious development across the life span. In D. L. Featherman, R. M. Lerner, and M. Perlmutter, eds., *Life-Span Development and Behavior: Conventional and Cognitive Developmental Approaches,* vol. 12. Hillsdale: Earlbaum.

Rizzuto, A.-M. 1979. *The Birth of the Living God: A Psychoanalytic Study.* Chicago: University of Chicago Press.

———. 1991. Religious development: A psychoanalytic point of view. Special Issue of *New Directions for Child Development,* vol. 52.

Scarlett, G. and L. Perriello. 1991. The development of prayer in adolescence. Special Issue of *New Directions for Child Development,* vol. 52.

Timpe, R. L. 1983. Epistemological and metaphysical limits to the integration of psychology and theology. *Journal of Psychology and Christianity,* vol. 2, no. 3.

Vergote, A. and A. Tamayo. 1980. *Parental Figures and the Representation of God: A Psychological and Cross-Cultural Study.* The Hague: Mouton.

Wulff, D. M. 1991. *Psychology of Religion: A Study of Classic and Contemporary Views.* New York: Wiley.

Contributors

Robert G. Goodman, Ed.D., is a fellow of the Clinical-Developmental Institute, Belmont, Massachusetts, and a licensed psychologist in the private practice of consultation and psychotherapy.

Thomas G. Gutheil, M.D., is associate professor of Psychiatry at the Massachusetts Mental Health Center, Harvard Medical School.

Rochelle G. K. Kainer, Ph.D., is on the teaching and supervisory faculty of the Washington School of Psychiatry, one of the founding members of the Washington Society of Psychoanalytic Psychology (WSPP), and coeditor of the WSPP journal, *Analytic Reflections*. She is in private practice in Washington, D.C.

Nancy Kehoe, RSCJ, Ph.D., is a Religious of the Sacred Heart and a clinical psychologist. She is an instructor in psychology in the Department of Psychiatry at The Cambridge Hospital, affiliated with Harvard Medical School. Dr. Kehoe has a private practice in Belmont, Massachusetts.

Tim Kochems, Ph.D., is a clinical psychologist in private practice in Newton Centre, Massachusetts. He is a supervising psychologist at Beth Israel Hospital, Harvard Medical School.

John McDargh, Ph.D., is associate professor of religion and psychology in the Department of Theology, Boston College. The author of *Psychoanalytic Object Relations Theory and the Study of Religion: On Faith and the Imaging of God,* he works extensively with mental health professionals on the interrelationship of psychotherapy and spirituality.

Gil G. Noam, Dipl. Psy., Ed.D., is assistant professor of psychology, Harvard Medical School, lecturer in human development and psychology at Harvard University and director, Hall-Mercer Laboratory of Developmental Psychology and Developmental Psychopathology, McLean Hospital. He practices and supervises adult and child psychotherapy at McLean Hospital and the Clinical-Developmental Institute.

Sharon Daloz Parks, Th.D., is the author of *The Critical Years: The Young Adult's Search for Meaning, Faith, and Commitment*. She is a senior research fellow at Harvard University—The Business School and The Kennedy School of Government. She is also a fellow at the Clinical Developmental Institute in Belmont, Massachusetts.

Mary Lou Randour, Ph.D., is a candidate at The Washington Psychoanalytic Institute, Washington, D.C. The author of *Women's Psyche, Women's Spirit: The Reality of Relationships,* she has written on the topics of psychoanalysis and religion, women's development, and psychotherapy. She has a private practice in Chevy Chase, Maryland.

Martha Robbins, Th.D., is associate professor of psychology and pastoral care at Pittsburgh Theological Seminary in Pittsburgh. She is author of *Mid-life Women and Death of Mother: A Study of Psychohistorical and Spiritual Transformation*.

Ana-Maria Rizzuto, M.D., is a training and supervisory analyst at the Psychoanalytic Institute of New England, East.

Maryanne Wolf, Ed.D., is an associate professor at the Elliot Pearson Department of Child Study, Tufts University. She conducts research that focuses on a neuroscience approach to language development. Dr. Wolf was the recipient of the 1991 American Psychological Association's award for Teacher of the Year.

Index